Choral Connections

Level 4 Mixed Voices

Teacher's Wraparound Edition

Teacher's Manual

GLENCOE
McGraw-Hill

New York, New York   Columbus, Ohio   Mission Hills, California   Peoria, Illinois

Meet the Authors

SENIOR AUTHOR
Mollie G. Tower - As Coordinator of Choral and General Music of the Austin Independent School District, Mollie Tower was recently nominated as "Administrator of the Year." She is very active in international, national, regional, and state music educators' organizations. Ms. Tower was contributing author, consultant, and reviewer for the elementary programs *Share the Music*, and *Music and You*. Senior author of *Música para todos, Primary and Intermediate Dual Language Handbooks for Music Teachers*, she has also written and consulted for many other publications. A longtime advocate of music education, Mollie is a popular clinician who conducts workshops across the country.

Milton Pullen
Professor of Music and Director of Choirs
After attending Texas A & I University where he acquired a Bachelor of Music Education in voice, Milton Pullen attended the University of Houston, where in 1976 he received a Master of Music in conducting. He has taught at the middle and high school levels for 24 years and for the last seven years has taught at the university level. He is now Professor of Music and Director of Choirs at Pepperdine University in Malibu, California.

Ken Steele
Director of Choral Activities
Ken Steele has taught secondary choral music for 22 years, having directed choirs at the middle school and high school levels. He received the Bachelor of Music degree from Stetson University in DeLand, Florida, and went on to the University of Texas in Austin to earn the Master of Music in Choral Literature and Conducting in 1971, studying with Dr. Morris J. Beachy. A member of Texas Music Educators Association, Texas Choral Directors Association, Texas Music Adjudicators Association, and a lifetime member of the American Choral Directors Association, he is currently the director of choral activities at L. C. Anderson High School, in Austin, Texas.

Gloria J. Stephens
Director of Choral Activities
With 23 years of teaching experience, Gloria Stephens is presently the Director of Choral Activities at Ryan High School in Denton, Texas. Mrs. Stephens earned her Bachelor of Music Education and Master of Music Education degrees from the University of North Texas in Denton. She has also done post-graduate work at Texas Woman's University in Denton, the University of Texas at Arlington, and Westminster Choir College in Princeton, New Jersey.

Contributing Writers
Dr. Susan Snyder has taught all levels of vocal music over the last 25 years. She holds a B.S. in music education from the University of Connecticut and an M.A. from Montclair State College. She holds a Ph.D. in curriculum and instruction from the University of Connecticut and advanced professional certificates from Memphis State University and the University of Minnesota. Teaching at Hunter College and City University of New York, Dr. Snyder was coordinating author of the elementary music program, *Share the Music*, and a consultant on *Music and You*. She has published many articles on music education and integrated curriculum and is an active clinician, master teacher, and guest conductor.

Vocal Development, Music Literacy
Katherine Saltzer Hickey, D.M.A.
University of California at Los Angeles
Los Angeles, California
Choir Director
Pacific Chorale Children's Choruses
Irvine, California

Glencoe/McGraw-Hill
A Division of The McGraw-Hill Companies

Send all inquiries to:
Glencoe/McGraw-Hill
15319 Chatsworth Street
Mission Hills, California 91345

ISBN 0-02-655535-2 (Student's Edition)
ISBN 0-02-655561-1 (Teacher's Wraparound Edition)

Printed in the United States of America.

2 3 4 5 6 7 8 9 MAL 02 01 00 99 98 97

Table of Contents

Authors and Contributors T2

Contents Teacher's Wraparound Edition T3

Program at a Glance T4

National Standards T6

Introduction T8

Program Philosophy T8

Organization and Flexibility T10

Level 4, Mixed Voices—Lesson Objectives T11

Student Text T13

Teacher's Wraparound Edition T14

Teacher's Resource Binder T15

Featured Listening Selections T16

SECTION		National Standards									Teacher's Resources	
Selection	**Concepts and Skills**											
TEACHING LESSONS		1	2	3	4	5	6	7	8	9		
The One Who Stands Alone	Beat; style; 3/4 and 4/4 meter.	a, b, c, e				a, b	b	a		c		
Siyahamba	Melodic leaps; register consistency; part independence; homophony; syncopated rhythms.	a, b, c, e				a, b	a, b		c	c		
The Prayer of Saint Francis	Tuning pitches; legato articulation; phrasing.	a, b, c, f				a, b	a, b, c	a	c	c		
Starlight Lullaby	Major tonality; changing keys; melody shared between voices.	a, b, c, f				a, b	a, b, c	a				
God Rest You Merry, Gentlemen	Minor tonality; ensemble precision; augmentation; round.	a, b, c, f			a	a, b	a, b, c	a		a, d		
Papillon, Tu Es Volage	Natural minor; French pronunciation.	a, b, c			a	a, b	a, b, c	a	c	d		
I Saw Three Ships	6/8 meter; consonant and dissonant chords.	a, b, c, e				a, b	a, b, c		c	d		
African Noel	Sight-singing using rhythm; conducting in 2/4 meter; changing meter.	a, b, c, e				a, b	a, b, c	a		a		
The Lord Is My Shepherd	Phrasing; upbeat entrances; sight-singing; tuning intervals.	a, b, c, e				a, b	a, b, c	a, b		a		
Forest Cool, Thou Forest Quiet	Phrasing; intensity; independent singing.	a, b, c, f				a, b	a, b, c, f	a, b, c	c	a		
Keep Your Lamps!	Written accents; syncopation; minor tonality.	a, b, c, f			b	a, b	a, b, c, f	a, b	c	a, b		
Blessed Are the Pure of Heart	Vocal tone color; polyphonic and homophonic texture; German pronunciation.	a, b, c, f				a, b	a, b, c, f	a, b	c	a		
V'amo di Core	Independent singing; round and canon; Italian language.	a, b, c, f				a, b	a, b, c, f	a, b	c	a		
I Will Lay Me Down in Peace	Independent singing; rhythmic interplay; melodic steps and skips; tone painting.	a, b, c, f				a, b	a, b, c, f	a, b	a, c	a		
The Cloths of Heaven	Tuning; melodic leaps; altered tones; staggered breathing.	a, b, c, f				a, b	a, b, c, f	a, b	a, c	a		

SECTION		National Standards									Teacher's Resources	
Selection	Concepts and Skills											
TECAHING LESSONS		1	2	3	4	5	6	7	8	9		
Ave Maria	Tuning; dissonant harmonies; role of the conductor; Latin pronunciation.	a, b, c, d, e, f				a, b, e	a, b, c, f	a, b	c	a, c		
HISTORICAL LESSONS												
Renaissance Period	Understanding the development of choral music during the Renaissance.						a, b, c, e, f	a	a, b, c, d, e	a, c, d, e		
Ave Regina Coelorum	Posture and breathing; rhythm; syncopation; vocal independence; Latin pronunciation.	a, b, c, f		c		a, b	a, b, c	a	c	a, c, d		
Baroque Period	Understanding the development of choral music during the Baroque period.						a, b, c, e, f	a	a, b, c, d, e	a, c, d, e		
Alleluia	Vocal independence; polyphony; melodic imitation; melodic sequences.	a, b, c, e, f				a, b, c	a, b, c, d, f	a		a, d		
Classical Period	Understanding the devel-opment of choral music during the Classical period.						a, b, c, d, e, f	a, b	a, b, c, d, e	a, c, d, e		
Come, Lovely Spring	Steady tempo; 6/8 meter; vocal independence; dynamics and tempo.	a, b, c, f			a	a, b, c, e	a, b, c, e, f	a		a, d		
Romantic Period	Understanding the development of choral music during the Romantic period.						a, b, c, e, f	a, b	a, b, c, d, e	a, c, d, e		
So Wahr Die Sonne Scheinet	Melodic steps and skips; shaping phrases with dynamics.	a, b, c, f				a, b	a, b, c, f	a	c	a, d		
Contemporary Period	Understanding the development of choral music during the Contemporary period.						a, b, c, d, e, f	a, b	a, b, c, d, e	a, c, d, e		
I Hear America Singing	Syncopated rhythm; accurate pitches; exuberant spiritual style.	a, b, c				a, b	a, b, c, e, f	a		a, d		

ADDITIONAL PERFORMANCE SELECTIONS
Over the Rainbow (SATB)
Three Canticles for Treble Voices (SA)
Who Is He in Yonder Stall? (TTBB)
42nd Street (SATB)
Blue Moon (SATB)
Desde el Fondo de Mi Alma (SA)
Georgia on My Mind (SATB)
Love Never Ends (SAT)

The folder icon indicates that Teacher Resources (such as listening maps, blackline masters, etc.) are available to support the learning process.

The transparency projector icon indicates that there are overhead transparencies available to enhance learning.

The headset icon indicates that there are listening selections specifically chosen to aurally illustrate the music of the period.

National Standards High School Grades 9–12

The National Standards for Music Education were developed by the Music Educators National Conference. Reprinted by permission.

MUSIC

The study of music contributes in important ways to the quality of every student's life. Every musical work is a product of its time and place, although some works transcend their original settings and continue to appeal to humans through their timeless and universal attraction. Through singing, playing instruments, and composing, students can express themselves creatively, while a knowledge of notation and performance traditions enables them to learn new music independently throughout their lives. Skills in analysis, evaluation, and synthesis are important because they enable students to recognize and pursue excellence in their musical experiences and to understand and enrich their environment. Because music is an integral part of human history, the ability to listen with understanding is essential if students are to gain a broad cultural and historical perspective. The adult life of every student is enriched by the skills, knowledge, and habits acquired in the study of music.

Every course in music, including performance courses, should provide instruction in creating, performing, listening to, and analyzing music, in addition to focusing on its specific subject matter.

1. **Content Standard:** Singing, alone and with others, a varied repertoire of music

Achievement Standard, Proficient:
Students
- **a.** sing with *expression and *technical accuracy a large and varied repertoire of vocal literature with a *level of difficulty of 4, on a scale of 1 to 6, including some songs performed from memory
- **b.** sing music written in four parts, with and without accompaniment
- **c.** demonstrate well-developed ensemble skills

Achievement Standard, Advanced:
Students
- **d.** sing with expression and technical accuracy a large and varied repertoire of vocal literature with a level of difficulty of 5, on a scale of 1 to 6
- **e.** sing music written in more than four parts
- **f.** sing in small ensembles with one student on a part

2. **Content Standard:** Performing on instruments, alone and with others, a varied repertoire of music

Achievement Standard, Proficient:
Students
- **a.** perform with expression and technical accuracy a large and varied repertoire of instrumental literature with a level of difficulty of 4, on a scale of 1 to 6
- **b.** perform an appropriate part in an ensemble, demonstrating well-developed ensemble skills
- **c.** perform in small ensembles with one student on a part

Achievement Standard, Advanced:
Students
- **d.** perform with expression and technical accuracy a large and varied repertoire of instrumental literature with a level of difficulty of 5, on a scale of 1 to 6

3. **Content Standard:** Improvising melodies, variations, and accompaniments

Achievement Standard, Proficient:
Students
- **a.** improvise stylistically appropriate harmonizing parts
- **b.** improvise rhythmic and melodic variations on given pentatonic melodies and melodies in major and minor keys
- **c.** improvise original melodies over given chord progressions, each in a consistent *style, *meter, and *tonality

Achievement Standard, Advanced:
Students
- **d.** improvise stylistically appropriate harmonizing parts in a variety of styles
- **e.** improvise original melodies in a variety of styles, over given chord progressions, each in a consistent style, meter, and tonality

4. **Content Standard:** Composing and arranging music within specified guidelines

Achievement Standard, Proficient:
Students
- **a.** compose music in several distinct styles, demonstrating creativity in using the *elements of music for expressive effect
- **b.** arrange pieces for voices or instruments other than those for which the pieces were written in ways that preserve or enhance the expressive effect of the music
- **c.** compose and arrange music for voices and various acoustic and electronic instruments, demonstrating knowledge of the ranges and traditional usages of the sound sources

Achievement Standard, Advanced:
Students
- **d.** compose music, demonstrating imagination and technical skill in applying the principles of composition

5. **Content Standard:** Reading and notating music

Achievement Standard, Proficient:
Students
- **a.** demonstrate the ability to read an instrumental or vocal score of up to four *staves by describing how the elements of music are used

Students who participate in a choral or instrumental ensemble or class

- **b.** sightread, accurately and expressively, music with a level of difficulty of 3, on a scale of 1 to 6

Achievement Standard, Advanced:

Students

- **c.** demonstrate the ability to read a full instrumental or vocal score by describing how the elements of music are used and explaining all transpositions and clefs
- **d.** interpret nonstandard notation symbols used by some 20th-century [*sic*] composers

Students who participate in a choral or instrumental ensemble or class

- **e.** sightread, accurately and expressively, music with a level of difficulty of 4, on a scale of 1 to 6

6. Content Standard: Listening to, analyzing, and describing music

Achievement Standard, Proficient:

Students

- **a.** analyze aural examples of a varied repertoire of music, representing diverse *genres and cultures, by describing the uses of elements of music and expressive devices
- **b.** demonstrate extensive knowledge of the technical vocabulary of music
- **c.** identify and explain compositional devices and techniques used to provide unity and variety and tension and release in a musical work and give examples of other works that make similar uses of these devices and techniques

Achievement Standard, Advanced:

Students

- **d.** demonstrate the ability to perceive and remember music events by describing in detail significant events[3] occurring in a given aural example
- **e.** compare ways in which musical materials are used in a given example relative to ways in which they are used in other works of the same genre or style
- **f.** analyze and describe uses of the elements of music in a given work that make it unique, interesting, and expressive

7. Content Standard: Evaluating music and music performances

Achievement Standard, Proficient:

Students

- **a.** evolve specific criteria for making informed, critical evaluations of the quality and effectiveness of performances, compositions, arrangements, and improvisations and apply the criteria in their personal participation in music
- **b.** evaluate a performance, composition, arrangement, or improvisation by comparing it to similar or exemplary models

Achievement Standard, Advanced:

Students

- **c.** evaluate a given musical work in terms of its aesthetic qualities and explaining the musical means it uses to evoke feelings and emotions

8. Content Standard: Understanding relationships between music, the other arts, and disciplines outside the arts

Achievement Standard, Proficient:

Students

- **a.** explain how elements, artistic processes (such as imagination or craftsmanship), and organizational principles (such as unity and variety or repetition and contrast) are used in similar and distinctive ways in the various arts and cite examples
- **b.** compare characteristics of two or more arts within a particular historical period or style and cite examples from various cultures
- **c.** explain ways in which the principles and subject matter of various disciplines outside the arts are interrelated with those of music[4]

Achievement Standard, Advanced:

Students

- **d.** compare the uses of characteristic elements, artistic processes, and organizational principles among the arts in different historical periods and different cultures
- **e.** explain how the roles of creators, performers, and others involved in the production and presentation of the arts are similar to and different from one another in the various arts[5]

9. Content Standard: Understanding music in relation to history and culture

Achievement Standard, Proficient:

Students

- **a.** classify by genre or style and by historical period or culture unfamiliar but representative aural examples of music and explain the reasoning behind their classifications
- **b.** identify sources of American music genres,[6] trace the evolution of those genres, and cite well-known musicians associated with them
- **c.** identify various roles[7] that musicians perform, cite representative individuals who have functioned in each role, and describe their activities and achievements

Achievement Standard, Advanced:

Students

- **d.** identify and explain the stylistic features of a given musical work that serve to define its aesthetic tradition and its historical or cultural context
- **e.** identify and describe music genres or styles that show the influence of two or more cultural traditions, identify the cultural source of each influence, and trace the historical conditions that produced the synthesis of influences

Terms identified by an asterisk (*) are explained further in the glossary of *National Standards for Arts Education*, published by Music Educators National Conference, © 1994.

3. E.g., fugal entrances, chromatic modulations, developmental devices
4. E.g., language arts: compare the ability of music and literature to convey images, feelings, and meanings; physics: describe the physical basis of tone production in string, wind, percussion, and electronic instruments and the human voice and of the transmission and perception of sound
5. E.g., creators: painters, composers, choreographers, playwrights; performers: instrumentalists, singers, dancers, actors; others: conductors, costumers, directors, lighting designers
6. E.g., swing, Broadway musical, blues
7. E.g., entertainer, teacher, transmitter of cultural tradition

INTRODUCTION

Choral Connections is a four-level series designed to build music literacy and promote vocal development for all students and voice categories in grades 6–12. The series is a multi-textbook program supported with print materials and audio listening components. This enables students to develop music skills and conceptual understanding, and provides teachers with a flexible, integrated program.

Choral Connections presents beginning, intermediate, and advanced-level literature for various voice groupings: mixed, treble, and tenor-bass. This comprehensive choral music program includes student texts, teacher's wraparound editions, teacher's resource binders, and optional audio recordings designed to enhance student learning while reducing teacher preparation time.

Choral Connections is a curriculum that provides your students with a meaningful, motivating choral music experience, and will help you and your students make many connections. This choral music program ...

Connects to . . . *the* National Standards

The National Standards are correlated to each lesson for quick-and-easy identification and reference. The performance standards related to singing and reading notations are explicit in each lesson, and by using the extension activities, teachers can connect the musical elements through improvisation and composition. Analysis and evaluation are an active and consistent component of lessons throughout the series. Additional student activities connect the lessons to the other arts, as well as provide a consistent historical and cultural context.

Connects to . . . Skill Development

Through vocal warm-ups and sight-singing exercises, students build vocal skills and master the vocal and sight-reading skills necessary to perform each piece. Rhythmic melodic and articulation skills are developed as needed for expressive interpretation. Students are encouraged to develop listening skills and use their perceptions to improve individual and group performance.

Connects to . . . Performance

Fundamental to a quality choral music program is the student performance of the literature. Student performance provides opportunities for young musicians to demonstrate musical growth, to gain personal satisfaction from achievement, and to experience the joy of music making. To help develop skills, *Choral Connections* provides exercises in warming-up and sight-singing which help prepare students to successfully sing each piece. Conceptual understanding is built throughout the teaching/learning sequence, as the performance is prepared.

Connects to . . . *the* Arts and Other Curriculum Areas

Choral music provides a rich opportunity to connect the musical experience to other art disciplines (dance, visual arts, theatre), and to enhance the learning in other subject areas. It also provides a vehicle to help students gain knowledge and understanding of historical and cultural contexts across the curriculum.

PROGRAM PHILOSOPHY

Responding to Trends in Choral Music Education

Choral Connections is consistent with current educational philosophy that suggests:

- Performance is a product which should be the end result of a sound educational process, building conceptual understanding and skills as the performance is prepared.
- Students are motivated through materials and concepts that are connected to their own lives and interests, and they should be exposed to high-quality, challenging musical literature.
- Students learn best when they are active participants in their learning, and when they clearly understand and help set the goals of the learning process.
- Students understand concepts better when they have background information and skills which allow them to place their learning into a larger context.
- Students need to actively manipulate musical concepts and skills through improvisation and/or composition in order to fully assimilate and understand them.
- Students improve when they receive fair, honest, and meaningful feedback on their successes and failures.
- Students should be encouraged to assess themselves individually and as a group, learning to receive and process constructive criticism, which leads to independent self-correction and decision making.

Scope and Depth of Music Literature

Most students are capable of performing more difficult material than they can sight-sing. Therefore, the literature in *Choral Connections* is drawn from many periods and styles of music. The wide range of composers and publishers ensures variety, and allows for various skills and concepts to be developed as each new piece is encountered. The high standards set in *Choral Connections* provides selections that are inherently powerful and exciting for students. Rather than working with contrived songs to teach skills or concepts, students learn through discovery and interaction with quality literature.

Addressing the National Standards

The National Standards for Arts Education, published in 1994 and reprinted with permission on pages T6–T7, launched a national effort to bring a new vision to arts education for all students. The National Standards provides a framework for achievement in music, with outcomes suggested for grades 4, 8, and 12. *Choral Connections* addresses the National Standards in several ways.

The most obvious and predominant National Standards addressed in choral ensemble are: (1) singing and (5) reading notation. However, good performance requires musical understanding which only occurs when all aspects of musical experience are incorporated. The preparation of vocal performance is enriched and deepened by involvement in all nine of the National Standards.

As you teach with *Choral Connections*, there will be frequent opportunities to deepen or extend student learning through: (2) playing through and creating accompaniments, (3) improvisation, (4) composition and arranging, (6) analyzing, (7) assessing, (8) linking with other arts and other academic disciplines, and (9) understanding historical and cultural contexts. The National Standards identified for each lesson and the Teacher's Wraparound extension activities help you become aware of the National Standards, and the depth of learning that will occur as you implement this choral music program.

Promoting Music Literacy

Choral Connections promotes music literacy. Literacy includes oral and aural aspects of music communication—reading, writing, singing, and listening. Each lesson begins with a *vocal warm-up* during which the student builds vocal skills through singing and listening. The lesson then proceeds to *sight-singing exercise(s)*, emphasizing reading development. These exercises may be rhythmic, melodic, harmonic, or a combination thereof; and emphasize the musical elements which are the objectives of the lesson. The sight-singing exercises lead directly into the *musical selection*. Students are encouraged to sight-sing in every lesson, and are assessed in an increasingly rigorous way as the text progresses from lesson to lesson. Sight-singing is approached as a challenge, and a means to the student's musical independence.

Literacy goes beyond reading pitch and rhythm and extends to the expressive elements of music and appropriate interpretation. Students are frequently asked to explore interpretive aspects of music making, and encouraged to suggest their own ideas for phrasing, dynamics, and so on. Through careful listening and constructive critique of their own work, they will gradually become more discriminating about the quality of performance, and the impact of that performance on the audience.

Including Authentic Student Assessment

The assessment in *Choral Connections* is systematic, objective, and authentic. There is ongoing *informal assessment* by teacher observation throughout the lessons. The text is written as a series of action steps for the student, so there are many opportunities for the director to hear and see the level of accomplishment.

Students will find objectives at the beginning of each lesson, and two types of assessment questions at the end. First, factual questions that check for understanding of concepts and skills are presented. Next, there are questions which require higher-level thinking through analysis, synthesis, and/or evaluation. The questions are always related directly to the lesson objectives, and allow students to demonstrate their understanding. By answering the questions, and demonstrating as suggested, students are involved in *self-assessment*. Many times students are involved in their own assessment, constructing rubrics or critiquing their performance, and identifying their next challenge.

The Teacher's Wraparound Edition includes lesson objectives and each lesson is taught so the concepts and skills are experienced, labeled, practiced, and reinforced, then measured through *formal assessment*. These assessment tasks match the lesson objectives, allowing students to demonstrate understanding of concepts and skills through performance, composition, or writing. Students are frequently required to produce audio or video tapes. This authentic assessment technique keeps testing of rote learning to a minimum, and allows measurement of higher-level application of knowledge and skills. A portfolio can be constructed for individual students, groups, or the whole ensemble; demonstrating growth over time.

Connecting the Arts and Other Curriculum Areas

Lessons in *Choral Connections* integrate many appropriate aspects of musical endeavor into the preparation of a piece. Students compose, improvise, conduct, read, write, sing, play, listen/analyze, and assess on an ongoing basis that builds understanding, as well as high standards. In this way, the many aspects of music are integrated for deeper learning.

As one of the arts, music can be linked to other arts through similarities and differences. Throughout the text, and particularly in the historical section, music is compared and contrasted with other arts to determine aspects of confluence, and the unique features of each art.

As one way of knowing about the world, music can be compared with concepts and skills from other disciplines as seemingly different as science or mathematics. The integrations between music and other disciplines are kept at the conceptual level, to maintain the integrity of both music and the other subjects. For example, mathematical sets of 2, 3, 4, 5, and 6 might be explored as a link to pieces with changing meter; or the text of a piece might become a starting point for exploration of tone painting. In Making Historical Connections, a time line connects music to social studies, and a list of authors for each period provides a link to language and literature.

Providing a Variety of Student Activities

Choral Connections begins with the choral experience, and builds understanding through active participation in a range of activities including singing, playing, improvising, composing, arranging, moving, writing, listening, analyzing, assessing, and connecting to cultures, periods, or disciplines. Lessons are written with the heading "Have students … ," so there is always an emphasis on learning by doing.

Fitting Your Classroom Needs

Effective classrooms are characterized by many features, including student participation, a positive environment, clear sense of purpose, challenging content, high motivation, and a sense of sharing between teacher and student. These probably describe your choral ensemble classroom, and *Choral Connections* will allow you to make the most of these characteristics.

With *Choral Connections*, your students will be clear about purpose and direction, have multiple routes to success, and be involved in their own learning. The lessons will guide you and your students to share in the excitement of music making, and help you to grow together. The lessons are written the way you teach, and allow you to maintain and strengthen your routines, while adding flexibility, variety, and depth.

ORGANIZATION AND FLEXIBILITY

Each *Choral Connections* text is divided into the following sections:

- Preparatory Materials
- Lessons
- Making Historical Connections
- Additional Performance Selections

Preparatory Materials

Preparatory Materials introduce such basic concepts as notes and their values, rests and their values, rhythm patterns, breathing mechanics, solfège and hand signs, frequently found intervals, and pitch. Activities provided in the Teacher's Wraparound Edition suggest ways to use these materials as beginning exercises if your students have little or no music background. If your students are familiar with choral music, these Preparatory Materials can be both a quick review and a convenient reference.

Lessons

The Lessons are designed to be taught over a period of time. Each lesson is developed around a piece of quality authentic music literature. The lesson includes warm-ups, sight-singing, and rhythmic or melodic drills, all of which are directly related to preparation of the piece. Objectives are clearly stated, and a motivational opening activity or discussion is provided. The Teacher's Wraparound Edition outlines a carefully sequenced approach to the piece, with multiple entry points, and clear assessment opportunities to document achievement and growth.

Making Historical Connections

Making Historical Connections provides narrative, listening, and choral experiences for each of the five main historical periods. A *narrative lesson* provides a brief and interesting exposition of the main characteristics of the period, leading from the previous period, and outlining the achievements and new styles that emerged. A time line guides the student to place the musical characteristics into a larger historical and cultural context. The *listening lesson* includes both vocal and instrumental listening selections from the period, with listening maps and teacher wraparound lessons to guide student listening. The third component, a *literature lesson*, rounds out the student experience through a preparation of a piece to be sung from the period.

Additional Performance Selections

Additional Performance Selections provide a range of additional literature featuring popular pieces and multicultural selections that can be used to enhance the repertoire of your choral music performance. Warm-up exercises and suggestions to help you guide your students through the score are given, as well as program tips.

Lesson Objectives

Each lesson has objectives that emphasize and build conceptual understanding and skills across the lessons. The objectives in this book are:

LESSON OBJECTIVES	
LESSON 1 The One Who Stands Alone	• Explore styles of performing. • Identify and perform with a steady beat. • Conduct in 3/4 and 4/4 meter.
LESSON 2 Siyahamba	• Identify and perform syncopated rhythms. • Sing melodic leaps with register consistency. • Sing independently in three homophonic parts.
LESSON 3 The Prayer of Saint Francis	• Recognize and sing legato articulation. • Identify out-of-tune singing, and tune pitches. • Determine effective breathing technique to perform correct phrasing.
LESSON 4 Starlight Lullaby	• Read and sing in major tonalities, changing keys. • Identify characteristics of a major scale. • Identify and sing melody lines that are shared between voice parts.
LESSON 5 God Rest You Merry, Gentlemen	• Identify and perform compositional devices of augmentation and round. • Read and sing in minor tonality. • Recognize characteristics of a minor scale. • Sing in an ensemble with precision.
LESSON 6 Papillon, Tu Es Volage	• Read and sing in natural minor. • Sing using correct French pronunciation.
LESSON 7 I Saw Three Ships	• Identify, read, and clap 6/8 meter. • Distinguish between consonant and dissonant chords. • Sing consonant and dissonant chords.
LESSON 8 African Noel	• Sight-read and sing focusing on rhythm. • Conduct in 2/4 meter. • Perform with a constant beat in changing meter.
LESSON 9 The Lord Is My Shepherd	• Identify and sing phrases using correct phrasing techniques. • Prepare and breathe correctly for upbeat entrances. • Sight-sing in major tonality. • Tune unison/octaves, thirds and sixths.
LESSON 10 Forest Cool, Thou Forest Quiet	• Identify and sing phrases using intensity. • Sing one part independently when four parts are being sung. • Sing using correct German pronunciation
LESSON 11 Keep Your Lamps!	• Identify and perform written accents. • Identify and perform accents created by syncopation. • Identify and sing in minor tonality.
LESSON 12 Blessed Are the Pure of Heart	• Sing using vocal tone colors drawn from mental images of sound. • Identify and perform a full, rich, Romantic period vocal sound. • Sing polyphonic and homophonic textures. • Sing with correct German pronunciation.
LESSON 13 V'amo di Core	• Sing independently. • Identify and sing in a round. • Distinguish between round and canon. • Sing with correct Italian pronunciation.
LESSON 14 I Will Lay Me Down in Peace	• Read and sing independent parts with rhythmic interplay. • Identify and sing melodic steps and skips accurately. • Identify the matching of text and music, or tone painting.

LESSON OBJECTIVES (continued)	
LESSON 15 The Cloths of Heaven	• Tune pitches accurately. • Read and sing melodic leaps with accuracy. • Read and sing altered tones using solfège syllables and hand signs or numbers. • Use staggered breathing.
LESSON 16 Ave Maria	• Tune pitches accurately. • Read and sing in dissonant harmonies accurately. • Follow the conductor. • Sing using correct Latin pronunciation.
RENAISSANCE PERIOD	• Identify specific performance characteristics used in Renaissance choral music as well as musical forms, figures, and developments of the Renaissance period. • Describe the relationship between music and the prevailing social, cultural, and historical events of the Renaissance in Europe. • Describe and compare characteristics of Renaissance art and music.
Ave Regina Coelorum	• Sing with correct posture and good breath support. • Read and perform rhythms including syncopation, eighth-sixteenth combinations, and dotted quarter-eighth note patterns. • Read and sing one part independently when four parts are sung in polyphonic texture. • Sing using correct Latin pronunciation.
BAROQUE PERIOD	• Identify musical forms, figures, developments of the Baroque period and specific performance characteristics of Baroque choral music. • Describe the relationship between music and the prevailing social, cultural, and historical events and ideas occurring in Europe during the Baroque period. • Describe and compare characteristics of Baroque art and music.
Alleluia	• Read and sing one part when five parts are sung in polyphony. • Identify and sing melodic imitation. • Identify and perform melodic sequences.
CLASSICAL PERIOD	• Identify musical forms, figures, and developments of the Classical period and specific performance characteristics to be used in Classical choral music. • Describe the relationship between music and the prevailing social, cultural, and historical events and ideas occurring in Europe during the Classical period. • Describe and compare characteristics of Classical art and music.
Come, Lovely Spring	• Maintain a steady tempo. • Read and sing accurately in 6/8 meter. • Sing one part independently when four parts are being sung. • Identify and interpret Classical dynamic and tempo markings.
ROMANTIC PERIOD	• Identify musical forms, figures, and developments of the Romantic period and specific performance characteristics to be used in Romantic choral music. • Describe the relationship between music and the prevailing social, cultural, and historical events and ideas occurring in Europe during the Romantic period. • Describe and compare characteristics of Romantic art and music.
So Wahr Die Sonne Scheinet	• Sing melodic steps and skips accurately. • Use dynamics to shape phrases. • Sing with correct German pronunciation.
CONTEMPORARY PERIOD	• Identify musical forms, figures, and developments of the Contemporary period and specific performance characteristics to be used in Contemporary choral music. • Describe the relationship between music and the prevailing social, cultural, and historical events and ideas during the Contemporary period. • Describe and compare characteristics of Contemporary art and music.
I Hear America Singing	• Identify and perform syncopated rhythms. • Sing pitches accurately. • Sing in exuberant spiritual style.

Lessons

The lessons, through which students systematically build musical skills and conceptual understanding, comprise the majority of the text. These lessons are structured as follows:

- **FOCUS** . . . tells the student the main concepts and skills addressed in the lesson. By having only a few main goals, students and teacher will keep focused on these objectives as work progresses.

- **SIGHT-SINGING EXERCISES** . . . build rhythmic, melodic, and expressive sight-singing skills through exercises that are directly related to some aspect of the upcoming musical selection. Through sight-singing practice every day, students gain confidence and skills to become independent readers.

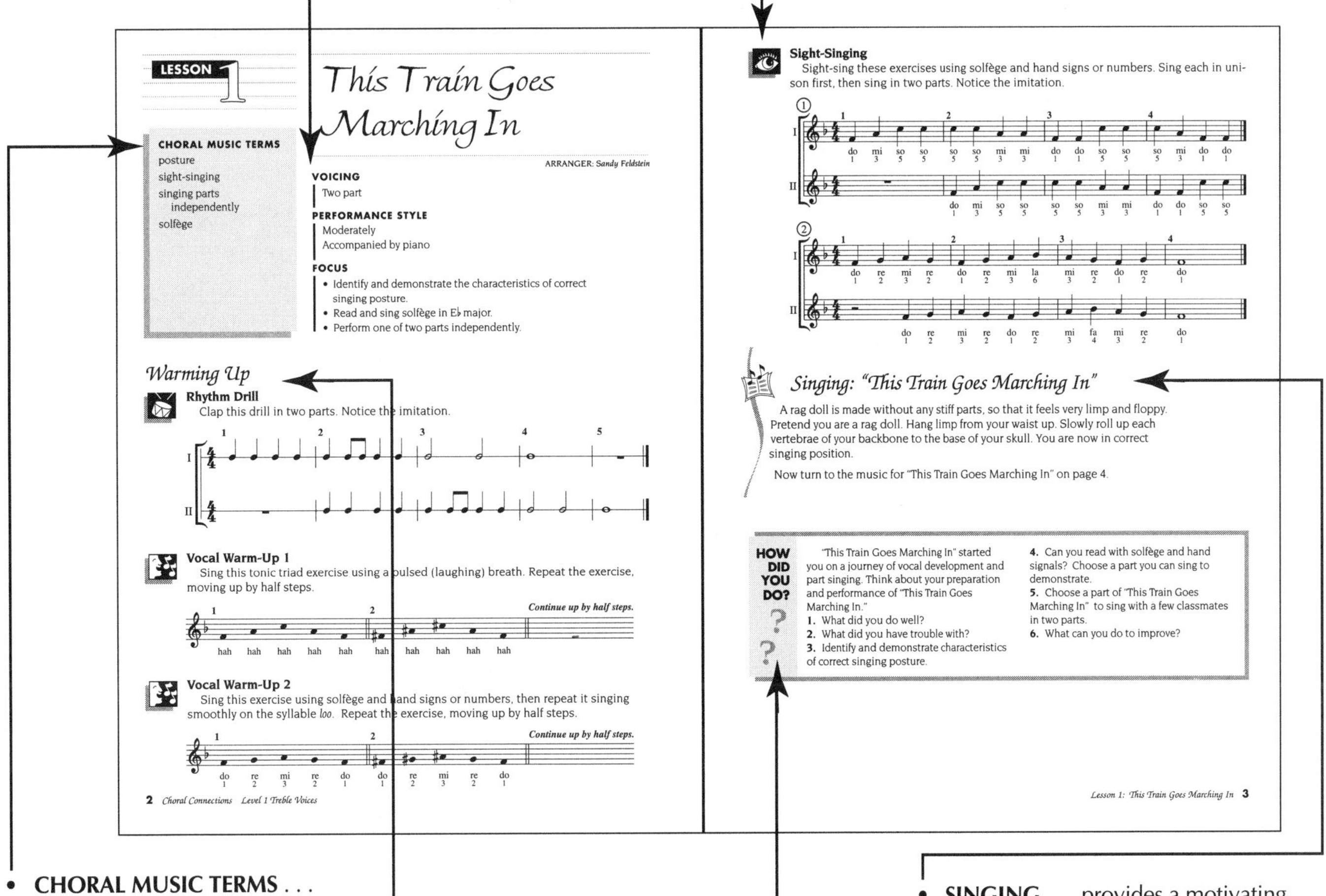

LESSON 1

This Train Goes Marching In

CHORAL MUSIC TERMS
posture
sight-singing
singing parts independently
solfège

ARRANGER: Sandy Feldstein

VOICING
Two part

PERFORMANCE STYLE
Moderately
Accompanied by piano

FOCUS
- Identify and demonstrate the characteristics of correct singing posture.
- Read and sing solfège in E♭ major.
- Perform one of two parts independently.

Warming Up

Rhythm Drill
Clap this drill in two parts. Notice the imitation.

Vocal Warm-Up 1
Sing this tonic triad exercise using a pulsed (laughing) breath. Repeat the exercise, moving up by half steps.

Continue up by half steps.

Vocal Warm-Up 2
Sing this exercise using solfège and hand signs or numbers, then repeat it singing smoothly on the syllable *loo*. Repeat the exercise, moving up by half steps.

Continue up by half steps.

2 *Choral Connections Level 1 Treble Voices*

Sight-Singing
Sight-sing these exercises using solfège and hand signs or numbers. Sing each in unison first, then sing in two parts. Notice the imitation.

Singing: "This Train Goes Marching In"

A rag doll is made without any stiff parts, so that it feels very limp and floppy. Pretend you are a rag doll. Hang limp from your waist up. Slowly roll up each vertebrae of your backbone to the base of your skull. You are now in correct singing position.

Now turn to the music for "This Train Goes Marching In" on page 4.

HOW DID YOU DO?

"This Train Goes Marching In" started you on a journey of vocal development and part singing. Think about your preparation and performance of "This Train Goes Marching In."

1. What did you do well?
2. What did you have trouble with?
3. Identify and demonstrate characteristics of correct singing posture.
4. Can you read with solfège and hand signals? Choose a part you can sing to demonstrate.
5. Choose a part of "This Train Goes Marching In" to sing with a few classmates in two parts.
6. What can you do to improve?

Lesson 1: This Train Goes Marching In 3

- **CHORAL MUSIC TERMS** . . . give the students an opportunity to build a musical vocabulary essential for clarity of thought in communicating about music to others.

- **SINGING** . . . provides a motivating introduction to the piece of music, related to the student's perspective, which begins with a familiar idea and asks the student to think about or explore some concept or skill. Through interest and active participation, the student is then led logically into the piece.

- **WARM-UP EXERCISES** . . . allow the students to warm-up their bodies, voices, and minds at the beginning of every class, while immediately exploring the main rhythmic, melodic, and skill issues that will arise in preparing the piece. These exercises are designed to sequentially build skills.

- **STUDENT SELF-ASSESSMENT—HOW DID YOU DO?** . . . gives the student ways to assess accomplishment, growth, and needs, for both self and group. Beginning with recall, comprehension and application questions, the final questions ask for analysis, synthesis, and evaluation, guiding the student to higher-level thinking and the ability to self-assess.

Making Historical Connections

The Historical section of the text provides a survey of Western music history through exploration of the culture and music of the five overarching periods: Renaissance, Baroque, Classical, Romantic, and Contemporary. Each period is addressed in the following ways:

- **Historical Narrative Lesson** . . . provides a brief, student-oriented historical context of the period through visual art, architecture, historical events, musical developments, artistic characteristics, musical personalities, and listening selections. Students are encouraged to imagine this time period as if they were living in it, and experience the music from the perspective of the period.
- **Historical Listening Lesson** . . . provides one choral and one instrumental listening selection, to give students an aural experience with the styles, sounds and forms of the period. Listening maps are provided in the Teacher's Resource Binder so the student can follow along as a visual guide to listening.
- **Historical Literature Lesson** . . . is paired with the narrative lesson for each period, and provides the opportunity to perform a piece with appropriate characteristics and performance style. The selected materials reflect the period, and provide a concrete example of those characteristics introduced in the previous narrative.

Additional Performance Selections

Each book provides additional performance selections which meet the various needs of the ensemble and director. Each selection is accompanied by a specifically designed warm-up to build appropriate vocal skills.

- **Patriotic Selections** . . . provide excellent openers and closers for concerts, and are particularly useful when performing at patriotic celebrations.
- **Holiday Selections** . . . acknowledge the need for performance literature appropriate for winter holidays and during the spring season.
- **Multicultural selections** . . . provide an opportunity for performance of music that has different criteria than Western art music, allowing exploration of different languages, vocal tone color, styles, movement, and cultural characteristics.
- **Proven Audience-Pleaser Selections** . . . allow you to round out your programs with appropriate rousing or sentimental pieces that provide a change of pace or variety.

Glossary

The glossary provides brief, accurate definitions of musical terms used in the text.

TEACHER'S WRAPAROUND EDITION

National Standards Connections

Choral Connections affords multiple opportunities to address the National Standards. Correlations between lesson content, extension activities, and bottom-page activities are listed to show the relationship between lesson activities and the standards.

Teaching Sequence

Each lesson is organized to follow a logical progression from warm-ups through assessment, while providing maximum flexibility of use for your individual situation. Each lesson is linked to one musical selection, and provides learning opportunities based on the inherent concepts and skills required to understand and perform the piece. The lessons of the Teacher Wraparound Edition are structured as follows:

- **Focus** . . . gives the teacher a brief overview of concepts and skills which form the content of the objectives and assessments in the lesson.
- **Objectives** . . . provides concrete, measurable objectives allowing an interconnected approach to lesson segments. Each objective will be assessed in three ways during the lesson.
- **Choral Music Terms** . . . identifies the terms used during the lesson to build understanding and skills.
- **Warming Up** . . . includes rhythm and vocal warm-up exercises, as well as sight-singing exercises. The vocal warm-ups are designed to sequentially develop vocal skills, and start each class immediately with singing. The sight-singing exercises are designed to systematically build sight-singing skills, and lead directly into the upcoming piece. The purpose of each exercise is stated clearly for the teacher and student at the beginning of the lesson. These exercises may all be done before the piece is introduced, or they may be presented cumulatively, one each day, and concurrent with developing understanding of the piece.
- **Singing** . . . provides motivation and an entree to the piece of literature. Many different approaches are utilized, but they all draw the student into the piece through active learning and thinking.

- **Suggested Teaching Sequence** . . . returns to each warm-up activity and reviews, then guides you directly from the warm-up into the piece of literature. In this way, you have multiple entry points, so your approach is new and different each day the ensemble works on the piece. Specific rehearsal techniques, based on sight-singing, sectional work, and analysis of difficulties build skills and conceptual understanding as the performance is refined day after day. Each lesson includes recommended steps for organizing students into small groups by voice part to sight-sing the song separately before coming together in full ensemble to perform the selection.
- **Assessment** . . . provides Informal Assessment, Student Self-Assessment, and Individual Performance Assessment. There is appropriate assessment for each lesson objective.

Assessment

Informal Assessment is accomplished through teacher observation during the lesson. Each objective is observable, and the text indicates the checkpoint for teacher assessment.

Student Self-Assessment is accomplished through oral or written response to questions in the Student Text.

Individual Performance Assessment requires the student to demonstrate a skill or understanding through individual assessment. This is frequently done through audio or video taping, creation of rubrics to assess the quality of the performance, or a written exercise to demonstrate understanding. Individual Performance Assessment can be done by the teacher, student, peers, or a combination thereof. The tapes may be compiled into a portfolio which shows growth and development of understanding.

Extensions and Bottom-Page Activities

Extensions and bottom-page activities in each lesson afford a plethora of background information, teaching strategies, and enrichment opportunities.

- **Enrichment activities** in the side columns provide opportunities for movement, improvisation, composition, and analysis based on lesson and selection content.
- **Vocal development strategies** give detailed information about specific techniques that facilitate vocal production, style, and negotiation of difficult passages within the piece.
- **Music literacy strategies** help students expand their ability to read and analyze music.
- **Teaching strategies** are available to reinforce concepts or skills that may be difficult for students, or elaborate on classroom management techniques suggested within the lesson.
- **More about** boxes provide background historical, cultural, and/or biographical information to give deeper understanding of the piece.
- **Curriculum connections** provide strategies to help students build bridges between music and other disciplines.

Performance Tips

In the Additional Performance Selection section, you are provided with performance suggestions that identify specific strategies that have worked successfully for choral music teachers, and potential "hot spots" you may need to address. Each selection is accompanied by a suggested program, including selections from the book. These recommendations should be extremely helpful for the beginning choral director, and provide many interesting alternatives for the experienced conductor.

TEACHER'S RESOURCE BINDER

The Teacher's Resource Binder contains teaching materials designed to reduce teacher preparation time and maximize students' learning. The following categories are provided to assist with meeting the individual needs and interests of your students.

Skill Masters. The *Skill Masters* provide sequential musical concepts that can be used to review and reinforce musical concepts in the areas of rhythm and pitch, music literacy, vocal development, and pronunciation guides.

Blackline Masters. The *Blackline Masters* are designed to enhance the concepts presented in the student text lessons.

Assessment. Assessment activities provide performance assessment criteria, rubrics, and other activity pages to help teachers with individual and group assessment.

Fine Art Transparencies. Full color overhead transparencies of the visual art pieces that introduce each of the historical sections are provided.

Listening Maps. Blackline masters of listening maps are provided and feature choral and instrumental selections. These help reinforce learning about the five major historical periods. Teachers may wish to make a transparency of the blackline master and have students follow along as the teacher points to the overhead transparency.

FEATURED LISTENING SELECTIONS

The Listening Program provides rich resources of sound to reinforce learning about the five major Western historical periods. Two selections for each period, one choral and the other instrumental, are accompanied by listening maps. At first, students listen as observers, watching the teacher guide their listening with a transparency of the map on the overhead projector. In the next listening, they then follow their own copies of the map, showing their ability to hear specific musical features. The Teacher's Wraparound Edition provides the CD number and track at point of use for each selection. Many more historical period examples are included on the CD sets than are referenced in the text. You're invited to use them to supplement and extend your lessons, or to have students create their own maps to creatively demonstrate understanding of musical and/or historical elements.

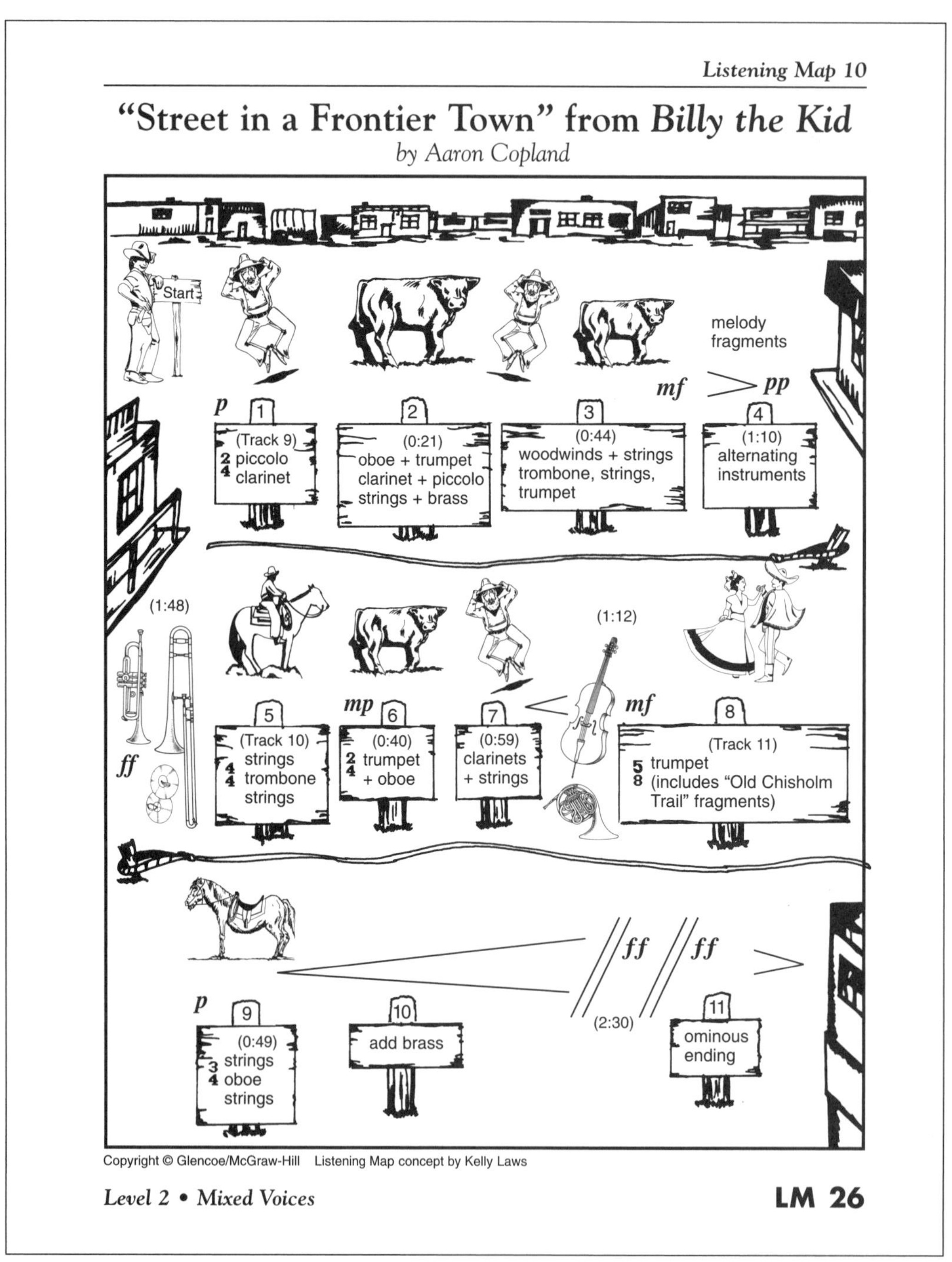

Choral Connections

Teacher's Wraparound Edition

LEVEL 4

MIXED VOICES

GLENCOE

McGraw-Hill

New York, New York
Columbus, Ohio
Mission Hills, California
Peoria, Illinois

Cover Photos: Peter Samels Photography

Glencoe/McGraw-Hill

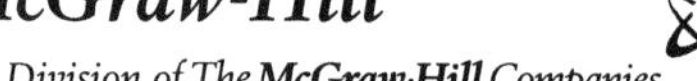

A Division of The **McGraw-Hill** Companies

Send all inquiries to:
Glencoe/McGraw-Hill
15319 Chatsworth Street
Mission Hills, California 91345

ISBN 0-02-655535-2 (Student's Edition)
ISBN 0-02-655561-1 (Teacher's Wraparound Edition)

Printed in the United States of America.

2 3 4 5 6 7 8 9 MAL 02 01 00 99 98 97

Meet the Authors

Senior Author
Mollie G. Tower—As Coordinator of Choral and General Music of the Austin Independent School District, Mollie Tower was recently nominated as "Administrator of the Year." She is very active in international, national, regional, and state music educators' organizations. Ms. Tower was contributing author, consultant, and reviewer for the elementary programs *Share the Music* and *Music and You*. Senior author of *Música para todos, Primary and Intermediate Dual Language Handbooks for Music Teachers*, she has also written and consulted for many other publications. A longtime advocate of music education, Mollie is a popular clinician who conducts workshops across the country.

Milton Pullen
Professor of Music and Director of Choirs
After attending Texas A & I University where he acquired a Bachelor of Music Education in voice, Milton Pullen attended the University of Houston, where in 1976 he received a Master of Music in conducting. He has taught at the middle and high school levels for 24 years and for the last seven years has taught at the university level. He is now Professor of Music and Director of Choirs at Pepperdine University in Malibu, California.

Ken Steele
Director of Choral Activities
Ken Steele has taught secondary choral music for 22 years, having directed choirs at the middle school and high school levels. He received the Bachelor of Music degree from Stetson University in DeLand, Florida, and went on to the University of Texas in Austin to earn the Master of Music in Choral Literature and Conducting in 1971, studying with Dr. Morris J. Beachy. A member of Texas Music Educators Association, Texas Choral Directors Association, Texas Music Adjudicators Association, and a lifetime member of the American Choral Directors Association, he is currently the director of choral activities at L. C. Anderson High School, in Austin, Texas.

Gloria J. Stephens
Director of Choral Activities
With 23 years of teaching experience, Gloria Stephens is presently the Director of Choral Activities at Ryan High School in Denton, Texas. Mrs. Stephens earned her Bachelor of Music Education and Master of Music Education degrees from the University of North Texas in Denton. She has also done post-graduate work at Texas Woman's University in Denton, the University of Texas at Arlington, and Westminster Choir College in Princeton, New Jersey.

Consulting Author

Dr. Susan Snyder has taught all levels of vocal music over the last 25 years. She holds a B.S. in music education from the University of Connecticut and an M.A. from Montclair State College. She holds a Ph.D. in curriculum and instruction from the University of Connecticut and advanced professional certificates from Memphis State University and the University of Minnesota. Teaching at Hunter College and City University of New York, Dr. Snyder was coordinating author of the elementary music program, *Share the Music*, and a consultant on *Music and You*. She has published many articles on music education and integrated curriculum and is an active clinician, master teacher, and guest conductor.

Consultants

Choral Music
Stephan P. Barnicle
Choir Director
Simsbury High School
Simsbury, Connecticut

Vocal Development, Music Literacy
Katherine Saltzer Hickey, D.M.A.
University of California at Los Angeles
Los Angeles, California
Choir Director
Pacific Chorale Children's Choruses
Irvine, California

Music History
Dr. Kermit Peters
University of Nebraska at Omaha
College of Fine Arts
Department of Music
Omaha, Nebraska

Contributors/Teacher Reviewers

Dr. Anton Armstrong
Music Director and Conductor, St. Olaf Choir
St. Olaf College
Northfield, Minnesota

Jeanne Julseth-Heinrich
Choir Director
James Madison Middle School
Appleton, Wisconsin

Caroline Lyon
Ethnomusicologist
University of Texas at Austin
Austin, Texas

Caroline Minear
Supervisor
Orange County School District
Orlando, Florida

Judy Roberts
Choir Director
Central Junior High School
Moore, Oklahoma

Dr. A. Byron Smith
Choir Director
Lincoln High School
Tallahassee, Florida

Table of Contents

PREPARATORY MATERIAL vii

LESSONS

1 The One Who Stands Alone *Joseph M. Martin* 2
2 Siyahamba *Arranger Donald Moore* 13
3 The Prayer of Saint Francis *René Clausen* 23
4 Starlight Lullaby *Philip Lane* 36
5 God Rest You Merry, Gentlemen *Arranger James Neal Koudelka* 45
6 Papillon, Tu Es Volage *Arranger Jonathan Thompson* 54
7 I Saw Three Ships *Arranger Edwin Fissinger* 62
8 African Noel *Arranger André J. Thomas* 71
9 The Lord Is My Shepherd *Allen Pote* 84
10 Forest Cool, Thou Forest Quiet *Johannes Brahms* 96
11 Keep Your Lamps! *André J. Thomas* 105
12 Blessed Are the Pure of Heart *Woldemar Voullaire* 111
13 V'amo di Core *Wolfgang Amadeus Mozart* 123
14 I Will Lay Me Down in Peace *Healey Willan* 127
15 The Cloths of Heaven *Adolphus Hailstork* 132
16 Ave Maria *Franz Biebl* 140

MAKING HISTORICAL CONNECTIONS

Renaissance Period 148
Renaissance Connections 154
Ave Regina Coelorum *Orlande de Lassus* 156

Baroque Period 164
Baroque Connections 168
Alleluia *Giovanni Battista Pergolesi* 170

Classical Period 178

Classical Connections 182

Come, Lovely Spring *Franz Joseph Haydn* 184

Romantic Period 194

Romantic Connections 198

So Wahr Die Sonne Scheinet *Robert Schumann* 200

Contemporary Period 210

Contemporary Connections 216

I Hear America Singing *André J. Thomas* 218

ADDITIONAL PERFORMANCE SELECTIONS

Over the Rainbow (SATB) *Harold Arlen*

Warm-Up 232

Literature 236

Three Canticles for Treble Voices (SSAA) *Paul Liljestrand*

Warm-Up 232

Literature 241

Who Is He in Yonder Stall? (TTBB) *Robert H. Young*

Warm-Up 233

Literature 248

42nd Street (SATB) *Harry Warren*

Warm-Up 233

Literature 254

Blue Moon (SATB) *Richard Rodgers*

Warm-Up 234

Literature 265

Desde el Fondo de Mi Alma (SSA) *Domingo Santa Cruz*

Warm-Up 234

Literature 273

Georgia on My Mind (SATB) *Hoagy Carmichael*

Warm-Up 235

Literature 276

Love Never Ends (SATB) *Elizabeth Volk*

Warm-Up 235

Literature 283

CHORAL MUSIC TERMS 291

Preparatory Material

Using the Preparatory Material

The preparatory material found on these pages is designed to build a basic rhythmic, melodic, and sight-singing vocabulary. By working through the challenges, students will build the skills required for successful work in the upcoming lessons.

- If your students have little or no music background, take a day or two to introduce this musical vocabulary. Have them sing a few rounds to get them familiar with basic conducting, breathing, and working together.
- If your students have a rich music background, and have participated in a solid elementary and/or middle-school music program, review these challenges quickly, stopping to answer questions and clarify any misunderstandings. Then proceed to Lesson 1. Refer back to these pages during lessons when necessary.

Notes and Rests

The alignment of notes and rests on this page show the relationship between notes or rests of different value. Encourage students to learn these concepts early.

Notes and Note Values

Rests and Rest Values

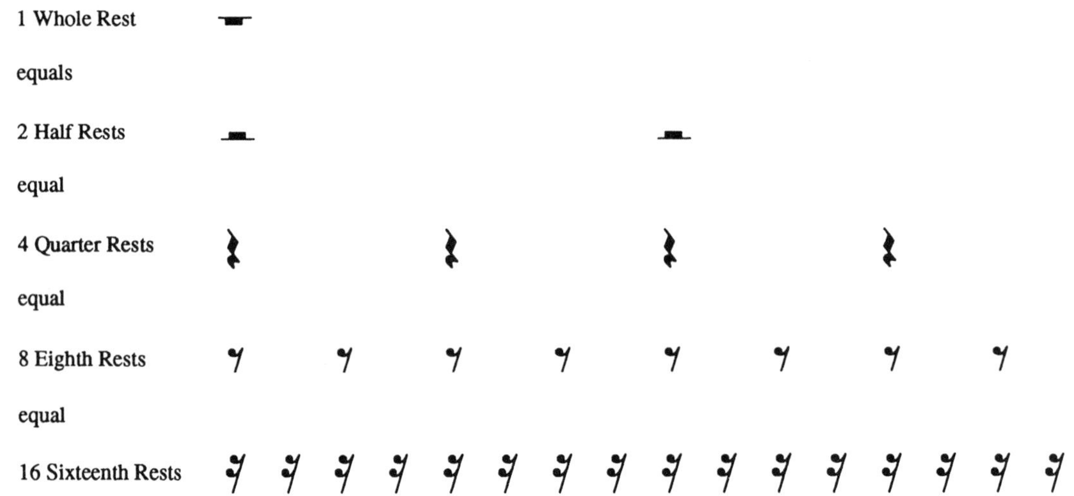

viii

Rhythm Challenge in 4/4 Meter

Directions: Accurately count and/or perform the following rhythms without stopping!

Rhythm Challenges

When presenting a rhythm challenge, allow students the chance to read through the whole challenge first, answering any questions, and helping them resolve any concerns. Then offer students the opportunity to perform the challenge without pressure.

At the beginning of the year, too much pressure for those with little or no previous experience might discourage them for the rest of their lives! Some techniques to consider are:

- Have students design a chart in the form of a graph with approximately 15 columns that represent the same number of trials. One or more trials can be attempted at the beginning of each class. After each trial, each student should record the number of the measure where the first mistake was made. After fifteen trials, most students should show, by a line graph, considerable improvement.
- Encourage students to design their own method of tracking their improvement. Students with access to computer programs might take it upon themselves to create a personalized chart for individuals or one for the entire class.

More Rhythm Challenges

To increase students' skill at reading rhythms, have them:

- Speak or clap each rhythm challenge as a group or in small ensembles, isolating and practicing measures and phrases that pose difficulty.
- Practice in small groups for a predetermined amount of time, such as 5 minutes. At the end of that time, assess rhythmic reading in one of the following ways: each student speaks and claps the pattern; each group speaks and claps the pattern; the whole class speaks and claps the pattern.
- Students should keep a record of their progress by recording the first measure where an error is made on each successive attempt.

Rhythm Challenge in 6/8 Meter

Directions: Accurately count and/or perform the following rhythms without stopping!

x

Breathing Mechanics

Singing well requires good breath control. Support for singing comes from correct use of the breathing mechanism. Deep, controlled breathing is needed to sustain long phrases in one breath. Also, correct breathing will support higher, more difficult passages.

Posture

Posture is very important in breath support.

- Keep your body relaxed, but your backbone straight.
- To stretch your back: Bend over and slowly roll your back upward until you are standing straight again. Do this several times.
- Hold your rib cage high, but keep your shoulders low and relaxed.
- Facing front, keep your head level. Imagine you are suspended by a string attached to the very top of your head.
- When you stand, keep your knees relaxed, but do not "lock" them by pushing them all the way back. Keep your feet slightly apart.
- When you sit, keep both feet flat on the floor and sit forward on the edge of your chair.

Inhaling

- Expand the lungs out and down, pushing the diaphragm muscle down.
- Inhale silently without gasping or making any other noise.
- Keep the throat and neck muscles relaxed to maintain a feeling of space in the back of the mouth (picture a reverse megaphone).
- Imagine taking a cool sip of air through a straw, lifting the soft palate.
- Expand your entire waistline, keeping the chest high, and the shoulders relaxed, feeling the breath low in the body.

Breath Control

To help you develop breath control do the following:

- Hold one finger about six inches from your mouth imagining that your finger is a birthday candle. Now blow out a steady stream of air to blow out the flame of the candle.

Summary

STANDING
Feet slightly apart, one slightly forward
Knees relaxed
Backbone straight
Rib cage high
Shoulders low
Head level

SITTING
Feet on the floor
Sit on edge of chair
Backbone straight
Rib cage high
Shoulders low
Head level

Breathing Mechanics

Remind students that vocal tone, resonance, and intonation are affected by posture and breathing. Basic singing posture is a relaxed, but firm, body stance. Have students read through the text on this page and practice correct posture and breathing.

Diaphragmatic Breathing

Have students:

- Feel the sensation of muscle expansion by placing thumbs above the small of the back with fingers pressing the top of the hips. Sip a long, deep breath and feel the action of the muscles.
- Feel the action of the diaphragm muscle by pressing the fingertips of both hands into the midsection of the torso just below the rib cage. Take a startled, quick surprise breath and feel the action of the muscle. Ask: How did the diaphragm react?
- Feel the diaphragm muscle expand outward as they sip a long, cool breath.
- Pant like a dog or bark like a dog (use *arf* and *woof*). Feel the action of the diaphragm.
- Use unvoiced consonants, such as *sh, f, p, t,* and *k* in different rhythms and tempos to create the diaphragmatic action.

What is Signing?

Signing in music describes the use of hand signals to represent relative sounds of pitches. The signs were used by Reverend John Curwen from a method developed by Sarah Glover of Norwich in the nineteenth century. The *do* is movable and was intended to teach beginners to sing accurate pitches. The system has been adopted by the Kodaly approach and Tonika-Do system in Germany.

Intervals

Help students remember intervals by relating them to the first two pitches of the following familiar songs:

Major 2nd —"Frère Jacques"
Major 3rd—"Taps"
Perfect 4th—"Here Comes the Bride"
Perfect 5th—"Twinkle, Twinkle Little Star"
Major 6th—"My Bonny Lies Over the Ocean"
Octave—"Somewhere, Over the Rainbow"

Have students:

- Challenge one another in pairs, one singing an interval, the other telling what interval was heard.
- Check any disagreements with another pair.
- Take turns singing intervals.

Composing with Frequently Found Intervals

Have students:

- Compose an exercise of eight measures, using at least three different intervals shown on this page.
- Notate their melodies.
- Describe their piece and perform it to a classmate.

Solfège and Hand Signs

Solfège is a system designed to match notes on the staff with specific interval relationships. Hand signs provide additional reinforcement of the pitch relationships.

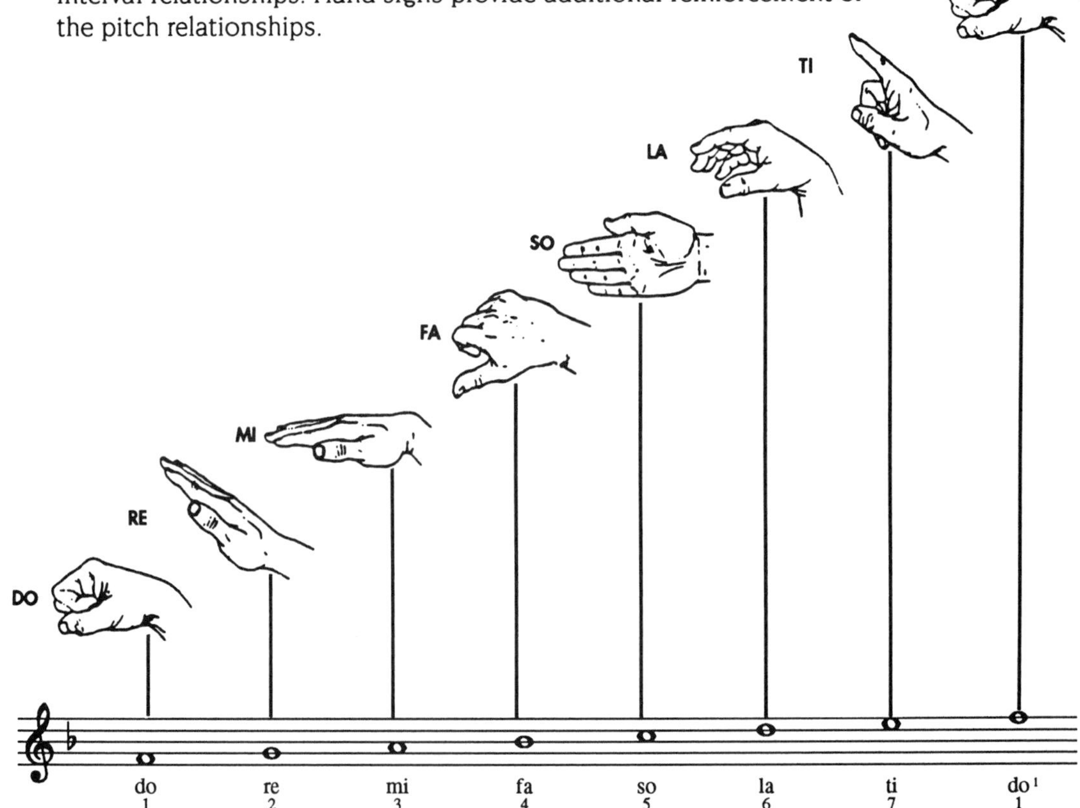

Frequently Found Intervals

An interval is the distance between two notes.

xii

Pitch Challenge

Directions: Accurately sing each measure on solfège using hand signs and without stopping! During the measure of rest, look ahead to the next challenge.

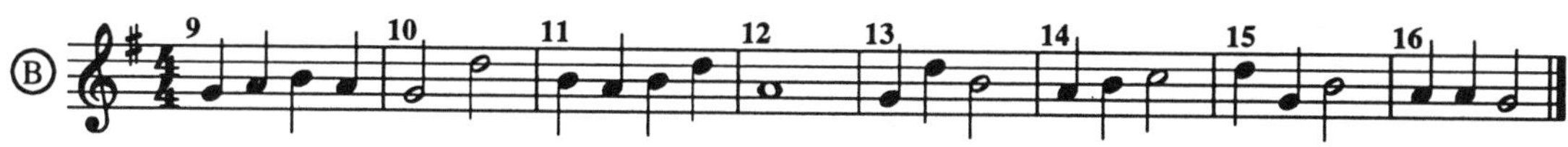

Testing Pitch Accuracy

The best way to get better at pitch accuracy is to get feedback about which pitches are sung flat or sharp. The following activity is excellent for both the singer and listener. However, use confident volunteers only, as students will be critiqued openly in front of peers.

Have students:

- Listen to volunteers who are willing to have their pitch accuracy assessed as they perform the Pitch Challenge on this page with a partner.
- If the pitch is accurate, listeners should point thumbs to the side; if sharp, point thumbs up; and if flat, point thumbs down.
- Repeat this activity with as many volunteers as time permits.

Lessons

LESSON 1

The One Who Stands Alone

COMPOSER: Joseph Martin
TEXT: J. Paul Williams and Joseph Martin

Focus

OVERVIEW
Beat; style; 3/4 and 4/4 meter.

OBJECTIVES
After completing this lesson, students will be able to:
- Explore styles of performing.
- Identify and perform with a steady beat.
- Conduct in 3/4 and 4/4 meter.

CHORAL MUSIC TERMS
Define the Choral Music Terms for students, giving pronunciation, and answering any questions that may arise.

Warming Up

Vocal Warm-Up
This Vocal Warm-Up is designed to prepare students to:
- Sing using solfège and hand signs or numbers.
- Sing together, feeling a common beat.
- Sing in different styles, including a heavy, strong beat.
- Sing vowel sounds.

Have students:
- Read through the Vocal Warm-Up directions.
- Sing, following your demonstration.

LESSON 1

The One Who Stands Alone

CHORAL MUSIC TERMS
4/4 meter
steady beat
style
3/4 meter

COMPOSER: *Joseph Martin*
TEXT: J. *Paul Williams and Joseph Martin*

VOICING
SATB

PERFORMANCE STYLE
With reverence, power, and great expression
Accompanied by piano

FOCUS
- Explore styles of performing.
- Identify and perform with a steady beat.
- Conduct in 3/4 and 4/4 meter.

Warming Up

Vocal Warm-Up
Sing this exercise using *vah*, *veh*, *vee*, *voh*, or *voo*. Move up or down by half steps on the repeats. Sing the exercise using different styles, for example: light, heavy, marked, staccato, legato, and majestically (maestoso).

Sight-Singing
With a partner, point to one note at a time as your partner sings the correct pitch. Help each other until you feel the pitches naturally. Begin with stepwise intervals, then try larger intervals as confidence builds. Now switch roles so both of you get to practice.

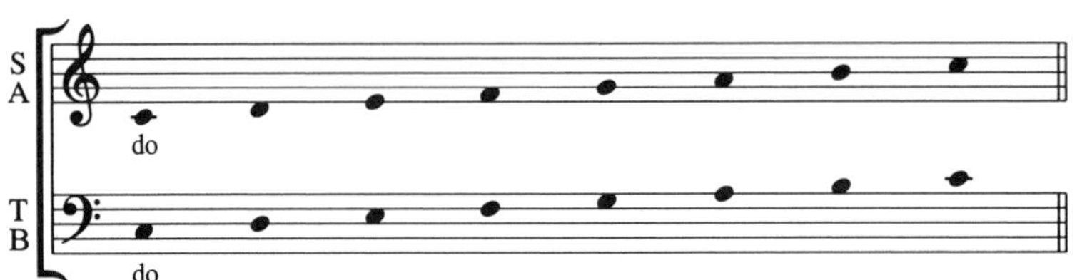

Sight-sing this exercise using solfège and hand signs or numbers. Notice the meter changes. Conduct in 3/4 and 4/4 as you sing.

TEACHER'S RESOURCE BINDER
Blackline Master 1, *Conducting Patterns in 3/4* and *4/4*, page 77

National Standards
This lesson addresses:
1. Singing, alone and with others, a varied repertoire of music. **(a, b, c, e)**
5. Reading and notating music. **(a, b)**
6. Listening to, analyzing, and describing music. **(b)**
7. Evaluating music and music performances. **(a)**
9. Understanding music in relation to history and culture. **(c)**

Singing: "The One Who Stands Alone"

The beat is not a sound, but a feeling.

You feel your heart beat, or the beat of a march. Beats are usually felt in sets. Here are the conducting patterns for beats in sets of 3 and 4. Practice these patterns so you can conduct "The One Who Stands Alone."

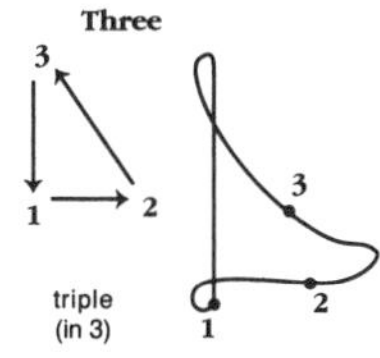

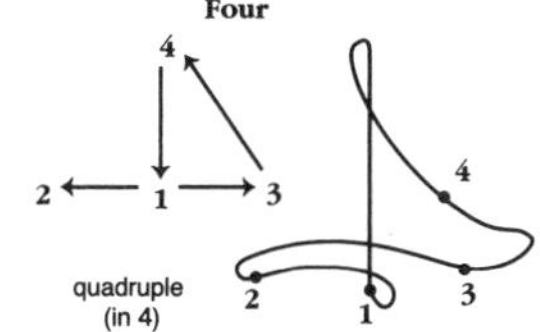

Now turn to the music for "The One Who Stands Alone" on page 4.

HOW DID YOU DO? ?

You've made a steady start with beats in sets of 3 and 4. Think about your preparation and performance of "The One Who Stands Alone."

1. Describe how the beats are organized in "The One Who Stands Alone."

2. Describe the style you used in "The One Who Stands Alone."

3. Sing the Sight-Singing exercise, conducting as you sing to show beats in sets of 3 and 4.

4. Do you think the composer made good use of beat, meter, and style in "The One Who Stands Alone"? Support your opinion with facts from the piece.

Sight-Singing

This Sight-Singing exercise is designed to prepare students to:

- Sight-sing pitches in a major key using solfège and hand signs or numbers.
- Sing together, feeling a common beat.
- Read in treble and bass clefs.
- Read, sing, and conduct in 3/4 and 4/4 meter.

Have students:

- Read through the Sight-Singing exercise directions.
- Read through each voice part rhythmically, using rhythm syllables.
- Sight-sing through each part separately using solfège and hand signs or numbers.
- Sing all parts together.

Singing: "The One Who Stands Alone"

Conduct beats in sets of 3 and 4.

Have students:

- Read the text on page 3.
- Distinguish clearly between the beat that is felt, and playing a sound on or with the beat.
- Learn the conducting patterns for beats in sets of 3 and 4, using Blackline Master 1, *Conducting Patterns in 3/4* and *4/4.*
- Look at the Sight-Singing exercise to decide when each pattern will be conducted, and then sing and conduct.
- Look at the notation for "The One Who Stands Alone," finding the meter signatures for 3/4 (measures 1 and 30) and 4/4 (measures 23 and 51).

Suggested Teaching Sequence

1. Review Vocal Warm-Up.
Explore different styles. Sing with reverence, power, and great expression.
Have students:

- Review the Vocal Warm-Up on page 2.
- Use a different vowel each time the exercise is done.
- Explore different styles, including light, heavy, marked, staccato, legato, and maestoso.
- Look at "The One Who Stands Alone" to determine the style intended by the composer. (with reverence, power, and great expression)
- Sing with reverence, power, and great expression.

2. Review Sight-Singing.
Read and sing using solfège and hand signs or numbers. Read, sing, and conduct in 3/4 and 4/4.
Have students:

- Review the Sight-Singing exercise on page 2.
- In pairs, point to one pitch at a time, first using stepwise intervals, then thirds, and so on.
- Read and sing the exercise.
- Practice the conducting patterns.
- Read, sing, and conduct the exercise.

The One Who Stands Alone

Music by Joseph M. Martin
Words by J. Paul Williams and Joseph M. Martin

SATB, Accompanied

Composer Joseph Martin

Joseph Martin is recognized internationally for his sacred choral compositions and piano recital skills. He received the Nina Plant Wideman Competition and performed with the Guadalajara Symphony Orchestra; one solo recital in Ex-convento del Carman was broadcast nationally. In addition to his compositional skills, he is Director of Church Music Marketing Development with Shawnee Press, Inc. He continues to perform throughout the country and participate in music conferences, festivals, and workshops.

Meet - ing ev - 'ry foe with cour - age brave - ly
march - ing through the night. There were those who died for
free - dom, Those who
molto cresc.
those who fell for li - ber - ty.
molto cresc.
molto cresc.

3. Sight-sing "The One Who Stands Alone" using solfège and hand signs or numbers.

Have students:

- Divide into voice sections (SATB) and read each part rhythmically, using rhythm syllables.
- Still in sections, sing with solfège and hand signs or numbers, identifying and working on problem areas.
- Sing the piece through, using solfège and hand signs or numbers, with full ensemble.
- Divide into sections and recite the text rhythmically for each voice part.
- Sing the piece through with text as a full ensemble.

4. Conduct and sing.

Have students:

- Review the conducting patterns for 3/4 and 4/4 meter on Blackline Master 1, *Conducting Patterns in 3/4 and 4/4.*
- Review the style of the piece. (with reverence, power, and great expression)
- Sing and conduct, with the conducting reflecting the style of the piece.
- Sing with reverence, power, and great expression as individual volunteers conduct.

MORE ABOUT

J. Paul Williams

Mr. Williams is a freelance lyricist in Little Rock, Arkansas. With extensive experience in church music, he collaborates with a large number of choral composers and has many compositions in print. He is a frequent guest clinician for church conferences throughout the Southwest.

DEVELOPING LEADERSHIP SKILLS

During the year, you will want to encourage leadership in many ways. Some possible suggestions are:

- Encourage students to make suggestions and/or decisions about performance style, tempo, and so on.
- Invite students to conduct pieces.

18

shout - ed from the moun - tains, "I have a dream,— I have a

dream. I have a dream."— *f* Hear their 23 voi - ces call like

thun - der down through time we hear their song. "Will you

TEACHING STRATEGY

Reading Rhythms and Pitches

If students are not familiar with the rhythm, pitches, or meters in the piece, have them:

- Use the Rhythm and Pitch Challenges on pages ix, x, and xiii to practice until they are familiar.

Posture and Breathing

Have students:

- Review correct posture and breathing for good singing.
- Discuss the problems of singing with reverence, power, and great expression as suggested in this piece, and still maintaining a quality sound.
- Identify the characteristic vocal sound they would like to achieve, and work toward it.

give your - self for free - dom and be the

p
one who stands a - lone."
p
p

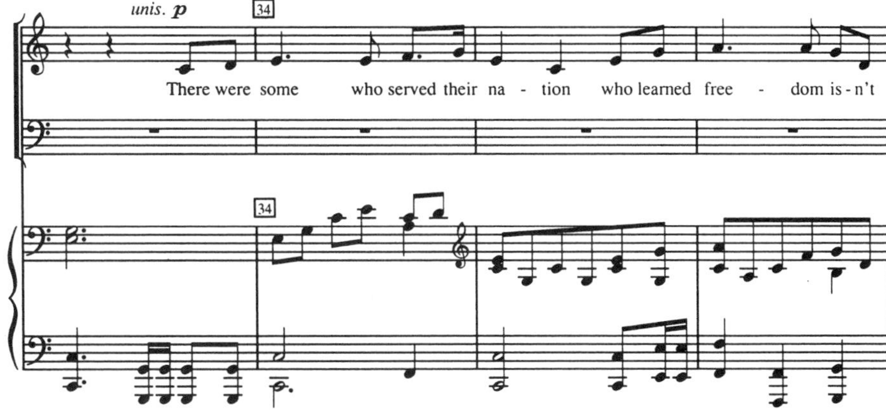
unis. p
34
There were some who served their na - tion who learned free - dom is - n't
34

VOCAL DEVELOPMENT

To encourage vocal development, have students:

- Demonstrate good vocal tone by singing with tall vowels and clear consonants.
- Energize sustained tones by increasing the breath support and dynamic level.
- Listen for diphthongs (two vowel sounds when one vowel sound is written) in such English words as *life* and *night.* Sing or sustain the first vowel sound and barely sing the second vowel sound with the next syllable.
- Demonstrate the correct singing of the *r* consonant after a vowel when singing in English. It should be almost silent, as in *there, were, marching, liberty, hear, thunder, served, war, surrender,* and *future.*
- Feel the arched contour of each musical phrase as it begins, builds, then tapers off. The dynamics should reflect the melodic contour.
- Perform the rhythms precisely; conduct and speak the rhythm or speak the text in rhythm.
- Balance the chords between the parts by listening to them. Try adding more weight to one part to determine the effect on the chord. Note when the voices join in unison.

CONNECTING THE ARTS

Visual Arts

Have students:

- Describe the characteristics of patriotic persons suggested in "The One Who Stands Alone."
- Discuss images, concrete or abstract, that might represent each of the characteristics or images mentioned in the piece. (This might include creating some art, using fine art from local or national museums, taking photographs, and so on.)
- Plan a slide show to accompany performance of the piece at concert time.

38

free.

Those who left their homes and fam - 'lies who knew

38

42

There were some who died for

war to bring us peace.

42

free - dom;

cry - ing

hear them shout with dy - ing breath,

molto cresc.

TEACHING STRATEGY

Performing to a Common Beat and Watching the Conductor

Have students:

- Each feel his or her pulse and pat it.
- Listen to all the pulses in the room, and slowly come to a common pulse which they all pat very softly.
- Stop patting and sing a familiar tune without a conductor, staying exactly together.
- Sing the same piece with you conducting, varying the tempo and dynamic levels, with them following exactly.
- Discuss the role of the conductor in keeping a group together, and the importance of watching the conductor.

Assessment

Informal Assessment

During this lesson, students showed the ability to:

- Perform together with a common steady beat throughout the lesson.
- Explore styles in the Vocal Warm-Up exercise.
- Conduct beats in sets of 3 and 4 in the Sight-Singing exercise.
- Sing with reverence, power, and great expression, conducting beats in sets of 3 and 4, in "The One Who Stands Alone."

Student Self-Assessment

Have students:

- Evaluate their performance with the How Did You Do? section on page 3.
- Answer the questions individually. Discuss them in pairs or small groups and/or write their responses on a sheet of paper.

Individual Performance Assessment

To further demonstrate accomplishment, have each student:

- In a group, conduct as others sing "The One Who Stands Alone," changing from 3 to 4 when indicated in the notation.
- Sing "The One Who Stands Alone," changing from moderate style to a style reflecting reverence, power, and great expression upon your signal.
- Write a paragraph describing the composer's use and organization of beat, style, and meter in "The One Who Stands Alone." Students' writing should tell why the composer's choices were or were not appropriate for the text, and support each description with an example from the piece, cited by measure.

Extension

Conductors

Have students:

- Watch conductors on television, multimedia computer encyclopedias, or local performing groups to identify specific well-known choral conductors.
- Be prepared to describe the conductors' style of conducting.

Harmonizing Patriotic Songs

Have students:

- Sing familiar songs that inspire patriotism, for example: "America the Beautiful," "Battle Hymn of the Republic," "God Bless America," "America," "Yankee Doodle Dandy," and so on.
- In small groups, aurally work out (improvise) harmony in 2, 3, or 4 parts for one of these songs, practicing until it becomes familiar and comfortable.

National Standards

The following National Standards are addressed through the Extension and bottom-page activities:

1. Singing, alone and with others, a varied repertoire of music. **(a, b, c, e)**
3. Improvising melodies, variations, and accompaniments. **(a)**
5. Reading and notating music. **(a, b)**
6. Listening to, analyzing, and describing music. **(a, b, c)**
8. Understanding relationships between music, the other arts, and disciplines outside the arts. **(c)**
9. Understanding music in relation to history and culture. **(a, b, c, d)**

thun - der down through time we hear their
song. "Will you stand and face the
63 Triumphant to the end
63 Triumphant and building
fu - ture, will you stand and face the

Patriotic Songs

Have students:

- Research a patriotic song from a country other than the United States.
- Demonstrate the piece by performing or playing a recording, and describing why it is considered a patriotic song in that country.
- Describe the musical characteristics of the piece, placing them on a chart.
- Compare the characteristics of all the researched pieces, and then compare them with the musical characteristics of "The One Who Stands Alone."
- Make any possible generalizations about the musical characteristics of patriotic songs.

ff
fu - ture, brave - ly stand and make a
ff
ff
fu - ture where no one
molto rit.
stands a - lone. Stands a - lone!
molto rit.
molto rit.

Siyahamba

South African Folk Song
ARRANGER: Donald Moore

CHORAL MUSIC TERMS
homophony
melodic leaps
register consistency
syncopated rhythm

VOICING
Three-part mixed

PERFORMANCE STYLE
Very rhythmic
Accompanied by piano with optional percussion

FOCUS
- Identify and perform syncopated rhythms.
- Sing melodic leaps with register consistency.
- Sing independently in three homophonic parts.

Warming Up

Rhythm Drill

Clap each of these rhythms, then combine them over an audible steady beat. Notice the syncopated rhythm that occurs when the emphasis is shifted off the beat.

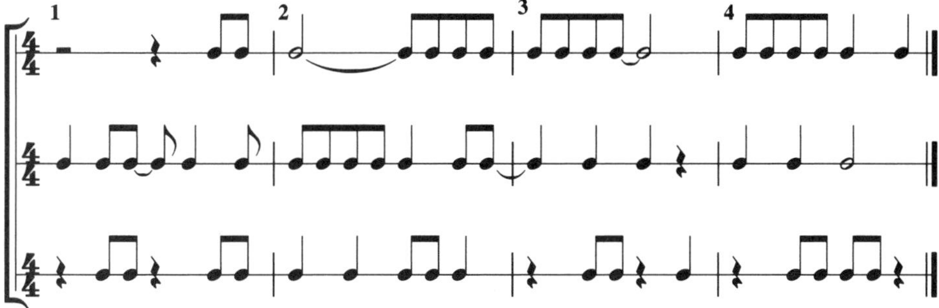

Vocal Warm-Up

Sing these scale passages on *nah*. Remember to use good breath support. Move up by half steps on the repeats. Keep the tone consistent from bottom to top and back again.

LESSON 2

Siyahamba

South African Folk Song
ARRANGER: Donald Moore

Focus

OVERVIEW

Melodic leaps; register consistency; part independence; homophony; syncopated rhythms.

OBJECTIVES

After completing this lesson, students will be able to:
- Identify and perform syncopated rhythms.
- Sing melodic leaps with register consistency.
- Sing independently in three homophonic parts.

CHORAL MUSIC TERMS

Define the Choral Music Terms for students, giving pronunciation, and answering any questions that may arise.

Warming Up

Rhythm Drill

This Rhythm Drill is designed to prepare students to:
- Read and perform syncopated rhythms.
- Perform parts independently.
- Maintain rhythmic independence.

Have students:
- Read through the Rhythm Drill directions.
- Perform the drill.

TEACHER'S RESOURCE BINDER

National Standards

1. Singing, alone and with others, a varied repertoire of music. **(a, b, c, e)**
5. Reading and notating music. **(a, b)**
6. Listening to, analyzing, and describing music. **(a, b)**
8. Understanding relationships between music, the other arts, and disciplines outside the arts. **(c)**
9. Understanding music in relation to history and culture. **(c)**

Vocal Warm-Up

The Vocal Warm-Up on page 13 is designed to prepare students to:

- Use correct breathing procedures.
- Sing with vocal flexibility on scale passages.
- Maintain consistent tone extending the range of an octave.

Have students:

- Read through the Vocal Warm-Up directions.
- Sing, following your demonstration.

Sight-Singing

This Sight-Singing exercise is designed to prepare students to:

- Sight-sing pitches in major using solfège and hand signs or numbers.
- Read in treble and bass clefs.
- Sing a part independently when three homophonic parts are sung.
- Tune chords.
- Identify syncopated rhythm.

Have students:

- Read through the Sight-Singing exercise directions.
- Read through each voice part rhythmically, using rhythm syllables.
- Sight-sing through each part separately using solfège and hand signs or numbers.
- Sing all parts together.

Singing: "Siyahamba"

Learn the cultural context of the song.

Have students:

- Read the text on page 14.
- Define homophonic texture (all parts moving chordally, with the same rhythm), and syncopated rhythms (rhythms that fall off the strong beat).
- Identify any music they may have heard that sounds like this. (Ladysmith Black Mombazo, and Paul Simon's recording of *Graceland* are examples of a group and a recording that are available commercially.)

Sight-Singing

Sight-sing this exercise using solfège and hand signs or numbers. First sing each part separately, then put them together. Tune each chord carefully. Notice the syncopation and sing it crisply once the pitches are in place.

Singing: "Siyahamba"

In South Africa, there has been a long struggle for equality. "Siyahamba" is a Zulu song that has served as a call for freedom. "Siyahamba" provides a symbol of both unity and determination. Characteristic of Zulu vocal music, homophonic texture and syncopated rhythms have gained this style of music worldwide popularity. Perhaps you have heard this style of music before.

Now turn to the music for "Siyahamba" on page 15.

HOW DID YOU DO?

Unity and determination are Zulu ideals that work well in learning a new piece of music. Think about your preparation and performance of "Siyahamba."

1. How do you keep register consistency when you sing melodic leaps? Demonstrate by singing the first three pitches of "Siyahamba."

2. How well could you hold your part in tune when there were three parts sounding at once? Choose two classmates and demonstrate, using the Sight-Singing exercise.

3. Describe how syncopated rhythms are different from other rhythms. Point some out in "Siyahamba."

4. Explain the cultural background of "Siyahamba." How does knowing the cultural background of the piece change the way you prepare or perform it? If you were going to do an authentic performance of "Siyahamba," what would you need to know about the Zulu style that you don't already know?

Siyahamba

South African Folk Song
Arranged by Donald Moore (ASCAP)

Three-part Mixed, Accompanied with Optional Percussion*

*Percussion may be found on insert.

Suggested Teaching Sequence

1. Review Rhythm Drill.
Identify and clap syncopated rhythms.
Have students:

- Review the Rhythm Drill on page 13.
- Identify the syncopated rhythms in each part. (There is no syncopation in the third part.)
- Clap all three parts together, listening to the interplay between them.
- Find the syncopated rhythm in measures 5–8 of "Siyahamba." (Measure 6 is syncopated and syncopation is over the bar line from measure 7 to 8.)

2. Review Vocal Warm-Up.
Sing scalewise passages using register consistency.
Have students:

- Review the Vocal Warm-Up on page 13.
- Place a hand horizontal to the bridge of the nose, and sing the exercise, imagining that the tone is always coming over the top of their hands.
- Describe how this helps maintain register consistency.
- Sing the first three pitches of "Siyahamba," a leap of a sixth upward, using the same technique.
- Repeat this activity with the leap of a minor 7th in measure 10.

"Siyahamba"

"Siyahamba" is a South African folk song. Fundamentally a straightforward arrangement, the percussion parts and accompaniment have been written to add a special rhythmic flavor to the ensemble.

3. Review Sight-Singing.

Read and sing in three parts using solfège and hand signs or numbers. Tune chords. Identify syncopation.

Have students:

- Review the Sight-Singing exercise on page 14.
- Sing each part, then put the parts together, singing slowly and tuning each part.
- Identify the syncopation in the second full measure, and sing it crisply.
- Look at the notation of "Siyahamba" to find the pitches of the Sight-Singing exercise. (measures 26–29)
- Identify what is different. (the rhythm)
- Read measures 26–29 of "Siyahamba" using solfège and hand signs or numbers.

4. Sight-sing "Siyahamba" using solfège and hand signs or numbers.

Have students:

- Divide into voice sections and read each part rhythmically, using rhythm syllables.
- Still in sections, sing with solfège and hand signs or numbers, identifying and working on problem areas.
- Sing the piece through, using solfège and hand signs or numbers, with full ensemble.

hamb' e ku - kha - nye - ni kwen - kos. ___ Si - ya -

9

hamb' ___ e - ku - kha - nye - ni kwen - kos. ___ Si - ya -

hamb' e ku - kha - nye - ni kwen - kos. ___ Si - ya -

TEACHING STRATEGY

Accent Articulation

Have students:

- Say the following words:

  \> chair \> bed \> seed \> tree

- Determine what parts of the body are involved in order to accent the words. (teeth, lips, mouth, diaphragm, tongue)
- Say the following words that begin with vowel sounds, accenting each:

  \> hour \> ant \> eat \> eye

- Determine what parts of the body are involved in order to accent the words. (diaphragm only)
- Discuss words in "Siyahamba" that are accented because of accent marks or because of syncopation, and in what manner each will be articulated.

13 ham - ba, hamba, oh,

ham - ba, ham - ba, ham - ba, oh, Si - ya -

13

hamb' e ku - kha - nye - ni kwen - kos. Si - ya -

1.

1.

2.

2.

*Use cue notes throughout only if range is a problem.

5. Learn the Zulu pronunciation.

Have students:

- Using a copy of the pronunciation guide at the bottom of this page, echo or read the pronunciation of the text slowly. (The pronunciation guide can also be written on the board.)
- Speak the Zulu text in rhythm.
- Sing the piece with the Zulu text, using correct pronunciation.

Pronunciation for "Siyahamba"

Use the following guide for pronunciation of the Zulu text in "Siyahamba":

Si - ya - hamb
See-yah-hahmb'

e - ku - kha - nye - ni
eh-koo-kah-nyeh-nee

kwen - kos
kwehn-kos

VOCAL DEVELOPMENT

To encourage vocal development, have students:

- Demonstrate good vocal tone by singing with tall vowels and clear consonants in the phonetic African language.
- Energize sustained tones by increasing the breath support and dynamic level.
- Listen for diphthongs (two vowel sounds when one vowel sound is written) in English words, as in *light.* Sing or sustain the first vowel sound and barely sing the second vowel sound with the next syllable.
- Demonstrate the correct singing of the *r* consonant after a vowel when singing in English. It should be almost silent, as in *marching.*
- Feel the arched contour of each musical phrase as it begins, builds, then tapers off. The dynamics should reflect the melodic contour.
- Perform the rhythms precisely at first; conduct and speak the rhythm or speak the text in rhythm.
- Balance the chords between the parts by listening to them. Try adding more weight to one part to determine the effect on the chord. Note when the voices join in unison.
- Relax the precision of the rhythm and pitch to emulate African folk style. "Scooping" of the voice is allowed!

light of God. We are march-ing in the light of God. 1. We are

march - ing, march - ing, oh,

[30] *ham - ba, ham - ba, oh,*

march - ing, march - ing, march - ing, oh, We are

ham - ba, ham - ba, ham - ba, oh, Si - ya -

[30]

1. 2. 3.

march - ing in the light of God. *2. We are

hamb' e ku - kha - nye - ni kwen - kos. (Optional Words) 3. 4. *Si - ya -*

1. 2. 3.

*Repeat as many times as desired

Assessment

Informal Assessment

During this lesson, students showed the ability to:

- Identify and clap syncopated rhythms in the Rhythm Drill.
- Learn and use register consistency in scales and upward leaps in the Vocal Warm-Up exercise.
- Sing one part independently when three parts are being sung in the Sight-Singing exercise.
- Sing independently, using syncopated rhythms and register consistency on upward leaps, in "Siyahamba."

Student Self-Assessment

Have students:

- Evaluate their performance with the How Did You Do? section on page 14.
- Answer the questions individually. Discuss them in pairs or small groups and/or write their responses on a sheet of paper.

Individual Performance Assessment

To further demonstrate accomplishment, have each student:

- Into a tape recorder, clap line 1 or 2 of the Rhythm Drill, demonstrating the ability to clap syncopated rhythm.
- Into a tape recorder, sing the first three pitches of "Siyahamba," demonstrating register consistency.
- In a trio or double trio, sing either measures 13–16 or 26–29 of "Siyahamba" into a tape recorder in an isolated space, demonstrating independent singing.

CURRICULUM CONNECTIONS

Zulu Culture, Its Music and Arts

Have students:

- Research the Zulu culture and its music, using any resources available, including knowledgeable community members.
- Include historical data, and information about the contemporary Zulus.
- Explore songs, instruments, and the range of styles of the Zulu tribes.
- Research other Zulu arts, including storytelling, dance, drama, and visual art.
- Compare the uses of characteristic elements, artistic processes, and organizational principles among the arts.
- Write an article for the school newspaper describing "Siyahamba" and giving background based on their research.

Extension

Movement

Have students:

- Develop body movements to accompany this piece, using a combination of stepping from side to side and hand claps. (The steps and swaying should be very natural, and not overexaggerated.)

Adding Instruments

Have students:

- Read and practice the instrument parts included in the score of "Siyahamba."
- Perform the piece with the percussion accompaniment.

or

- In a small group, improvise a drum, shaker, and stick accompaniment to the piece using ostinato patterns, and changing patterns for different sections of the piece.

A Cappella Style Singing

Have students:

- Sing the piece in full ensemble, a cappella.
- Sing the piece in smaller groups, a cappella.
- Find a way to extend the form of the piece by adding an a cappella section, either with the full ensemble or a small group.

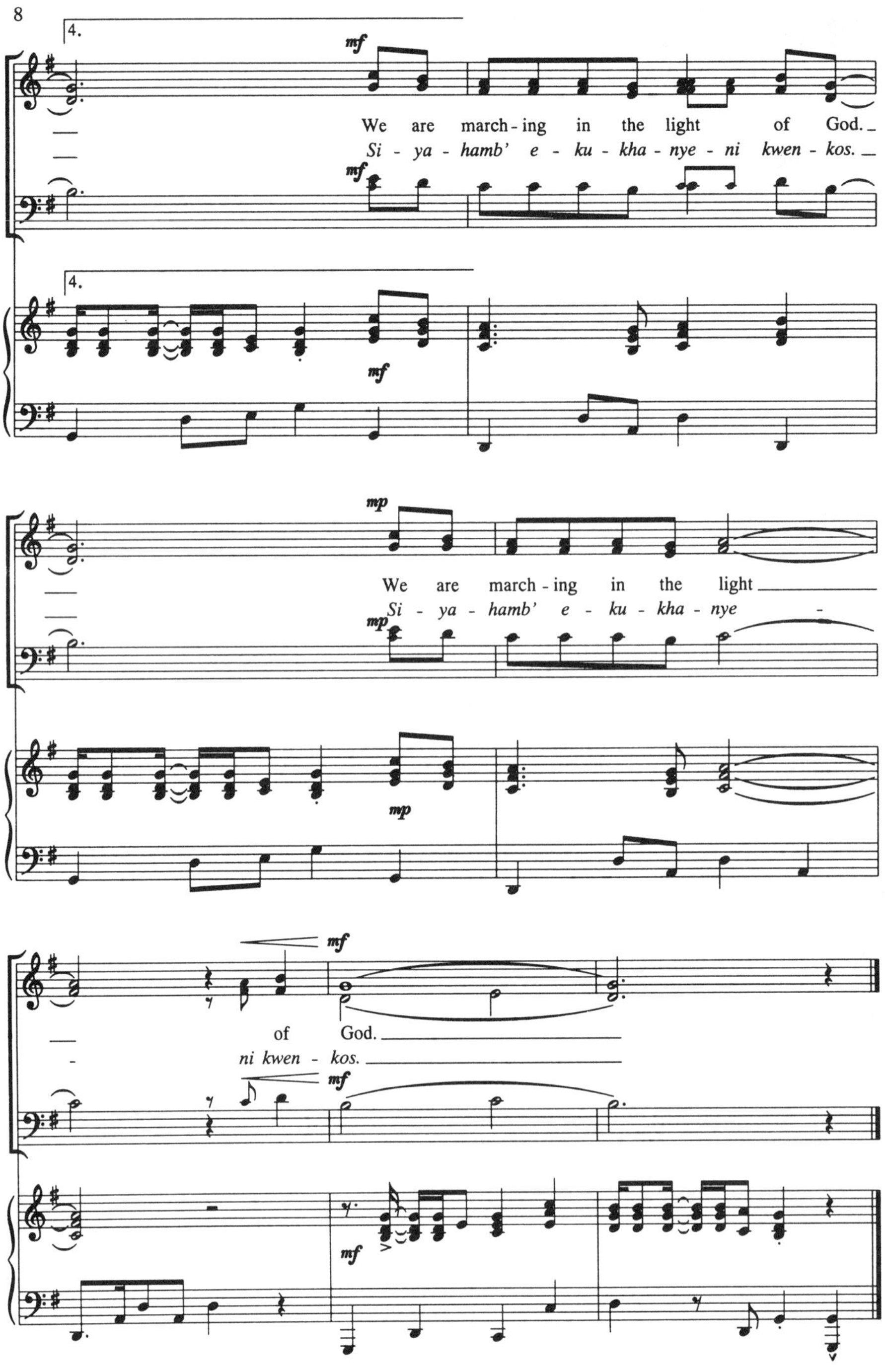

8

4.

mf

We are march - ing in the light of God. _

Si - ya - hamb' e - ku - kha - nye - ni kwen - kos. _

mp

We are march - ing in the light

Si - ya - hamb' e - ku - kha - nye -

mf

of God.

ni kwen - kos.

National Standards

The following National Standards are addressed through the Extension and bottom-page activities:

1. Singing, alone and with others, a varied repertoire of music. **(a, b, c, e)**
2. Performing on instruments, alone and with others, a varied repertoire of music. **(b)**
4. Composing and arranging music within specified guidelines. **(a, b, c)**
5. Reading and notating music. **(a, b)**
6. Listening to, analyzing, and describing music. **(a, b, c, e)**
8. Understanding relationships between music, the other arts, and disciplines outside the arts. **(a, b, c, d)**
9. Understanding music in relation to history and culture. **(a, b, c, d)**

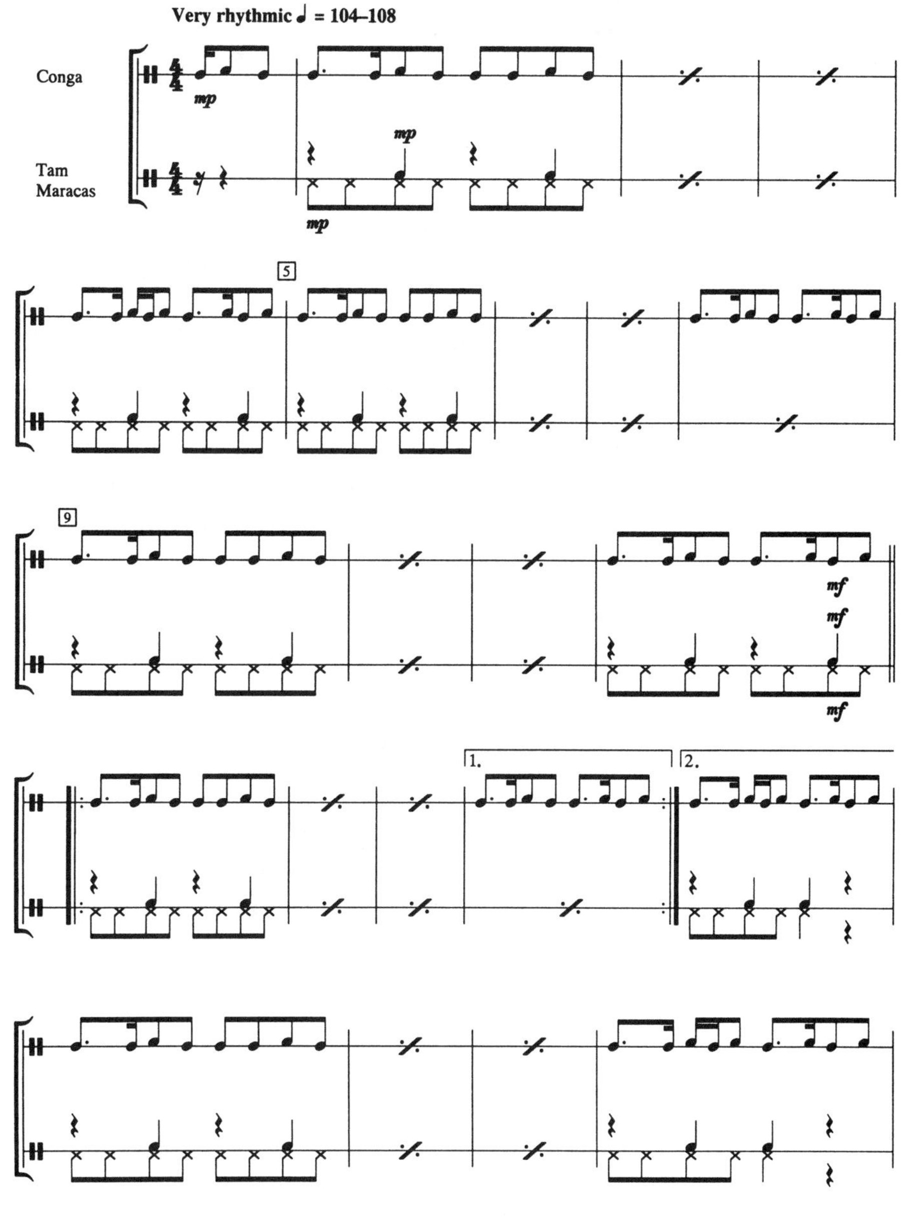

Composing in the Zulu Style

Have students:

- Identify the characteristics of this piece that they feel are important to the style of "Siyahamba." (stepwise melody with some large leaps, harmony in 3rds and 6ths, homophony, syncopated rhythms)
- Compose a melody that has the tonal and rhythmic characteristics identified, using a major key. (Words can be chosen first, and the rhythm determined by the text, or vice versa.)
- Experiment and finally determine harmony in three parts that moves mostly in 3rds and 6ths with the melody, following the "Siyahamba" model.
- Add rhythmic percussion parts, and sing a cappella with rhythmic percussion accompaniment.

Comparing Style and Function Across Cultures

Have students:

- Describe the function and musical characteristics that determine the styles of "The One Who Stands Alone" (Lesson 1) and "Siyahamba."
- Compare and contrast both the purpose of each piece within its society, and the use of musical materials including melodic, rhythmic, harmonic, and textural elements.
- Write a paragraph that compares both the use of musical materials and the function of the pieces in the two styles.

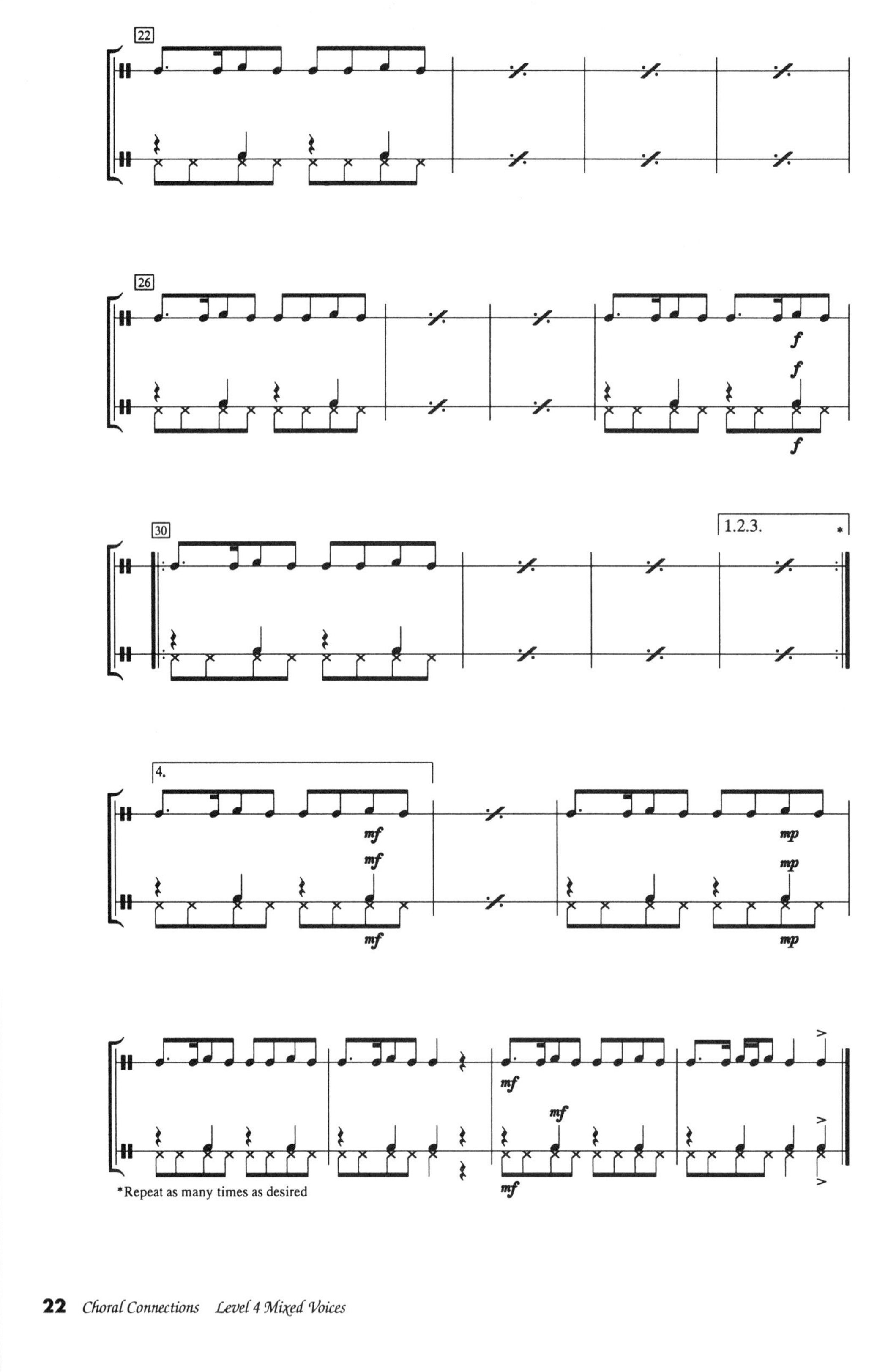
22
26
30
1.2.3.
4.
f
mf
mp
*Repeat as many times as desired

The Prayer of Saint Francis

CHORAL MUSIC TERMS
legato articulation
phrasing
tuning

COMPOSER: *René Clausen*
TEXT: St. *Francis of Assisi*
(*Giovanni Francesco Bernardone*, 1182–1226)

VOICING
SATB

PERFORMANCE STYLE
Gently flowing
Accompanied by piano

FOCUS
- Recognize and sing using legato articulation.
- Identify out-of-tune singing, and tune pitches.
- Determine effective breathing technique to perform correct phrasing.

Warming Up

Vocal Warm-Up

Sing this exercise on *loo* using legato articulation. Move up a half step on each repeat. Vary the places where you breathe, for example: after each measure; after each two measures; after three measures; singing the last three on one breath. Now sing the whole phrase on one breath.

LESSON 3

The Prayer of Saint Francis

COMPOSER: René Clausen
TEXT: St. Francis of Assisi (Giovanni Francesco Bernardone, 1182–1226)

Focus

OVERVIEW
Tuning pitches; legato articulation; phrasing.

OBJECTIVES
After completing this lesson, students will be able to:
- Recognize and sing using legato articulation.
- Identify out-of-tune singing, and tune pitches.
- Identify effective breathing technique and perform correct phrasing.

CHORAL MUSIC TERMS
Define the Choral Music Terms for students, giving pronunciation, and answering any questions that may arise.

Warming Up

Vocal Warm-Up
This Vocal Warm-Up is designed to prepare students to:
- Use legato articulation.
- Extend the breath through a phrase.

Have students:
- Read through the Vocal Warm-Up directions.
- Sing, following your demonstration.

TEACHER'S RESOURCE BINDER
Blackline Master 2, *Singing Pitches in Tune*, page 78

National Standards

1. Singing a varied repertoire of music. **(a, b, c, f)**
5. Reading and notating music. **(a, b)**
6. Listening to, analyzing, and describing music. **(a, b, c)**
7. Evaluating music and music performances. **(a)**
8. Understanding relationships between music, the other arts, and disciplines outside the arts. **(c)**
9. Understanding music in relation to history and culture. **(c)**

Sight-Singing

This Sight-Singing exercise is designed to prepare students to:

- Sight-sing in four parts using solfège and hand signs or numbers, tuning pitches.
- Read in treble and bass clefs.
- Read and sing with rhythmic independence.
- Sing independently when four parts are sung.

Have students:

- Read through the Sight-Singing exercise directions.
- Read through each voice part rhythmically, using rhythm syllables.
- Sight-sing through each part separately using solfège and hand signs or numbers.
- Sing all parts together.

Singing: "The Prayer of Saint Francis"

Experience the power of the text. Have students:

- Read the text on page 24.
- Discuss types of texts they might use as a composer. (humorous, joyful, heart-wrenching, full of emotion)
- Read the song text, identifying the meaning.
- Identify the negative and positive qualities related to peace mentioned in the text. (hatred/love, injury/pardon, doubt/faith, despair/hope, darkness/light, sorrow/joy, to be consoled/giving consolation, to be understood/understanding)
- Discuss situations where each might be found in the world today.

Sight-Singing

Sight-sing this exercise using solfège and hand signs or numbers. Notice the sound of the full harmonies, and that each section moves against other parts, creating dissonances for resolution. Tune each pitch carefully. Use legato articulation, and breathe at the phrase markings.

Singing: "The Prayer of Saint Francis"

When composers begin with a text, they look for some meaning that can be enhanced by a musical setting. What type of text would you look for if you were a composer? Read aloud the text of "The Prayer of Saint Francis." What meaning does this text hold? Identify the negative and positive qualities related to peace mentioned in the text. Are they meaningful in the world today? How?

Now turn to the music for "The Prayer of Saint Francis" on page 25.

HOW DID YOU DO?

The composer set the text to music, and you have brought the combination of text and music to life with your performance. Think about your preparation and performance of "The Prayer of Saint Francis."

1. Describe legato articulation, and demonstrate it in the first phrase of "The Prayer of Saint Francis."

2. Can you tell whether pitches are in tune or not? Sing the Sight-Singing exercise in a quartet to demonstrate your ability to sing in tune.

3. How do you know where a phrase begins and ends? What does breathing have to do with phrasing? Demonstrate how you sing a phrase, using any phrase of "The Prayer of Saint Francis" you wish.

4. How did the composer enhance Saint Francis's ideas about qualities related to peace through music? Give specific examples, and describe the compositional devices and techniques used by the composer.

TEACHING STRATEGY

Supporting the Phrase Line During the Vocal Warm-Up

If you feel comfortable, or have a student who is proficient at the keyboard, improvise arpeggios and extra rhythmic interest in the piano accompaniment to the Vocal Warm-Up exercise on page 23. Change the style of the exercise to provide variety and interest, exploring staccato as well as legato articulation, exotic flowing style, and others.

Commissioned by the Borger H.S. Varsity Choir, Johnny Miller, Director, for their performance at the Texas Music Educators Association Convention, February 6, 1992: Dedicated to his father, Bob Miller.

The Prayer of Saint Francis

By René Clausen

Suggested Teaching Sequence

1. Review Vocal Warm-Up.
Sing with legato articulation. Breathe to perform phrases.
Have students:

- Review the Vocal Warm-Up on page 23.
- Identify and use legato articulation.
- Explore breathing at different places in the phrase.
- Sing the whole phrase using one breath.

2. Review Sight-Singing.
Sight-sing in four parts using solfège and hand signs or numbers. Tune pitches. Use legato articulation. Sing through phrases.
Have students:

- Review the Sight-Singing exercise on page 24.
- Using Blackline Master 2, *Singing Pitches in Tune,* signal when they hear pitches out of tune, pointing downward for flat pitches, and upward for sharp pitches.
- Listen as you sing each line, raising a hand when you sing pitches out of tune.
- Sight-sing for each other, indicating when pitches are out of tune, and adjusting the pitch.
- Identify the dissonances and resolutions.

"The Prayer of Saint Francis"

This piece was commissioned by the Borger High School Varsity Choir, Johnny Miller, Director, for their performance at the Texas Music Educators Association Convention in February, 1992.

3. Sight-sing "The Prayer of Saint Francis" using solfège and hand signs or numbers.

Have students:

- Divide into voice sections (SATB) and read each part rhythmically, using rhythm syllables, adding dynamics to shape the phrases.
- Still in sections, sing with solfège and hand signs or numbers, identifying and working on problem areas.
- Sing the piece through, using solfège and hand signs or numbers, with full ensemble.
- Divide into sections and recite the text rhythmically for each voice part.
- Sing the piece through with text as a full ensemble, using techniques of phrasing and legato articulation and tuning pitches carefully.

4. Identifying the musical word painting of negative and positive qualities.

Have students:

- Review the negative and positive qualities related to peace found in the text.
- Listen to and describe the chords occurring where negative words occur. (minor, diminished, dissonant)
- Listen to and describe the chords occurring where positive words appear. (major, bright, open)
- Identify this musical technique as word painting.

Composer René Clausen

René Clausen, composer and conductor of the Concordia Choir, Concordia College, Moorhead, Minnesota, is a graduate of St. Olaf College, Northfield, Minnesota. He holds a master's degree in conducting performance from the University of Illinois, and is currently pursuing the degree of Doctor of Musical Arts in Choral Conducting from the University of Illinois.

Prior to his appointment as conductor of the Concordia Choir in 1986, he served as the Director of Choral Activities at West Texas State University, and as an assistant professor of choral music at Wichita State University. He is known throughout the United States for his compositions and choral clinics.

VOCAL DEVELOPMENT

To encourage vocal development, have students:

- Create a gentle, introspective sound by singing with hushed intensity and using tall vowels and clear consonants.
- Arch or lift the tone on melodic leaps by increasing the space in the mouth and pharynx.
- Energize sustained tones by increasing the breath support and dynamic level.
- Sustain phrases by staggering the breathing and moving forward through the phrases.
- Listen for diphthongs (two vowel sounds when one vowel sound is written) in such English words as *light, joy, I, dying,* and *life.* Sing or sustain the first vowel sound and barely sing the second vowel sound with the next syllable.

TEACHING STRATEGY

Tuning Pitches

Have the students sing the piece on *loo,* with attention to intonation, finding and isolating problem spots and having only those part lines involved sing the intervals in question.

30
there is des - pair, let me bring hope.
there is des - pair, let me, let me bring hope.
faith, let me bring love, let me bring hope.
faith, let me bring love, let me bring hope.

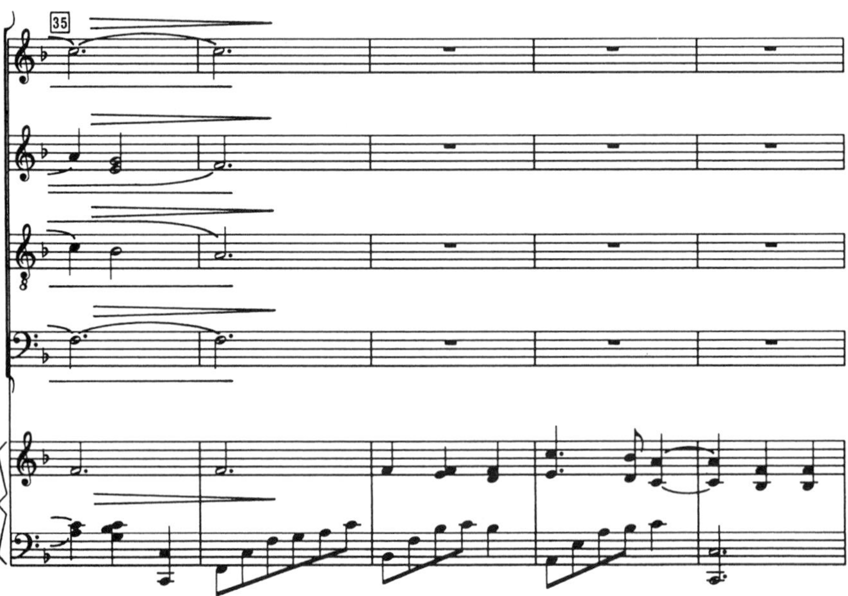
35

Signing

Signing in music describes the use of hand signals to represent relative sounds of pitches. The signs were used by Reverend John Curwen from a method developed by Sarah Glover of Norwich in the nineteenth century. The *do* is movable and was intended to teach beginners to sing accurate pitches. The system has been adopted by the Kodaly approach and *Tonika-Do* system in Germany.

VOCAL DEVELOPMENT

To encourage vocal development, have students:

- Demonstrate the correct singing of the *r* consonant after a vowel when singing in English. It should be almost silent, as in *Lord, injury, pardon, there, darkness, understand, pardoned, born, eternal,* and *your.*
- Feel the arched contour of each musical phrase as it begins, builds, then tapers off. The dynamics should reflect the melodic contour. Plan the dynamic contrasts.
- Analyze the linear melodic intervals and tune them carefully.
- Balance the chords between the parts by listening to them. Try adding more weight to one part to determine the effect on the chord. Note where the voices sing in unison.

CURRICULUM CONNECTIONS

Biography

Have students:

- Research Saint Francis of Assisi (Giovanni Francesco Bernardone, 1182–1226) to discover what contributions he made to society.
- Research the times in which Saint Francis lived, and what was happening historically.
- Compare issues of Saint Francis's time to those of today.
- Speculate on the types of music available in the time of Saint Francis to set this text, and what elements used in this piece are the same or different than what would have existed then.

Assessment

Informal Assessment

During this lesson, students showed the ability to:

- Use legato articulation and breathe to shape phrases in the Vocal Warm-Up exercise.
- Sing one part independently, tuning pitches, when four parts are being sung in the Sight-Singing exercise.
- Sing independently, using legato articulation, tuning pitches carefully, and shaping phrases through breathing in "The Prayer of Saint Francis."

Student Self-Assessment

Have students:

- Evaluate their performance with the How Did You Do? section on page 24.
- Answer the questions individually. Discuss them in pairs or small groups and/or write their responses on a sheet of paper.

Individual Performance Assessment

To further demonstrate accomplishment, have each student:

- Listen to and follow any voice part line of "The Prayer of Saint Francis," signaling when a pitch is sung out of tune by pointing downward for a flat pitch, and upward for a sharp pitch.
- In a quartet or double quartet, sing measures 5–35 of "The Prayer of Saint Francis" into a tape recorder in an isolated space, demonstrating legato articulation, in-tune singing, and correct phrasing.

TEACHING STRATEGY

Legato Articulation

Have students:

- Pretend to play the beginning of "The Prayer of Saint Francis" on a violin, using legato bowing.
- Discuss the need for longer bowing action on longer notes.
- Discuss the change in bowing direction on shorter notes, which creates a slight stress.
- Sing the piece, using these clues to help the legato articulation, and think about the bowing action as they sing.
- Discuss how this piece would be different played by a trumpet, and whether a trumpet or a violin is more appropriate.

Extension

Dynamics and Tempo

Have students:

- Identify dynamic and tempo markings in the notation for "The Prayer of Saint Francis."
- Perform the piece, attending to the dynamic and tempo markings, for increased expression.

Evaluating a Performance

Have students:

- Discuss the outcome of effective performance of this piece, including musical satisfaction for the performer, "goose bumps" for the listener, and effective transmission of the composer's message through interpretation.
- Discuss pieces they have heard performed that have had this effect and what the characteristics were that contributed to it.
- Listen to a tape or video of their performance and compare it to the models they have suggested.
- Assess their performance through comparison, suggesting improvements and changes to make their performance more effective.

National Standards

The following National Standards are addressed through the Extension and bottom-page activities:

1. Singing, alone and with others, a varied repertoire of music. **(a, b, c)**
4. Composing and arranging music within specified guidelines. **(b, c)**
5. Reading and notating music. **(a, b)**
6. Listening to, analyzing, and describing music. **(a, b, c, e)**
7. Evaluating music and music performances. **(a, b, c)**
8. Understanding relationships between music, the other arts, and disciplines outside the arts. **(a, b, c, d)**
9. Understanding music in relation to history and culture. **(a, c, e)**

Arranging "The Prayer of Saint Francis" for Instrumental Ensemble or MIDI/Keyboard

Have students:

- Discuss the character and mood of this piece, and then decide which instruments would convey the same mood as the vocal setting.
- Arrange the piece for instrumental ensemble or keyboard/synthesizer.
- Perform the new arrangement.
- Discuss what effect the removal of words had on the musical impact of the piece.

love, to love.
love, to love, to love.
love, to love, to love.
loved, to love, to love.
love, to love,
mp
For it is in giv - ing that we re - ceive, and in pard - 'ning that we are
For it is in giv - ing that we re - ceive, and in pard - 'ning that we are
For it is in giv - ing that we re - ceive, and in pard - 'ning that we are
For it is in giv - ing, and in pard - 'ning,
80
85

p
90
rit.
par - doned. For in dy - ing we are born to e - ter - nal
p
rit.
par - doned. For in dy - ing we are born to e - ter - nal
p
rit.
par - doned. For in dy - ing we are born to e - ter - nal
p
rit.
For in dy - ing born to e - ter - nal
p
a tempo
95
life. make me an in - stru-ment of your
mp
life. Lord, make me an in - stru-ment of your
mp
life. Lord, make me an in - stru-ment of your
mp
life. Lord, make me an in - stru-ment of your
mp

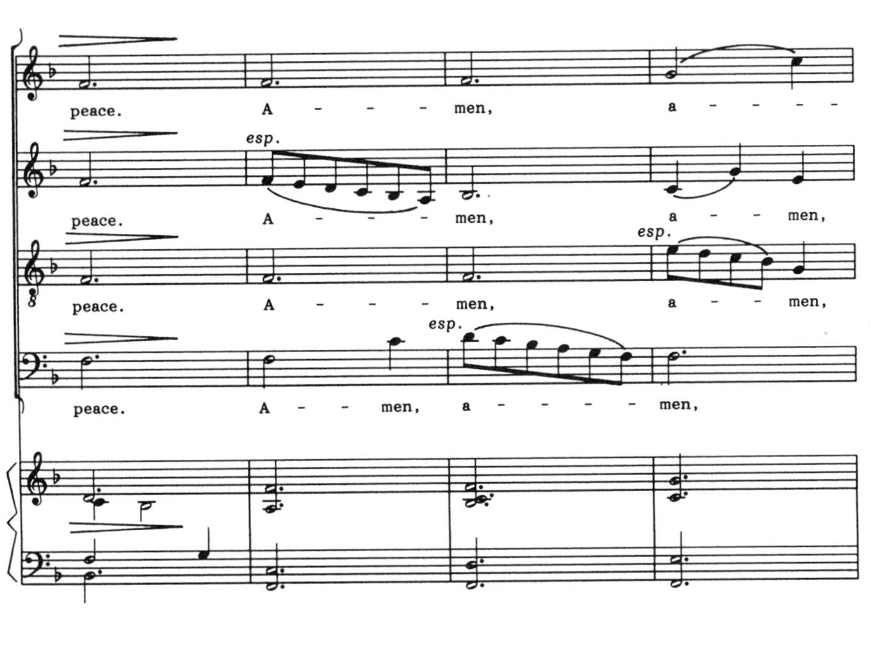
esp.
esp.
esp.
peace. A - - - men, a - - - -
peace. A - - - men, a - - men,
peace. A - - - men, a - - men,
peace. A - - men, a - - - - - men,

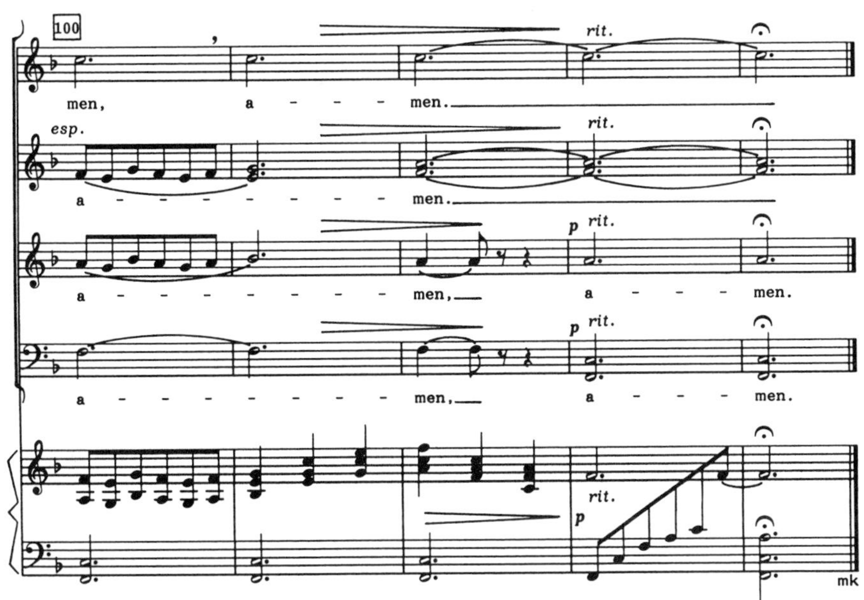
100
rit.
esp.
p
men, a - - - men.
a - - - - - - - - men.
a - - - - - - - men, a - - - men.
a - - - - - - - - men, a - - - men.
mk

Starlight Lullaby

COMPOSER: Philip Lane
TEXT: Peter Lawson

Focus

OVERVIEW
Major tonality; changing keys; melody shared between voices.

OBJECTIVES
After completing this lesson, students will be able to:

- Read and sing in major tonalities, changing keys.
- Identify characteristics of a major scale.
- Identify and sing melody lines that are shared between voice parts.

CHORAL MUSIC TERMS
Define the Choral Music Terms for students, giving pronunciation, and answering any questions that may arise.

Warming Up

Vocal Warm-Up

This Vocal Warm-Up is designed to prepare students to:

- Hear and sing in major tonality.
- Go from articulated connected singing on shorter values to legato singing on longer values.
- Sing with different vowel and initial consonant sounds.
- Feel subdivided rhythms at slower and faster tempos.

Have students:

- Read through the Vocal Warm-Up directions.
- Sing, following your demonstration.

LESSON 4

Starlight Lullaby

COMPOSER: *Philip Lane*
TEXT: *Peter Lawson*

CHORAL MUSIC TERMS
changing keys
half step
major tonalities
major scale
melody line
voice parts
whole step

VOICING
SATB

PERFORMANCE STYLE
Andante
Accompanied by piano

FOCUS

- Read and sing in major tonalities, changing keys.
- Identify characteristics of a major scale.
- Identify and sing melody lines that are shared between voice parts.

Warming Up

Vocal Warm-Up

Sing this exercise on *loo* using legato articulation on the quarter notes, and good diaphragmatic action to articulate the eighth notes. What other syllables might you use to sing this exercise? How do they feel different from *loo*?

Sight-Singing

Sight-sing this exercise using solfège and hand signs or numbers. Count carefully as you sing. Notice the homophonic and polyphonic styles. Did you sing all the tones of the major scale? Does the same part have the melody throughout the exercise? Try sharing the melody between voice parts.

TEACHER'S RESOURCE BINDER
Blackline Master 3, *The Major Scale*, page 79
Skill Master 21, *Circle of Fifths*, page 45

National Standards

Through involvement with this lesson, students will develop the following skills and concepts:

1. Singing, alone and with others, a varied repertoire of music. **(a, b, c, f)**
5. Reading and notating music. **(a, b)**
6. Listening to, analyzing, and describing music. **(a, b, c)**
7. Evaluating music and music performances. **(a)**

Singing: "Starlight Lullaby"

A composer must make many choices. One is the tonal set to use. The major scale is a popular and comfortable tone set, made up of the following arrangement of steps:

whole whole half whole whole whole half

In C major, match these steps to the notes:

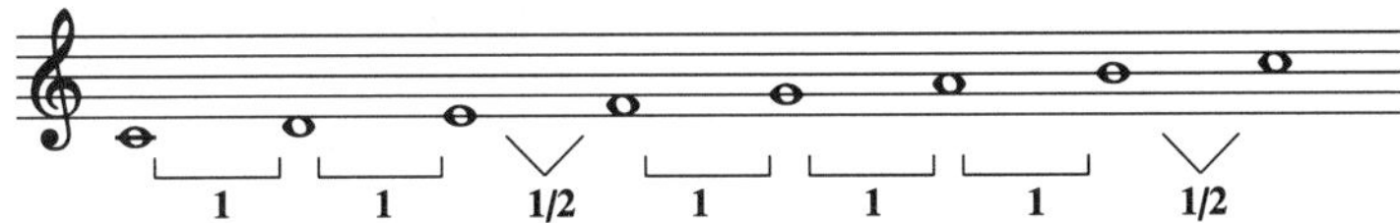

Other major scales have different pitches, but always the same arrangement of whole and half steps.

Now turn to the music for "Starlight Lullaby" on page 38.

HOW DID YOU DO?

Each time you learn a new concept or skill, you take a step toward better musicianship. Think about your preparation and performance of "Starlight Lullaby."

1. Write a major scale and show the arrangement of whole and half steps.

2. How well can you sight-sing in major? If you were given a never-before-seen melody, what might be a problem for you?

3. Write a melody in C major, then give it to a classmate. Have the classmate read your melody by sight, and you read theirs. How well did you do? What could you do better?

4. When a melody line is shared between voice parts, what problems can occur? What can you do to solve these problems?

Sight-Singing

This Sight-Singing exercise is designed to prepare students to:

- Sight-sing in four parts using solfège and hand signs or numbers for the major diatonic scale.
- Read in treble and bass clefs.
- Read and sing in homophonic and polyphonic styles.
- Identify the melody.

Have students:

- Read through the Sight-Singing exercise directions.
- Read through each voice part rhythmically, using rhythm syllables.
- Sight-sing through each part separately using solfège and hand signs or numbers.
- Sing all parts together.

Singing: "Starlight Lullaby"

Identify characteristics of a major scale.

Have students:

- Read the text on page 37.
- Using Blackline Master 3, *The Major Scale,* identify the same whole and half step relationships in several major scales, sight-sing using solfège and hand signs or numbers, and construct major scales.
- Look at the notation for "Starlight Lullaby," identifying where key changes occur. (measures 15, 28, 45, and 69)

Suggested Teaching Sequence

1. Review Vocal Warm-Up.
Sing with legato articulation and diaphragmatic articulation. Use different syllables and tempo.
Have students:

- Review the Vocal Warm-Up on page 36.
- Identify legato articulation caused by tongue motion when singing a consonant, and diaphragmatic pushes for sustained syllables.
- Suggest and sing the exercise with other consonant/vowel combinations. Discuss the difference between these and *loo.*
- Sing at different tempos.

2. Review Sight-Singing.
Read and sing in four parts using solfège and hand signs or numbers. Identify tones of the C major scale. Sing the melody sharing voice parts.
Have students:

- Review the Sight-Singing exercise on page 36.
- Identify homophonic and polyphonic elements of the exercise.
- Identify the C major syllables their voice part includes.
- Identify where the melody occurs in the exercise. (The melody is mostly in the upper treble voice, although the polyphonic treatment in measure 3 allows the men to imitate the melody for a while.)
- Write out just the melody line, then assign different parts of it to each section, singing in their own range, for example: measure 1, sopranos; measure 2, tenors; measure 3, altos; measure 4, basses; and so on.
- Discuss the difficulty of finding the beginning pitch when the melody is shared between voice parts at different registers, and how to listen for clues in the part before.

To Ian Tracey and the Royal Liverpool Philharmonic Choir

Starlight Lullaby

Philip Lane
Peter Lawson

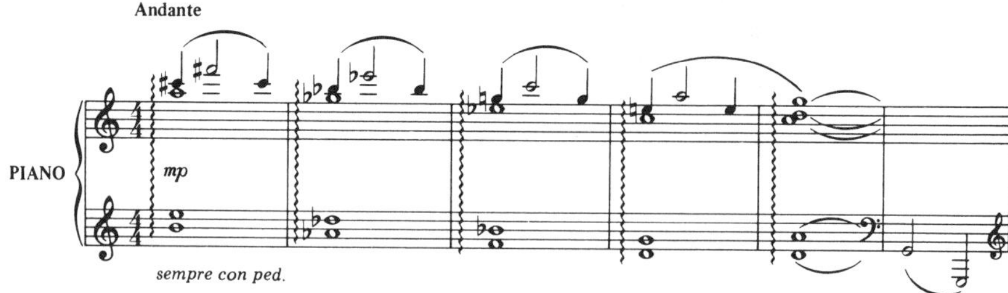

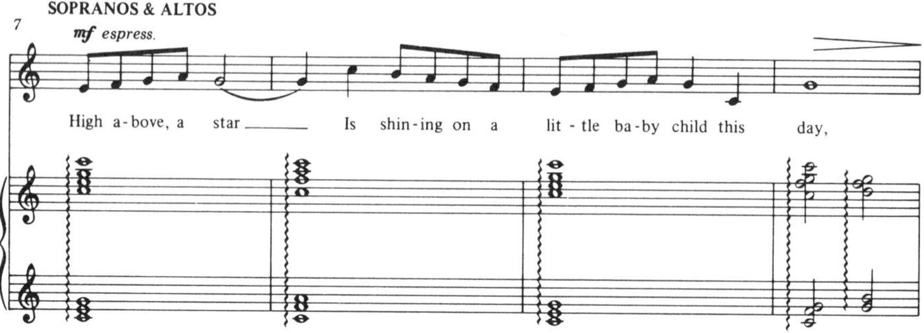

An orchestral version of the accompaniment is available for hire, scoring: 2.2.2.2 – 2.0.0.0 – hp. cel. str.

This piece is no. 2 of *Three Christmas Pictures*, a short choral and/or orchestral suite which may be performed separately or together. *Sleighbell Serenade* (no. 1) is also available separately (X357), and no. 3, *Christmas Eve Waltz*, is orchestral only.

"Starlight Lullaby"

This piece is the second of *Three Christmas Pictures*, a choral and/or orchestral suite; the other two pieces in the work are "Sleighbell Serenade" and "Christmas Waltz" (orchestra only). The three sections may be performed separately or together. There is an orchestral accompaniment for this piece available from the publisher (Oxford Press).

15 S.A: (Hum) (Hum)

TENOR: Cho-rus from a-bove sing soft-ly 'Al-le-lu-ia!' An-gel voi-ces sing-ing

B: (Hum) (Hum)

19 (Hum)

'Peace on earth,' Sweet-ly ca-rol-ling, with heav'n-ly mirth, To ce-le-brate our

(Hum)

23 (Hum.)

(Hum.)

Sa-viour's birth, No time can dim, Star-light lul-la-by for him.

(Hum) (Hum.)

3. Sight-sing "Starlight Lullaby" using solfège and hand signs or numbers.

Have students:

- Divide into voice sections (SATB) and read each part rhythmically, using rhythm syllables, adding dynamics to shape the phrases.
- Still in sections, sing with solfège and hand signs or numbers, identifying and working on problem areas, including preparing key changes by singing the last pitch in the old key, and then the first pitch in the new one.
- Discuss problems caused by sudden modulations. (ones with no preparation or common chord)
- Sing the piece through, using solfège and hand signs or numbers, with full ensemble.
- Divide into sections and recite the text rhythmically for each voice part.
- Sing the piece through with text as a full ensemble, using techniques of phrasing and legato articulation, and tuning pitches carefully.

TEACHING STRATEGY

Dynamics and Tempo

Have students:

- Identify dynamic and tempo markings in the notation for "Starlight Lullaby."
- Perform the piece, attending to the dynamic and tempo markings for increased expression.

4. Sharing the melody with accuracy.

Have students:

- Identify sections where their voice part has the melody.
- Identify ways to begin their sections with pitch accuracy (using a pitch from the previous section as a clue).
- Define dynamic considerations when their section does not have the melody.
- Sing the piece on *loo,* listening for intonation, blend, rise and fall of melodic lines, and pitch accuracy at the key changes.

41

Star-light lul-la-by for him.

(Hum) (Hum.)

No time can dim, (Hum.)

(Hum) (Hum.)

45

Ah Ah

T.B. unis.

Gold, frank-in-cense and myrrh, to-kens from a-far, Gi-ven to the ho-ly child,

49

Kings, fol-low-ing a star, Come un-to the sta-ble bare.

Ah Ah

VOCAL DEVELOPMENT

To encourage vocal development, have students:

- Demonstrate good vocal tone by singing tall vowels and alter (or modify) the vowel sounds when necessary, as in *above* and *Alleluia.*
- Energize sustained tones by increasing the breath support and dynamic level.
- Sing a resonating hum by creating a large space inside the mouth and closing the lips with an *mm* sound. The "buzz" should be felt in the nose and forehead.
- Listen for the uniformity of the vowel sound when singing the *Ah.*
- Sustain phrases by staggering the breathing and moving forward through the phrases.
- Demonstrate the correct singing of the *r* consonant after a vowel. It should be almost silent, as in *star, far, earth, mirth, our, birth, Virgin, Mary,* and *mother.*
- Listen for diphthongs (two vowel sounds when one vowel sound is written) in words such as *high, shining, day, lay, finds, voices, time, myrrh, bare, marvel, mild,* and *there.* Sing or sustain the first vowel sound and barely sing the second vowel sound with the next syllable.
- Identify intervals and chords between the parts and tune them carefully.
- Plan the dynamics to reflect the contour of the melodic line and the rise and fall of each musical phrase. Energize *forte* and *piano* singing with full breath support.

CONNECTING THE ARTS

Enhancing the Story Line with Visual Art, Dance, or Theater

The text of the piece adds a few characters or images of the Christmas story at a time. Have students:

- Consider ways to create this additive tableau in one of the other arts—dance, drama, or visual art. (shadow screen tableau, framed live tableau, puppets, slides or transparencies that overlay reproducing student-created fine art in puzzle style, etc.)
- Find a way to include their ideas in the performance of the piece in a way that is sensitive and enhances the mood.
- Consider how much can be done without taking away from the vocal performance.

Assessment

Informal Assessment

During this lesson, students showed the ability to:

- Identify and use legato articulation in the Vocal Warm-Up exercise.
- Sing one part independently, tuning pitches, when four parts are being sung in the Sight-Singing exercise.
- Sing a shared melody between voice parts in the Sight-Singing exercise.
- Identify characteristics of a major scale in the Singing section.
- Sing independently, using legato articulation, tuning pitches carefully, and sharing the melody line between voice parts in "Starlight Lullaby."

Student Self-Assessment

Have students:

- Evaluate their performance with the How Did You Do? section on page 37.
- Answer the questions individually. Discuss them in pairs or small groups and/or write their responses on a sheet of paper.

Individual Performance Assessment

To further demonstrate accomplishment, have each student:

- Write and sing a major scale on a pitch chosen by you.
- Sing through "Starlight Lullaby" in full ensemble, signaling with thumbs up in front of the body (hidden from the view of others) when singing the melody, and not signaling when singing a supporting harmony part.
- In a quartet or double quartet, sing measures 35–69 of "Starlight Lullaby" into a tape recorder in an isolated space, demonstrating legato articulation, in-tune singing, shared melody line, and change of key.

65 In - fant in a low - ly crib

unis.

In - fant in a — low - ly crib 'mid hum - ble — stall. —

In - fant in a low - ly crib

69 *mp espress.* High a - bove, a star — is shin - ing on a lit - tle ba - by child this day,

p Ah — Ah —

p Ah — Ah —

73 *mp* Cho - rus from a - bove — sing soft - ly 'Al - le - lu - ia,' *mf* An - gel voi-ces sing-ing

Extension

Sharing the Melodic Line

Have students:

- Choose a familiar melody and write it down.
- Rewrite the melody on two (women/men) or four (SATB) staves, shifting to a different part for each measure of the melody.
- Sing the melody in this fragmented form, sharing the melody.
- Repeat, improvising a harmonic accompaniment when their voice part does not have the melody.

How Many Major Keys Are There?

This would be a good time to review the circle of fifths, and the key signatures for all major keys. Have students:

- Review Skill Master 21, *Circle of Fifths,* in the TRB, that has the circle of fifths and the key signatures for each key.
- Review hand signs for pitches of the diatonic scale, including those above and below the octave *do*s.
- Write short melodies in several keys, sharing them with classmates to practice reading flexibly in different keys.

Write an Instrumental Obligato

Have students:

- Compose a single line obligato for tone chimes or handbells to be played as the ensemble sings the piece.
- Use the major scale and the specified harmonies in the piano accompaniment as a guideline for the obligato.

National Standards

The following National Standards are addressed through the Extension and bottom-page activities:

1. Singing, alone and with others, a varied repertoire of music. **(a, b, c, f)**
3. Improvising melodies, variations, and accompaniments. **(a, c)**
4. Composing and arranging music within specified guidelines. **(b, c)**
5. Reading and notating music. **(a, b)**
6. Listening to, analyzing, and describing music. **(a, b, c, e)**
7. Evaluating music and music performances. **(a, b, c)**
8. Understanding relationships between music, the other arts, and disciplines outside the arts. **(a, b)**
9. Understanding music in relation to history and culture. **(c)**

Understanding the Major Scale Through Improvisation

Students at this level should be very comfortable reading melodies in the major scale, and singing pitches in tune. However, they may not be as comfortable with improvising melodies that flow naturally.

Have them:

- Echo as you lead improvised melodies, using stepwise and skipwise melodic motion, and shaping phrases with repetition and contrast. (Lead four short patterns which, when sung in sequence, create a complete melody. The students echo each pattern, then sing all four in sequence from memory.)
- Discuss what makes a good melody, including use of stepwise motion and skips, beginning and ending on the tonic, using shorter motifs that either repeat or contrast within the longer melody, and possibly following a harmonic skeleton, using chord tones and passing tones to construct the melody.
- Improvise melodies in the major scale, first with only one of these characteristics in mind, then adding others as they become comfortable.
- Echo lead their own improvised melodies in short motifs as you did, with the whole group combining each four echo patterns to sing a melody.

Having Your Performance Evaluated by a Professional

Have students:

- Discuss the role of an adjudicator at a choral festival.
- Discuss how they feel about being observed by an adjudicator as they are performing.
- Discuss how the adjudicator sees her or his role.
- Identify the reasons and positive outcomes that can come from going to a choral festival and being adjudicated.

77

'Peace on earth,' Ah Ah To ce - le - brate our

Sweet - ly ca - rol-ling with heav'n - ly mirth,

81

Sa - viour's birth, Ah

Sa - viour's birth, No time can dim,

Allargando al fine

Star - light lul - la - by,

Ah

85

Star - light lul - la - by for him.

Reproduced and printed by Halstan & Co. Ltd., Amersham, Bucks., England

Creating an Assessment Rubric for "Starlight Lullaby"

Have students:

- Discuss the characteristics of a desirable performance of this piece, using all their knowledge of performance.
- Identify the criteria by which they think an adjudicator might assess the performance of the piece.
- For each criterion, decide what characteristics will comprise an adequate, good, very good, and excellent performance.
- Create a rubric chart and reproduce it for each student.
- Use the rubric to assess quartets or double quartets performing all or part of "Starlight Lullaby."

God Rest You Merry, Gentlemen

CHORAL MUSIC TERMS

augmentation
ensemble precision
half step
minor scale
minor tonality
round
whole step

Traditional English Carol
ARRANGER: *James Neal Koudelka*

VOICING

SATB

PERFORMANCE STYLE

Briskly
Accompanied by keyboard

FOCUS

- Identify and perform compositional devices of augmentation and round.
- Read and sing in minor tonality.
- Recognize characteristics of a minor scale.
- Sing in an ensemble with precision.

Warming Up

Rhythm Drill

Read and clap this rhythm with precision. Now divide into two groups. Half clap the rhythm as written, half clap it in augmentation, twice as slowly. Now clap it as a round, with Group 2 beginning four beats after Group 1.

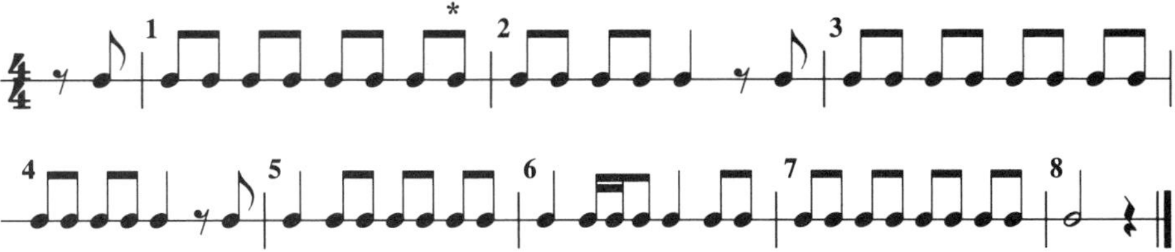

Vocal Warm-Up

Sing this exercise slowly at first, tuning each note as you go. When the pattern is familiar, move up a half step on each repeat. Use different articulations and styles to keep it interesting, and challenge yourself.

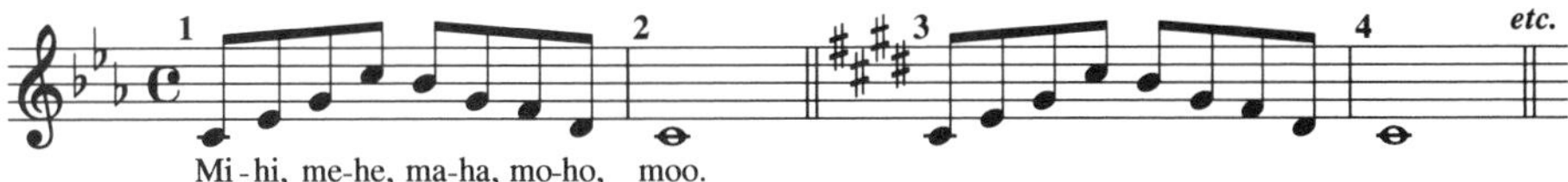
Mi-hi, me-he, ma-ha, mo-ho, moo.
etc.

TEACHER'S RESOURCE BINDER

Blackline Master 4, *The Minor Scale,* page 80
Skill Master 21, *Circle of Fifths,* page 45

National Standards

1. Singing a varied repertoire of music. **(a, b, c, f)**
4. Composing and arranging music within specified guidelines. **(a)**
5. Reading and notating music. **(a, b)**
6. Listening to, analyzing, and describing music. **(a, b, c)**
7. Evaluating music and music performances. **(a)**
9. Understanding music in relation to history and culture. **(a, d)**

LESSON 5

God Rest You Merry, Gentlemen

Traditional English Carol
ARRANGER: James Neal Koudelka

Focus

OVERVIEW

Minor tonality; ensemble precision; augmentation; round.

OBJECTIVES

After completing this lesson, students will be able to:

- Identify and perform compositional devices of augmentation and round.
- Read and sing in minor tonality.
- Recognize characteristics of a minor scale.
- Sing in an ensemble with precision.

CHORAL MUSIC TERMS

Define the Choral Music Terms for students, giving pronunciation, and answering any questions that may arise.

Warming Up

Rhythm Drill

This Rhythm Drill is designed to prepare students to:

- Read and clap rhythms with precision.
- Identify and perform augmented rhythms.
- Identify and clap in a round.

Have students:

- Read through the Rhythm Drill directions.
- Perform the drill.

Vocal Warm-Up

The Vocal Warm-Up on page 45 is designed to prepare students to:

- Hear and sing in harmonic minor.
- Read and sing the intervals in the exercise with confidence.
- Explore articulations and styles.

Have students:

- Read through the Vocal Warm-Up directions.
- Sing, following your demonstration.

Sight-Singing

This Sight-Singing exercise is designed to prepare students to:

- Sight-sing in four parts using solfège and hand signs or numbers for the harmonic minor scale.
- Read in treble and bass clefs.
- Identify and sing *si*.
- Listen for a precise ensemble sound.

Have students:

- Read through the Sight-Singing exercise directions.
- Read through each voice part rhythmically, using rhythm syllables.
- Sight-sing through each part separately using solfège and hand signs or numbers.
- Sing all parts together.

Singing: "God Rest You Merry, Gentlemen"

Identify characteristics of a minor scale.

Have students:

- Read the text on page 46.
- Using Blackline Master 4, *The Minor Scale,* identify the same whole and half step relationships in several minor scales, sight-sing using solfège and hand signs, and construct minor scales.
- Look at the notation for "God Rest You Merry, Gentlemen," and sight-sing the melody line beginning at measure 10 in minor.

Sight-Singing

Sight-sing this exercise using solfège and hand signs or numbers. Notice the minor key, and sing accurately all *si's* (D♯). This raised tone will feel like *ti* in a major key. Sing using both legato and staccato articulation, working for a precise ensemble sound. Once you know the exercise, sing with your eyes closed to hear the ensemble sound better.

Singing: "God Rest You Merry, Gentlemen"

Many traditional tunes are in minor tonality. There are three different kinds of minor scales: natural, harmonic, and melodic. The natural minor scale is made up of the following arrangement of steps:

whole half whole whole half whole whole

In E minor, match these steps to the notes:

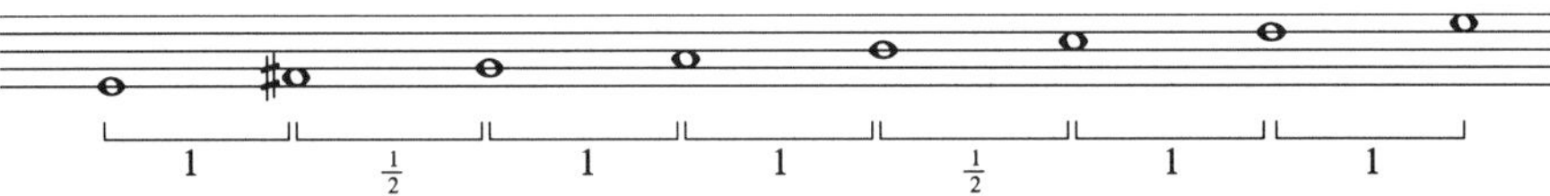

In minor, the tonal center is *la*. You use the pitch names of the relative major scale, in this case G major, to read the pitches in minor. In the harmonic minor, the seventh pitch is raised a half step. Instead of *so*, you will call it *si*.

Now turn to the music for "God Rest You Merry, Gentlemen" on page 47.

HOW DID YOU DO? ? ?

Sometimes, pieces in minor can provide quite a challenge. Think about your preparation and performance of "God Rest You Merry, Gentlemen."

1. How precise is your singing? Sing the Sight-Reading exercise with three classmates to show your skill at singing with precision.
2. Write a minor scale and show the arrangement of whole and half steps.
3. How well can you sight-sing in minor? If you were given a never-before-seen melody, what might be a problem for you?
4. Write a melody in E minor, then give it to a classmate. Have them read your melody by sight, and you read theirs. How well did you do? What could you do better?
5. Describe the compositional devices used by the arranger for each of the three verses of "God Rest You Merry, Gentlemen."

Arranger James Neal Koudelka

James Neal Koudelka is a music educator in Lincoln, Nebraska, where he has a large private voice and piano studio. Koudelka has worked since 1979 for the Lincoln public schools as a professional piano accompanist and choral director. He also has been musical director at the Okoboji, Iowa, summer theater since 1988.

As a composer, Koudelka has choral works published with Alfred Publishing Company, Carl Fischer, Inc., and G. Schirmer. He is an active member of the New Tuners Musical Theatre Workshop in Chicago, developing works for the American stage.

To Duane Nichols and the Lincoln, NE, Northeast High School Concert Choir

God Rest You Merry, Gentlemen

Traditional English Carol
Arranged by James Neal Koudelka

SATB Voices and Keyboard

TEACHING STRATEGY

Staggered Breathing

The introduction for "God Rest You Merry, Gentlemen" has an indication for staggered breathing. Have students:

- Practice holding out chord tones, each person breathing at a different time than either neighbor, and then joining back in without any accent.
- Continue to hold the chord indefinitely, each section changing their pitch as indicated by the teacher, but sustaining the tone through staggered breathing.

(Note: By changing tones one at a time, you can help students become accustomed to sustaining dissonant relationships between parts, then resolving them.)

Suggested Teaching Sequence

1. Review Rhythm Drill.
Read and clap rhythms. Identify and clap augmentation and round.
Have students:

- Review the Rhythm Drill on page 45.
- In two groups, first identify augmentation as going half as fast, and then clap with one group going half as fast as the other. Notice that the faster group repeats the pattern twice.
- Still in two groups, perform the rhythm as a round.
- Be sure to switch parts, so both groups have the opportunity to perform each task.
- Review the notation of "God Rest You Merry, Gentlemen," finding the augmentation (verse 2, measure 21) and round (verse 3, measure 34).

2. Review Vocal Warm-Up.
Read and sing in minor. Tune pitches. Use different articulations and styles.
Have students:

- Review the Vocal Warm-Up on page 45.
- Tune each pitch carefully until the pattern becomes familiar.
- Suggest different articulations (staccato, legato, and marcato) and styles (jazz, classical, hip, dramatic), changing the rhythm as appropriate to fit each style.

3. Review Sight-Singing.
Read and sing in harmonic minor. Use legato and staccato articulation. Work for precise ensemble sound.
Have students:

- Review the Sight-Singing exercise on page 46.
- Identify the raised *so,* and label it *si.*
- Use different articulations.
- Close their eyes and sing with eyes closed, listening carefully to the ensemble sound.

4. Sight-sing "God Rest You Merry, Gentlemen" using solfège and hand signs or numbers.

Have students:

- Divide into voice sections (SATB) and read each part rhythmically, using rhythm syllables, adding dynamics to shape the phrases.
- Still in sections, sing with solfège and hand signs or numbers, identifying and working on problem areas.
- Sing the piece through, using solfège and hand signs or numbers, with full ensemble.
- Divide into sections and recite the text rhythmically for each voice part.
- Sing the piece through with text as a full ensemble.

5. Work toward a precise ensemble sound.

Have students:

- Sing the entire piece on the staccato syllable *doot* for ensemble rhythmic accuracy.
- Give strict attention to pitch and rhythmic placement.
- Identify the compositional devices used by the composer— verse 1: soprano melody and ATB accompaniment; verse 2: TB melody with SA augmented melody; verse 3: strict round.
- Review all dynamic and tempo markings.
- Perform the piece, refining the ensemble sound.

16

ti - dings of com - fort and joy, com-fort and joy, O, ti - dings of com - fort and

mf

19 dim. unis. mp 21

joy. God rest you, mer - ry,

dim. unis. mf

In Beth-le-hem, in Jew - ry, This

dim. mp

22

gen - tle - men, let noth - ing you dis - may, To

bless - ed Babe was born. And laid with-in a man - ger up - on this bless-ed morn, To

VOCAL DEVELOPMENT

To encourage vocal development, have students:

- Demonstrate good vocal tone by singing with tall vowels and clear consonants.
- Create a rich resonant sound on the *loo* syllables by increasing the space in the mouth and pharynx.
- Modify vowel sounds in words such as *God, from,* and *Son,* to create a resonant *awh* sound rather than an *uh* sound.
- Energize sustained tones and accented notes by increasing the breath support and dynamic level.
- Sustain phrases by staggering the breathing and moving forward through the phrases.
- Listen for diphthongs (two vowel sounds when one vowel sound is written) in English words such as *day, astray, tidings, joy, mind, find,* and *rejoiced.* Sing or sustain the first vowel sound and barely sing the second vowel sound with the next syllable.
- Demonstrate the correct singing of the *r* consonant after a vowel when singing in English. It should be almost silent, as in *merry, remember, Savior, born, comfort, manger, mother, Mary, certain,* and *shepherds.*
- Feel the arched contour of each musical phrase as it begins, builds, then tapers off. The dynamics should reflect the melodic contour.
- Balance the chords between the parts by listening to them. Try adding more weight to one part to determine the effect on the chord.
- Note the augmentation of the melody with the verse at measure 21 and the canon of the melody at measure 33.

CONNECTING THE ARTS

Dance

Have students:

- Identify the style of this piece as a traditional English tune with three verses.
- Learn some English country dances to gain a repertoire of familiar steps and formations.
- Explore traditional English country dance movements that might fit with the melody.
- Explore variations of that movement that would show both augmentation and round through dance.
- Create a dance with formation and steps that are stylistically matched to the piece, and illustrate the augmentation of the second verse, and round in the third verse.

Assessment

Informal Assessment

During this lesson, students showed the ability to:

- Identify and perform augmentation and round in the Rhythm Drill.
- Tune pitches and use different articulations and styles in the Vocal Warm-Up exercise.
- Sing one part independently in harmonic minor when four parts are being sung in the Sight-Singing exercise.
- Work toward a precise ensemble sound in the Sight-Singing exercise.
- Identify characteristics of a minor scale in the Singing section.
- Sing independently, using legato articulation, tuning pitches carefully, and sharing the melody line between voice parts in "God Rest You Merry, Gentlemen."

Student Self-Assessment

Have students:

- Evaluate their performance with the How Did You Do? section on page 46.
- Answer the questions individually. Discuss them in pairs or small groups and/or write their responses on a sheet of paper.

Individual Performance Assessment

To further demonstrate accomplishment, have each student:

- Write and sing a minor scale on a pitch you choose in both natural and harmonic form.
- Sing through "God Rest You Merry, Gentlemen" in a group of at least 16 students while being videotaped, showing characteristics of precision ensemble performance.
- In a quartet or double quartet, sing verses 2 and 3 of "God Rest You Merry, Gentlemen," into a tape recorder in an isolated space, demonstrating the ability to perform augmentation and round.

34

grad cresc. to m. 46

God our heav'n-ly Fa - ther, A bless-ed an - gel came, And un - to cer-tain shep - herds brought

(slightly detached) *unis.* *mp* *grad. cresc. to m. 46*

From God our heav'n-ly Fa - ther, A bless-ed an - gel came, And

grad. cresc. to m. 46

37

più legato

ti-dings of the same, How that in Beth - le - hem was born The Son of God by name; O —

un - to cer-tain shep-herds brought ti-dings of the same, How that in Beth-le - hem was born the

40

ti - dings of com - fort and joy, com-fort and joy. O, — ti - dings of com - fort and

più legato

Son of God by name; O — ti - dings of com - fort and joy, com-fort and joy, O —

piu legato

Extension

Exploring the Rhythm Drill Through Articulation, Style, and Melody

Have students:

- Discuss ways they could expand the idea of the Rhythm Drill through articulation, style and/or melody.

—**articulation:** Perform the drill with a combination of articulations that are practiced and refined.

—**style:** Perform the drill in a specific style, adding scat syllables, text, or changing the rhythm to accommodate the style.

—**melody:** Create a melody for the rhythm that has a pitch from the tonic chord on each strong beat. In this way, they will still be able to perform augmentation and canon without too much dissonance.

- In small groups or individually, create a new arrangement of the Rhythm Drill, adding one or more of the preceding suggestions.
- Perform their new drill for the ensemble.
- Identify any drills that demonstrate imagination or technical skill that warrants more refinement and work.
- Refine and expand any identified works into compositions.

National Standards

The following National Standards are addressed through the Extension and bottom-page activities:

1. Singing, alone and with others, a varied repertoire of music. **(a, b, c)**
3. Improvising melodies, variations, and accompaniments. **(b)**
4. Composing and arranging music within specified guidelines. **(b, c, d)**
5. Reading and notating music. **(a, b)**
6. Listening to, analyzing, and describing music. **(a, b, c)**
7. Evaluating music and music performances. **(a, b, c)**
8. Understanding relationships between music, the other arts, and disciplines outside the arts. **(a, b, d)**
9. Understanding music in relation to history and culture. **(a, d)**

Understanding the Minor Scale Through Improvisation

Students at this level might be comfortable reading melodies in minor and singing pitches in tune. However, they may not be as comfortable with improvising melodies that flow naturally. Have them:

- Echo as you lead improvised melodies, using stepwise and skipwise melodic motion, and shaping phrases with repetition and contrast. (Lead four short patterns that, when sung in sequence, create a complete melody. Students echo each pattern, and then sing all four in sequence from memory.)
- Discuss what makes a good melody, including use of stepwise motion and skips, beginning and ending on the tonic, using shorter motifs that either repeat or contrast within the longer melody, and possibly following a harmonic skeleton, using chord tones and passing tones to construct the melody.
- Improvise melodies in the minor scale, first with only one of these characteristics in mind, then adding others as they become comfortable.
- Echo lead their own improvised melodies in short motifs as you did, with the whole group combining each four echo patterns to sing a melody.

52 *Choral Connections Level 4 Mixed Voices*

How Many Minor Keys Are There?

There are parallel and relative minor keys for each major key in the circle of fifths.

Have students:

- Use Skill Master 21, *Circle of Fifths,* in the TRB to review the circle of fifths and the key signatures for each key.
- Identify relative minor as the key that uses the same tone set as a major (G major and E minor), and parallel minor as the key that uses the same pitches as major (G major and G minor).
- Review hand signs for pitches of the natural and harmonic minor keys.
- Write short melodies in several minor keys, sharing them with classmates to practice reading flexibly in different keys.

Papillon, Tu Es Volage

French Canadian Folk Song
ARRANGER: Jonathan Thompson

Focus

OVERVIEW
Natural minor; French pronunciation.

OBJECTIVES
After completing this lesson, students will be able to:
- Read and sing in natural minor.
- Sing using correct French pronunciation.

CHORAL MUSIC TERMS
Define the Choral Music Terms for students, giving pronunciation, and answering any questions that may arise.

Warming Up

Vocal Warm-Up

This Vocal Warm-Up is designed to prepare students to:
- Identify, hear, and sing in natural minor.
- Sing with buoyancy.

Have students:
- Read through the Vocal Warm-Up directions.
- Sing, following your demonstration.

Papillon, Tu Es Volage

French Canadian Folk Song
ARRANGER: *Jonathan Thompson*

CHORAL MUSIC TERMS
lentemente
natural minor

VOICING
SATB

PERFORMANCE STYLE
Sweetly
A cappella

FOCUS
- Read and sing in natural minor.
- Sing using correct French pronunciation.

Warming Up

Vocal Warm-Up

Sing this exercise using solfège and hand signs or numbers. Bounce on your toes as you sing, and keep your singing bouncy as well. What tonality is this exercise written in?

Sight-Singing

Sight-sing this exercise using solfège and hand signs or numbers. Notice that all parts are written in the treble clef, but each may be sung in your vocal register. Choose any part you wish as you read and sing together. How would you describe these vocal parts in relationship to one another? Continue until you have sung all three parts.

TEACHER'S RESOURCE BINDER

Blackline Master 5, *Translation and Pronunciation Guide for "Papillon, Tu Es Volage,"* page 82

National Standards

1. Singing a varied repertoire of music. **(a, b, c)**
4. Composing and arranging music. **(a)**
5. Reading and notating music. **(a, b)**
6. Listening to, analyzing, and describing music. **(a, b, c)**
7. Evaluating music and music performances. **(a)**
8. Understanding relationships between music, the other arts, and disciplines outside the arts. **(c)**
9. Understanding music in relation to history and culture. **(d)**

Singing: "Papillon, Tu Es Volage"

Imagine a beautiful butterfly flitting from flower to flower. What might this butterfly symbolize in life? Read the text of "Papillon, Tu Es Volage" in English. What does the butterfly symbolize in this text?

Now turn to the music for "Papillon, Tu Es Volage" on page 56.

HOW DID YOU DO?

When you learn a new piece, are you like a butterfly trying one thing and then another, or do you focus on one learning issue until it is mastered? Think about your preparation and performance of "Papillon, Tu Es Volage."

1. Describe how you read in natural minor, then sing either the Vocal Warm-Up or Sight-Singing exercise to demonstrate your ability.

2. Write a melody in a natural minor, then give it to a classmate. Have your classmate read your melody by sight, and you read theirs. How well did you do? What could you do better?

3. How is your French pronunciation? What is easy? What is difficult? Demonstrate your French pronunciation by reading aloud the first verse of "Papillon, Tu Es Volage."

4. Write a short essay describing the symbolism of the butterfly in "Papillon, Tu Es Volage."

"Papillon, Tu Es Volage"

"Papillon, Tu Es Volage," similar to many of Quebec's folk songs, is of French origin. In the present choral arrangement, all five verses of the folk song are set. The arranger suggests that dynamic indications are followed carefully in order so that the style of the song, with its poignancy and elegance, is communicated effectively. The first eleven measures may be sung by either a soprano soloist, a few sopranos, or the full section. The use of soloist is favored by the arranger on the grounds that it would lend variety to the performance. It is important that the folk melody be allowed to predominate a little in each verse so that the dialogue between the girl and her fickle lover is conveyed clearly.

Sight-Singing

This Sight-Singing exercise is designed to prepare students to:

- Sight-sing in three parts using solfège and hand signs or numbers.
- Read and sing in natural minor.
- Sing independently.

Have students:

- Read through the Sight-Singing exercise directions.
- Read through each voice part rhythmically, using rhythm syllables.
- Sight-sing through each part separately using solfège and hand signs or numbers.
- Sing all parts together.

Singing: "Papillon, Tu Es Volage"

Discuss the symbolism of the butterfly.

Have students:

- Read the text on page 55.
- Imagine a butterfly and describe its actions.
- Discuss what these actions, and the butterfly, might symbolize in life. (Accept any thoughtful answer at this point.)
- Use Blackline Master 5, *Translation and Pronunciation Guide for "Papillon, Tu Es Volage,"* to read the English text of the piece, and then identify the butterfly as a symbol of an unfaithful lover or a free spirit that will not be tied down to one person.
- Identify who is speaking in each verse, and discover that it is a dialogue between a girl and her fickle lover. Discuss the mood and tone of voice of each character.

Suggested Teaching Sequence

1. Review Vocal Warm-Up.
Identify, read, and sing in natural minor. Use a bouncy tone. Hear the difference between major and minor.
Have students:

- Review the Vocal Warm-Up on page 54.
- Bounce on their toes on the strong beats of each measure, using a bouncy tone.
- Identify the tonality as D natural minor.

2. Review Sight-Singing.
Read and sing in natural minor. Sing independently.
Have students:

- Review the Sight-Singing exercise on page 54.
- Repeat, singing a different part on each repeat until they are all familiar.
- Describe the relationship between the lines: Part 1 is the melody, and Parts 2 and 3 are accompaniment parts, written in fifths.

Papillon, Tu Es Volage

Arranged by
Jonathan Thompson

SATB

TEACHING STRATEGY
Identifying a Key as Minor

Have students:

- Discuss and identify strategies for determining whether a piece is in major or minor, and, if minor, what type of minor key it might be. Some possible strategies include:

—Look at the key signature, and determine the possible major key.
—Look at the notation, especially the beginning chord, and the chords at the ends of phrases, identifying the tonal center.
—Determine if the tonal center matches the major key, or is a third below, indicating the relative minor.
—If minor, look for altered tones. If there are none, it is natural minor. If there are

3. Sight-sing "Papillon, Tu Es Volage" using solfège and hand signs or numbers.

Have students:

- Divide into voice sections (SATB) and read each part rhythmically, using rhythm syllables, adding dynamics to shape the phrases.
- Remember that the text of the piece is like a dialogue, and notice that the melody falls with either the men or women in relation to the text.
- Still in sections, sing with solfège and hand signs or numbers, identifying and working on problem areas.
- Sing the piece through, using solfège and hand signs or numbers, with full ensemble.

4. Learn the French pronunciation.

Have students:

- Using Blackline Master 5, *Translation and Pronunciation Guide for "Papillon, Tu Es Volage,"* echo the text in short phrases.
- Echo in this order: all voice parts on measures 1–10; basses on measures 11–21; sopranos and altos on measures 22–32; all voice parts on measures 33–44; sopranos and altos on measures 44–55.
- Read through the entire piece, speaking the French text in rhythm.
- Sing the piece with correct French pronunciation.

altered tones, it is possibly harmonic minor.

—Acknowledge that sometimes pieces shift between keys, so keep aware of unusual changes.

—Use the historical period in which the piece was written to guide expectations.

Early pieces might be modal, or have key shifts. Classical pieces are more straightforward. Romantic pieces are usually in a key, but have altered tones, and can shift. Contemporary pieces may even be atonal, or use chromatic or whole tone scales.

VOCAL DEVELOPMENT

To encourage vocal development, have students:

- Demonstrate good vocal tone by singing with tall vowels and clear consonants.
- Create a rich resonant sound on the *oh* syllables by increasing the space in the mouth and pharynx. Try using an *oo* sound.
- Articulate the French text precisely with rhythmic accuracy.
- Energize sustained tones by increasing the breath support and intensity.
- Sustain phrases by staggering the breathing and moving forward through the phrases.
- Feel the arched contour of each musical phrase as it begins, builds, then tapers off. Plan the dynamics to reflect the melodic contour and meaning of the text.
- Balance the chords between the parts by listening carefully. Analyze the chords and listen for major and minor chord tonalities.
- Articulate the staggered entrances of each voice at measures 22 and 33 with precise rhythm and text pronunciation.
- French text pronunciation includes sounds not used in English, such as mixed vowels, nasal vowels, the enya (ɲ) and glide (ɥ). Pay close attention to the stressing patterns and practice the text aloud in rhythm.

CONNECTING THE ARTS

Creative Dance

Have students:

- Identify the style of this piece as a folk tune with five verses in dialogue form.
- Discuss what style of dance would be appropriate to express the same mood as the piece. (probably symbolic or creative modern dance)
- Create a dance that symbolically expresses the message of each verse, without being literal.
- Perform the dance with the piece.

Assessment

Informal Assessment

During this lesson, students showed the ability to:

- Identify and sing in natural minor in the Vocal Warm-Up.
- Read and sing one part independently in natural minor when three parts are being sung in the Sight-Singing exercise.
- Work toward a precise ensemble sound in the Sight-Singing exercise.
- Sing independently in natural minor, using correct French pronunciation, in "Papillon, Tu Es Volage."

Student Self-Assessment

Have students:

- Evaluate their performance with the How Did You Do? section on page 55.
- Answer the questions individually. Discuss them in pairs or small groups and/or write their responses on a sheet of paper.

Individual Performance Assessment

To further demonstrate accomplishment, have each student:

- Write and sing a natural minor scale on a pitch chosen by you.
- Compose a melody in natural minor and sing it using solfège and hand signs.
- Sing a self-chosen phrase or verse of "Papillon, Tu Es Volage" into a tape recorder in an isolated space, demonstrating the ability to use correct French pronunciation.

Extension

Aurally Distinguishing Between Major and Minor Melodies

Have students:

- Listen to the C major scale.
- Listen to "Three Blind Mice" in C major.
- Listen to the A natural minor scale.
- Listen to "Three Blind Mice" in A minor.
- Listen to or sing other familiar melodies ("Row, Row, Row Your Boat" or "Frère Jacques"), identifying whether they are major or minor, and then altering them to the other.

Aurally Distinguishing Between Major and Minor Triads

Have students:

- Look at C major and A minor keys drawn on the board.
- Listen to each chord, signaling thumbs up for major and thumbs down for minor.
- Listen to other chords, signaling for major or minor. (Begin with only root position triads, then gradually include inversions.)

National Standards

The following National Standards are addressed through the Extension and bottom-page activities:

1. Singing, alone and with others, a varied repertoire of music. **(a, b, c)**
3. Improvising melodies, variations, and accompaniments. **(b, c)**
4. Composing and arranging music within specified guidelines. **(b, c, d)**
5. Reading and notating music. **(a, b)**
6. Listening to, analyzing, and describing music. **(a, b, c)**
8. Understanding relationships between music, the other arts, and disciplines outside the arts. **(a, c, d)**
9. Understanding music in relation to history and culture. **(a, d)**

45
Soprano
mour a - vait des ai - les, ai -
Alto
p
Com - me toi, beau pa - pil -

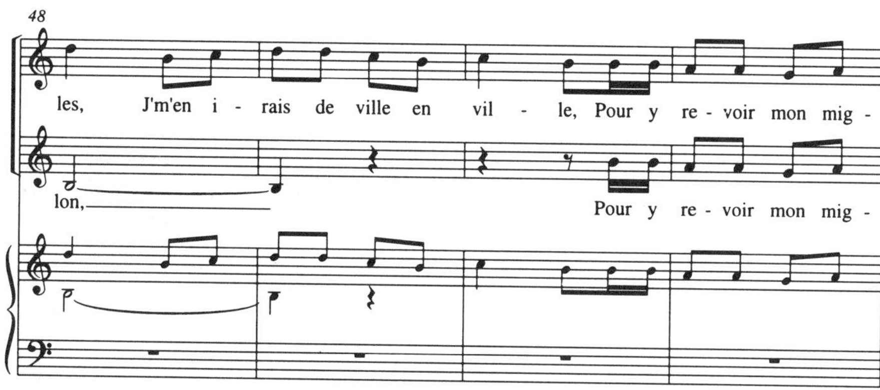
48
les, J'm'en i - rais de ville en vil - le, Pour y re - voir mon mig -
lon,
Pour y re - voir mon mig -

52
non, Y cueil- ler les fleurs de la bell' sai - son!
non, Y cueil- ler les fleurs bell' sai - son!

Improvising Over a Shifting Chord Accompaniment

The Sight-Singing exercise has an interesting accompaniment of i–vii shifting chords. This is an interesting accompaniment over which to improvise.

Have students:

- Listen to the accompaniment chords, and identify them as the A minor and G major chords, without the thirds.
- Build the chords on the board.
- Improvise chord tone melodies over the accompaniment, gradually including passing tones, and adding rhythmic complexity. (Half of the students will sing the accompaniment as the other half improvises. Then switch.)

The Butterfly in the Arts

The butterfly is a loved character in many cultures. Have students:

- Explore the butterfly as it is presented in the arts, across periods and cultures.
- Share information with one another, forming generalizations about the butterfly in the arts.
- Create a multimedia presentation, including this choral piece, that demonstrates artistic representations of the butterfly in dance, visual art, literature, and music.
- Add to the repertoire by creating their own artistic representations of the butterfly.

MORE ABOUT

Animals as Symbols

Have students:

- Research other animals that act as symbols in different cultures.
- Find animals that symbolize different human characteristics, including bravery, cowardice, determination, adaptability, loyalty, independence, and so on.
- Find musical compositions that are named for animals, and listen to see if the composer captured the essence of the animal musically, and how.

I Saw Three Ships

Traditional Carol
ARRANGER: Edwin Fissinger

Focus

OVERVIEW
6/8 meter; consonant and dissonant chords.

OBJECTIVES
After completing this lesson, students will be able to:
- Identify, read, and sing in 6/8 meter.
- Distinguish between consonant and dissonant chords.
- Sing consonant and dissonant chords.

CHORAL MUSIC TERMS
Define the Choral Music Terms for students, giving pronunciation, and answering any questions that may arise.

Warming Up

Vocal Warm-Up
This Vocal Warm-Up is designed to prepare students to:
- Sing using good posture.
- Feel the pulse in 6/8 meter.
- Sing with legato articulation.

Have students:
- Read through the Vocal Warm-Up directions.
- Sing, following your demonstration.

LESSON 7

I Saw Three Ships

Traditional Carol
ARRANGER: *Edwin Fissinger*

CHORAL MUSIC TERMS
consonant
dissonant
6/8 meter

VOICING
SATB

PERFORMANCE STYLE
Rocking, swaying
A cappella

FOCUS
- Identify, read, and clap in 6/8 meter.
- Distinguish between consonant and dissonant chords.
- Sing consonant and dissonant chords.

Warming Up

Vocal Warm-Up

Stand and raise both hands over your head, then stretch upward. Lower your arms gradually, keeping them straight and extended. Sing this exercise using *koo*, keeping this posture to allow plenty of room for your breath. Move up by half steps on repeats, using legato articulation.

Sight-Singing

First clap the rhythm of each line to review 6/8 meter. Now sight-sing each line using solfège and hand signs or numbers. All four lines may be sung together. Try various ways to combine them.

TEACHER'S RESOURCE BINDER

National Standards

1. Singing, alone and with others, a varied repertoire of music. **(a, b, c, e)**
5. Reading and notating music. **(a, b)**
6. Listening to, analyzing, and describing music. **(a, b, c)**
8. Understanding relationships between music, the other arts, and disciplines outside the arts. **(c)**
9. Understanding music in relation to history and culture. **(d)**

Singing: "I Saw Three Ships"

What do you think is the difference between consonant and dissonant sounds? If all the bells on Earth rang at the same time, and you could hear them all, would the sound be consonant or dissonant? Listen to several sounds played together, and decide if the chord is consonant or dissonant. What intervals are more and less consonant to your ears?

Now turn to the music for "I Saw Three Ships" on page 64.

HOW DID YOU DO? ? ? ?

If you worked together in harmony, you created dissonance in this piece. Think about your preparation and performance of "I Saw Three Ships."

1. You should be able to read and sing easily in 6/8 meter by now. How good are you at reading in this meter? Are there any patterns that you still find difficult? What can you do to improve?

2. Describe the difference between a consonant and dissonant chord, then demonstrate the difference in a small group.

3. Describe any dissonance in "I Saw Three Ships" and why these sounds are considered dissonant.

4. Write an essay describing the use of dissonant harmonies in "I Saw Three Ships," identifying where this occurs, and why the composer might have chosen this compositional device.

Sight-Singing

This Sight-Singing exercise is designed to prepare students to:

- Sight-sing in four parts using solfège and hand signs or numbers.
- Read and sing in 6/8 meter.
- Sing independently.

Have students:

- Read through the Sight-Singing exercise directions.
- Read through each voice part rhythmically, clapping the rhythm to review 6/8 meter.
- Sight-sing through each part separately using solfège and hand signs or numbers.
- Sing all parts together.

Singing: "I Saw Three Ships"

Compare consonant and dissonant chords.

Have students:

- Read the text on page 63.
- Discuss possible definitions of consonant and dissonant sounds. (whether the sound combinations are pleasing or grating, and different opinions of these occurring at different historical periods and with different aural experiences)
- Discuss whether all bells sounding at the same time would be consonant or dissonant. (There may be different opinions, based on the definition of consonant and dissonant.)
- Explore playing any three or four pitches (a chord) on a keyboard, deciding whether they are consonant or dissonant, and why.
- Identify 2nds and 7ths as more dissonant that 3rds, 5ths, and 6ths.

Suggested Teaching Sequence

1. Review Vocal Warm-Up.
Use correct posture. Sing in 6/8 meter.
Have students:

- Review the Vocal Warm-Up on page 62.
- Review correct posture and how it affects breathing.
- Identify 6/8 meter and legato articulation.

2. Review Sight-Singing.
Read and sing in 6/8 meter. Sing independently.
Have students:

- Review the Sight-Singing exercise on page 62.
- Repeat, singing a different part on each repeat until they are all familiar.
- Arrange a piece using the four lines in different combinations, adding dynamic variation.

I Saw Three Ships

Traditional Carol
Arranged by Edwin Fissinger

SATB, A cappella

TEACHING STRATEGY

6/8 Meter

At this level, 6/8 meter should be quite familiar to students; however, they may need experience improvising in 6/8.
Have students:

- Echo as you clap improvised rhythmic patterns in 6/8 meter, using the basic rhythms of the meter and shaping phrases with repetition and contrast. (Lead four short patterns that, when clapped in sequence, create a complete phrase. The students echo each pattern, and then clap back all four in sequence from memory.)

3. Sight-sing "I Saw Three Ships" using solfège and hand signs or numbers.

Have students:

- Divide into voice sections (SATB) and read each part rhythmically, using rhythm syllables, adding dynamics to shape the phrases.
- Still in sections, sing with solfège and hand signs or numbers, identifying and working on problem areas.
- Sing the piece through, using solfège and hand signs or numbers, with full ensemble.
- Divide into sections and recite the text rhythmically for each voice part.
- Sing the piece through with text as a full ensemble.

4. Identify dissonant chords in "I Saw Three Ships."

Have students:

- Listen as sopranos and altos sing measures 39–42 using solfège and hand signs, and determine that the chords are consonant.
- Listen as tenors and basses add their parts to measures 39–42, and determine that the new chords are dissonant.
- Discuss why the addition of the tenor/bass parts produces dissonant chords. (the 2nds and 7ths created by the combination of pitches)
- Discuss why the arranger chose these chords for the text of this verse. (The text is about all the bells on Earth ringing. The sound is meant to represent the different kind of harmony that occurs when all voices and pitches are present, and that this may require a different kind of listening.)

- Discuss what makes a good rhythmic phrase, including use of short motifs that either repeat or contrast within the longer rhythm, and building tension and release across the phrase.
- Improvise rhythmic phrases in 6/8 meter, first using a few rhythmic elements, then adding others as they become comfortable.
- Echo lead their own improvised rhythms in short motifs as you did, with the whole group combining each four echo patterns to clap the entire phrase.

VOCAL DEVELOPMENT

To encourage vocal development, have students:

- Demonstrate good vocal tone by singing with tall vowels and clear consonants.
- Arch or lift the tone on melodic leaps by increasing the space in the mouth and pharynx.
- Energize sustained tones by increasing the breath support and dynamic level.
- Sustain phrases by staggering the breathing and moving forward through the phrases.
- Listen for diphthongs (two vowel sounds when one vowel sound is written) in some English words such as *I, day, rejoice,* and *pray.* Sing or sustain the first vowel sound and barely sing the second vowel sound with the next syllable.
- Demonstrate the correct singing of the *r* consonant after a vowel when singing in English. It should be almost silent, as in *morning, our, Savior, whither, earth,* and *Lord.*
- Feel the arched contour of each musical phrase as it begins, builds, then tapers off. The dynamics should reflect the melodic contour.
- Sing with full breath support and a relaxed voice at measure 39 in the high tessitura. Find the high notes by using "the call" or hooting sounds without tightness or strain in the voice. Keep the palate lifted to create an easy resonance space.
- Analyze the linear melodic intervals and tune them carefully.
- Balance the chords between the parts by listening to them. Try adding more weight to one part to determine the effect on the chord.

Assessment

Informal Assessment

During this lesson, students showed the ability to:

- Sing in 6/8 meter in the Vocal Warm-Up exercise.
- Read and sing one part independently in 6/8 meter when four parts are being sung in the Sight-Singing exercise.
- Identify characteristics of consonant and dissonant chords in the Singing section.
- Sing independently in 6/8 meter, with consonant and dissonant harmonies, in "I Saw Three Ships."

Student Self-Assessment

Have students:

- Evaluate their performance with the How Did You Do? section on page 63.
- Answer the questions individually. Discuss them in pairs or small groups and/or write their responses on a sheet of paper.

Individual Performance Assessment

To further demonstrate accomplishment, have each student:

- Into a tape recorder in an isolated space, clap all four lines of the Sight-Singing exercise to demonstrate the ability to read in 6/8 meter.
- Write a paragraph describing consonant and dissonant chords, how they are formed, how they are used in "I Saw Three Ships," and whether there is any disagreement about what is considered consonant and dissonant sound.
- In full ensemble, sing the entire piece, signaling by placing two fingers in front of the right shoulder when the chords are consonant, and one finger on the right shoulder when the chords are dissonant.

Extension

Ensemble Size

This piece will feel very different when performed by either a large or a small ensemble.

Have students:

- Record their performance in full ensemble.
- Record performances by quartets or double quartets.
- Discuss the difference in feeling of the performances, and decide why and under what circumstances each might be appropriate.
- Choose between them, or combine them, to construct the final performance style.

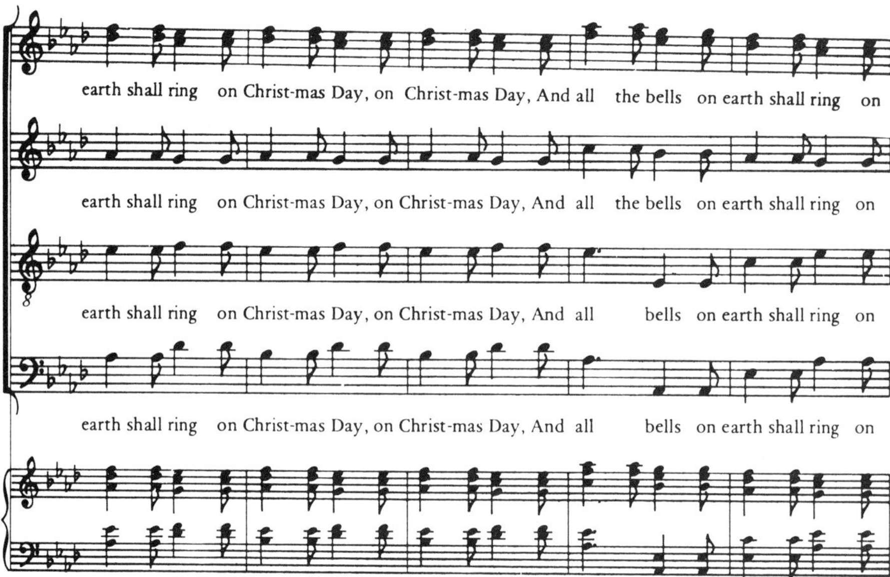

68 *Choral Connections Level 4 Mixed Voices*

National Standards

The following National Standards are addressed through the Extension and bottom-page activities:

1. Singing, alone and with others, a varied repertoire of music. **(a, b, c, e, f)**
3. Improvising melodies, variations, and accompaniments. **(b, c)**
5. Reading and notating music. **(a, b)**
6. Listening to, analyzing, and describing music. **(a, b, c)**
8. Understanding relationships between music, the other arts, and disciplines outside the arts. **(a, b, c, e)**
9. Understanding music in relation to history and culture. **(a, d)**

47
mf
Christ- mas Day in the morn- ing. Then let us all__ re- joice__ a- main! On
Christ- mas Day in the morn- ing. Then let us all__ re- joice__ a- main! On
Christ- mas Day in the morn- ing. Then let us all__ re- joice__ a- main! On
Christ- mas Day in the morn- ing. Then let us all__ re- joice__ a- main! On

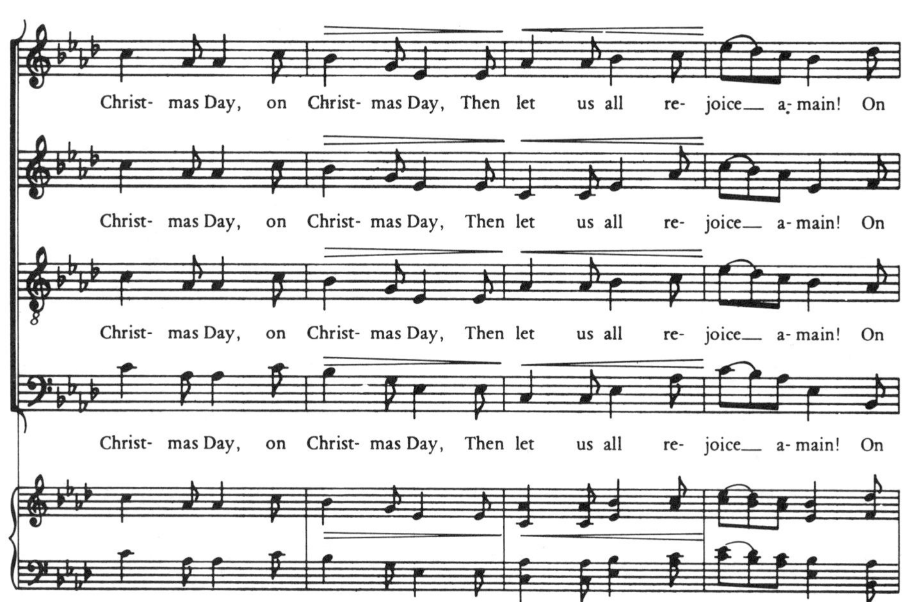
Christ- mas Day, on Christ- mas Day, Then let us all re- joice__ a- main! On
Christ- mas Day, on Christ- mas Day, Then let us all re- joice__ a- main! On
Christ- mas Day, on Christ- mas Day, Then let us all re- joice__ a- main! On
Christ- mas Day, on Christ- mas Day, Then let us all re- joice__ a- main! On

Dissonance as a Matter of Opinion

Have students:

- Research definitions of consonance and dissonance using dictionaries and thesauruses.
- Discuss the traditional meaning of these terms used in music. (chords that are pleasing and those that are grating)
- Discuss possible other opinions of what is considered consonant or dissonant, based on historical, cultural, or social perspectives. (The concept of dissonance changes during different periods of history, is different depending upon culture, and is very different based on what one is used to hearing in the environment.)
- Listen to some twentieth-century orchestral or choral music (by Stravinsky, Berg, Britten, Bartók) and record their impression of the dissonance in the piece after listening one time, three times, and ten times.
- Listen to the music of non-European cultures to identify dissonance, and track their perception of dissonance over repeated listenings.

Dissonance in the Arts

The dissonance in twentieth-century music is reflected in all contemporary arts, and reflects a feeling of dissonance in the society. Have students:

- Explore dissonance in the arts during this century.
- Share information with one another, discussing how the manifestation of dissonance is the same and different across arts.
- Create a multimedia presentation, including creation of music, visual art, drama, and dance, centered around a social theme (ecology, homelessness, inequality, waste, pollution, and so on), that demonstrates artistic representations of that theme.
- Present a performance that incorporates all these arts to draw awareness to the issue they have chosen.

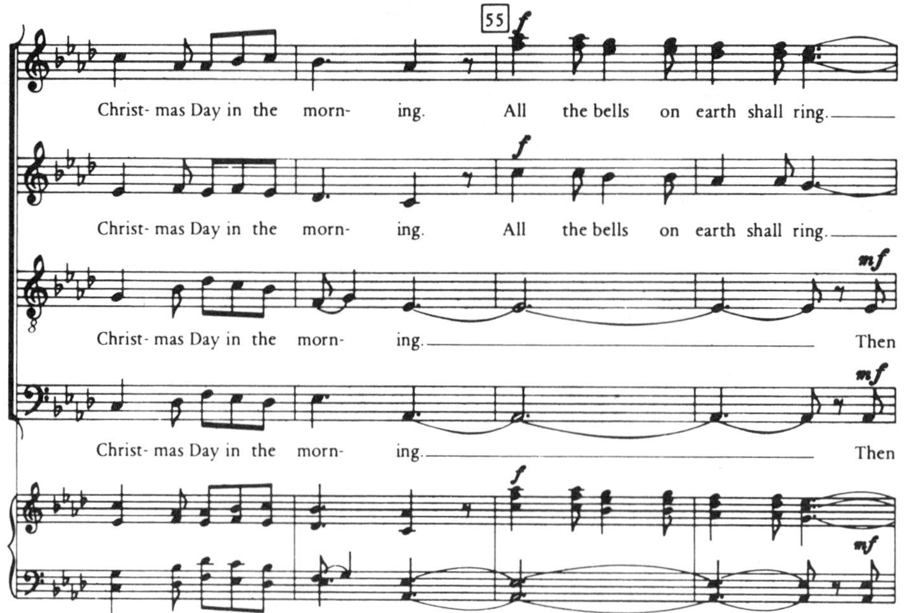

Dissonance in the Twentieth Century

Have students:

- Listen to and write down the sounds around them for 10 minutes.
- Share lists, and categorize the sounds as environmental or human-made, consonant or dissonant.
- Discuss sound pollution as one aspect of environmental concern.
- Invite an ear specialist to discuss any immediate dangers to people's hearing within the community.
- Research and find music that uses or explores environmental sounds, such as "An American in Paris" by Gershwin, "Doot Doot" by Mannheim Steamroller, "And God Created Great Whales" by Hovhaness, and so on.

African Noel

ARRANGER: André J. Thomas

CHORAL MUSIC TERMS
changing meter
constant beat
rhythm
sight-reading
2/4 meter

VOICING

Four-part chorus

PERFORMANCE STYLE

Rhythmically, joyously
A cappella with optional unpitched percussion

FOCUS

- Sight-read and sing focusing on rhythm.
- Conduct in 2/4 meter.
- Perform with a constant beat in changing meter.

Warming Up

Vocal Warm-Up

Sing this exercise using *doo* or whatever syllables come spontaneously to mind. The brisk motion and quick rhythms require clear articulation. While singing, roll the shoulders, shake out the arms, loosen the neck area, and do it rhythmically with the music. Move up and down by half steps on each repeat. Notice the tied note, and feel the syncopation as you sing.

African Noel

ARRANGER: André J. Thomas

Focus

OVERVIEW

Sight-singing using rhythm; conducting in 2/4 meter; changing meter.

OBJECTIVES

After completing this lesson, students will be able to:

- Sight-read and sing, focusing on rhythm.
- Conduct in 2/4 meter.
- Perform with a constant beat in changing meter.

CHORAL MUSIC TERMS

Define the Choral Music Terms for students, giving pronunciation, and answering any questions that may arise.

Warming Up

Vocal Warm-Up

This Vocal Warm-Up is designed to prepare students to:

- Sing using clear rhythmic articulation.
- Loosen the upper torso for a more relaxed tone.
- Move rhythmically while singing.

Have students:

- Read through the Vocal Warm-Up directions.
- Sing, following your demonstration.

TEACHER'S RESOURCE BINDER

Blackline Master 6, *Sight-Reading Rhythms*, page 84
Skill Master 19, *Conducting Patterns*, page 42

National Standards

1. Singing, alone and with others, a varied repertoire of music. **(a, b, c, e)**
5. Reading and notating music. **(a, b)**
6. Listening to, analyzing, and describing music. **(a, b, c)**
7. Evaluating music and music performances. **(a)**
9. Understanding music in relation to history and culture. **(a)**

Sight-Reading

This Sight-Reading exercise is designed to prepare students to:

- Sight-read rhythm.
- Conduct in 2/4 meter.

Have students:

- Read through the Sight-Reading exercise directions.
- Read each voice part rhythmically, using rhythm syllables.
- Sing the exercise using their choice of pitches.
- Sing, using different combinations of *doo-bee-doot*.

Singing: "African Noel"

Focus on rhythmic sight-reading.
Have students:

- Read the text on page 72.
- Objectively assess individual and group sight-singing abilities.
- Discuss strategies for good rhythmic sight-reading, including using a system, setting a beat internally before beginning, constantly looking ahead for trouble spots, and conducting as they read.
- Sight-read the rhythm of their voice part of "African Noel" from the beginning through measure 56 once each day, tracking their own improvement.

Sight-Reading

Rhythm is one of the keys to sight-singing success. Make a plan before you begin reading, choose a tempo, and look ahead for upcoming problem spots. Really focus and do your best the first time through. After speaking and clapping this rhythm, sing it using pitches of your choice from the B♭ major tonic chord (B♭, D, F). Sing using different combinations of *doo-bee-doot*.

Singing: "African Noel"

Imagine that your first reading of a piece was evaluated.

Would your sight-reading skills be considered good? excellent?

To read well, you must be able to read rhythms. What "system" do you use for rhythmic reading? What other ways do you help yourself read rhythms well?

Now turn to the music for "African Noel" on page 73.

HOW DID YOU DO? ?

Good reading skills lead to good performance. Think about your preparation and performance of "African Noel."

1. Did your ability to sight-read rhythm improve during this lesson? How? How do you know?

2. Read and speak the Sight-Reading exercise, conducting in 2/4 meter.

3. The meter changes from 2/4 to 3/8 to 2/8 to 4/4 during "African Noel." Describe how these meter changes work, then clap the tenor line rhythm from measure 53 to the end to show your ability to perform changing meters.

For Anton Armstrong and the St. Olaf Choir

African Noel

Arranged by André J. Thomas

Four-part Chorus of Mixed Voices, A cappella

♩ = 100

Soprano *f* Sing No - el, sing No - el, No - el, No - el,

Alto *f* Sing No - el, sing No - el, No - el, No - el,

Tenor *f* Sing No - el, sing No - el, No - el, No - el,

Bass *f* Sing No - el, sing No - el, No - el, No - el,

♩ = 100

Piano (for rehearsal only)

5 *p* sing No - el, sing No - el, No - el, No - el,

p sing No - el, sing No - el, No - el, No - el,

p sing No - el, sing No - el, No - el, No - el,

p sing No - el, sing No - el, No - el, No - el,

Arranger André Thomas

André J. Thomas is Director of Choral Activities and Associate Professor of Music Education (choral) at the Florida State University School of Music. Previously, he served on the faculty of the University of Texas Department of Music at Austin.

Dr. Thomas is frequently in demand as a choral adjudicator, clinician, and director of honor choirs and all-state choirs throughout the United States, Europe, and Australia. Besides his extensive conducting credits, he has distinguished himself as a composer/arranger. In the 1992–93 academic year, Dr. Thomas was awarded the University Award for Excellence in Teaching. He currently serves as the President-Elect of the Florida American Choral Directors Association.

Suggested Teaching Sequence

1. Review Vocal Warm-Up.
Sing with clear articulation. Move rhythmically to loosen the upper torso.
Have students:

- Review the Vocal Warm-Up on page 71.
- Use their own spontaneous syllables to add interest.
- Add the suggested movement to produce a relaxed tone.
- Notice the tied notes, identify the syncopation, and then find similar syncopation on the first page of "African Noel."

2. Review Sight-Reading.
Sight-read rhythms.
Have students:

- Review the Sight-Reading exercise on page 72.
- Review the strategies to enhance sight-reading.
- Read the exercise only once each day, conducting in 2/4 meter as they read.
- Monitor and track their success each day, noting improvement over time.

3. Sight-read and sight-sing measures 1–56 of "African Noel."
Have students:

- Divide into voice sections and read each part of measures 1–56 rhythmically, using rhythm syllables and conducting in 2/4 meter.
- Still in sections, sight-sing the measures with solfège and hand signs or numbers, identifying and working on problem areas.
- Sight-sing the piece through, using solfège and hand signs or numbers, with full ensemble, conducting in 2/4 meter.
- Sing measures 1–56 through with full ensemble.

4. Sight-read and sight-sing measures 57–end of "African Noel."

Have students:

- Look at measures 57–end, analyzing the multiple metric changes and rhythmic complexities.
- Discuss how the shift from 2/4 to 3/8 works. (The quarter note remains constant; therefore, the eighth notes in 3/8 have the same value as the eighth notes in 2/4.)
- Divide into voice sections and read each part of measures 57–end rhythmically, using rhythm syllables.
- In sections, read the rhythm of measures 57–71, using rhythm syllables.
- Still in sections, sight-sing measures 57–71 with solfège and hand signs or numbers, identifying and working on problem areas.
- Sight-sing measures 57–71 with solfège and hand signs or numbers, identifying and working on problem areas.
- Sing measures 57–71 through with full ensemble.
- Repeat the above process for measures 72–end.

9 *mp*

sing No - el, sing No - el, No - el, No - el,

sing No - el, sing No - el, No - el, No - el,

sing No - el, sing No - el, No - el, No - el,

sing No - el, sing No - el, No - el, No - el,

13 *mf*

sing No - el, sing No - el, No - el, No - el,

sing No - el, sing No - el, No - el, No - el,

sing No - el, sing No - el, No - el, No - el,

sing No - el, sing No - el, No - el, No - el,

TEACHING STRATEGY

Sight-Reading Rhythms

When sight-reading and sight-singing are formally assessed, both pitch and rhythm are factors taken into consideration.

Have students:

- Discuss the following reasons why reading rhythm correctly minimizes sight-reading mistakes: Even if the pitch suffers, the rhythm is correct. Missing the rhythm of a sight-reading exercise in order to resolve a pitch problem maximizes the mistake. If the rhythm is wrong the pitch is automatically wrong because it is in the wrong place in time. Negotiating the correct rhythm increases the singer's chance of recovering the pitch in subsequent measures of the sight-reading material.

17

Sing we all— No - el,— sing we all— No - el,—

Sing we all— No - el,— sing we all— No - el,—

Sing we all— No - el,— sing we all— No - el,—

Sing we all— No - el,— sing we all— No - el,—

21

sing we all— No - el,— sing we all— No - el,—

sing we all— No - el,— sing we all— No - el,—

sing we all— No - el,— sing we all— No - el,—

sing we all— No - el,— sing we all— No - el,—

5. Sing "African Noel" with full ensemble.

- Discuss transitions from section to section, particularly where the meter changes.
- Practice these transitions in isolation.
- Perform the entire piece with full ensemble.

MUSIC LITERACY

Is "African Noel" Really African?

Have students:

- Remember that the broad term *African* represents many cultures and many styles.
- List musical characteristics of African music they know.
- List musical characteristics of "African Noel."
- Compare the two lists, identifying the aspects of "African Noel" that seem African.
- Discuss whether this piece is African, in an African style, or European.

VOCAL DEVELOPMENT

To encourage vocal development, have students:

- Sing with a firm, articulated tone. Lift the soft palate and stretch the opening of the throat to create large spaces for resonance.
- Use principles of good English by singing with tall, open vowels and clearly articulated consonants with adequate breath support.
- Articulate the rhythm precisely. Speak the text in rhythm while tapping the beat.
- Conduct and speak. Note the meter changes.
- Energize the sustained notes by increasing breath support and dynamic intensity. Be precise about the rhythm.
- Attack and release consonants with precision.
- Demonstrate the correct singing of the *r* consonant after a vowel in English; it should be almost silent, as in *gather, here, hear, cheer,* and *born.*
- Balance the voice parts by listening to each part. Adjust the weight or loudness of each part to achieve a balanced blend of the voices.
- Plan the dynamics to reflect the imitation and repetition found in the music. Vary the dynamics for added interest, using crescendos and decrescendos within phrases.

33

p

sing No - el, sing No - el, No - el, No - el,

p

sing No - el, sing No - el, No - el, No - el,

p

sing No - el, sing No - el, No - el, No - el,

p

sing No - el, sing No - el, No - el, No - el,

37

mp

sing No - el, sing No - el, No - el, No - el,

mp

sing No - el, sing No - el, No - el, No - el,

mp

sing No - el, sing No - el, No - el, No - el,

mp

sing No - el, sing No - el, No - el, No - el,

TEACHING STRATEGY

Conducting in 2/4 Meter

By now, students should be familiar with conducting patterns; however, if necessary, have them refer to Skill Master 19, *Conducting Patterns,* in the TRB.

Assessment

Informal Assessment

During this lesson, students showed the ability to:

- Sing in 2/4 meter in the Vocal Warm-Up exercise.
- Sight-read rhythms in 2/4 meter in the Sight-Reading exercise.
- Identify and perform the changing meters of measures 57–71 in "African Noel."
- Sing independently in 2/4 meter, and with changing meters, in "African Noel."

Student Self-Assessment

Have students:

- Evaluate their performance with the How Did You Do? section on page 72.
- Answer the questions individually. Discuss them in pairs or small groups and/or write their responses on a sheet of paper.

Individual Performance Assessment

To further demonstrate accomplishment, have each student:

- Using Blackline Master 6, *Sight-Reading Rhythms,* sight-read and conduct an exercise chosen by you with 80 percent accuracy, to demonstrate rhythmic sight-reading ability in 2/4 meter.
- Read and conduct the Sight-Reading exercise to demonstrate the ability to conduct in 2/4 meter.
- Into a tape recorder in an isolated space, rhythmically speak the tenor line from measures 53–77 in "African Noel," demonstrating the ability to maintain a constant pulse when there are changing meters.

49

sing, Oh

sing, Oh

f sing No - el, sing No - el, No - el, No - el,

f sing No - el, sing No - el, No - el, No - el,

53

sing, *sub.p* O

sing, *sub.p* O

sing No - el, sing No - el, No - el, No - el, *sub.p* O

sing No - el, sing No - el, No - el, No - el, *sub.p* O

Extension

Add Percussion Accompaniment

Have students:

- Add the percussion parts for conga drum and tambourine as provided on page 83.
- Use this accompaniment in performance.

Building Sight-Reading Skills

Sight-reading and sight-singing are skills that require development over time.

Have students:

- Practice sight-reading every day, working sequentially from rhythmic exercises that are easy to more difficult ones, using segments of pieces from each section of this text and any additional available octavos.
- Discuss and develop strategies for sight-singing both individually and when in an ensemble.
- Challenge each other and the group by taping and assessing each attempt.
- Establish a policy of learning from mistakes, analyzing, and developing strategies to avoid repeating past errors through drill and practice.
- Acknowledge accomplishments and growth.
- Learn analysis cues based on period, composer, notational cues, and by scanning the whole score to build expectations before reading actually commences.
- Occasionally read easier pieces to experience success and build self-esteem.

National Standards

The following National Standards are addressed through the Extension and bottom-page activities:

1. Singing, alone and with others, a varied repertoire of music. **(a, b, c, e, f)**

3. Improvising melodies, variations, and accompaniments. **(b, c)**

5. Reading and notating music. **(a, b, c)**

6. Listening to, analyzing, and describing music. **(a, b)**

8. Understanding relationships between music, the other arts, and disciplines outside the arts. **(c)**

9. Understanding music in relation to history and culture. **(a, d)**

Improvising Melodies to a Rhythm

Have students:

- Read the Sight-Reading exercise on page 72 on one pitch, using scat or rhythm syllables.
- Decide on a scale using that pitch as the tonal center, either major, minor (natural or harmonic), or pentatonic.
- Sing up and down the scale a few times to refamiliarize themselves with the pitches.
- Read the Sight-Reading exercise, improvising a melody in the chosen scale.
- Optional: Choose a chord progression to follow as they improvise.
- Volunteer to sing their melodies to the ensemble.
- Discuss any particularly effective melodic passages created through improvisation.

Sight-Reading with Style

Have students who are good sight-readers:

- Read in small ensembles to build independence.
- Work on sight-reading with interpretive sensitivity, anticipating phrasing, dynamics, tempo changes, and stylistic articulation as they sing.
- Discuss and analyze their reading critically in order to improve.

67
Lamb of God is born to - day in Beth - le - hem.
Lamb of God is born to - day in Beth - le - hem.
Lamb of God is born to - day in Beth - le - hem.
Lamb of God is born to - day in Beth - le - hem.
72
cresc.
ff
Sing No - el, Sing No -
Sing No - el, Sing No -
Sing No - el, No - el, sing No - el, No - el, No - el,
Sing No - el, No - el, sing No - el, No - el, No - el,

77
ff
el,
sing No - el. Oh
ff
el,
sing No - el. Oh
ff
sing, No - el, sing No - el, No - el, No - el,
Oh
ff
sing, No - el, sing No - el, No - el, No - el,
Oh
81
(spoken)
sing No-el, No-el, sing No-el, No-el, sing
No-el.
(spoken)
sing No-el, No-el, sing No-el, No-el, sing
No-el.
(spoken)
sing No-el, No-el, sing No-el, No-el, sing
No-el.
(spoken)
sing No-el, No-el, sing No-el, No-el, sing
No-el.

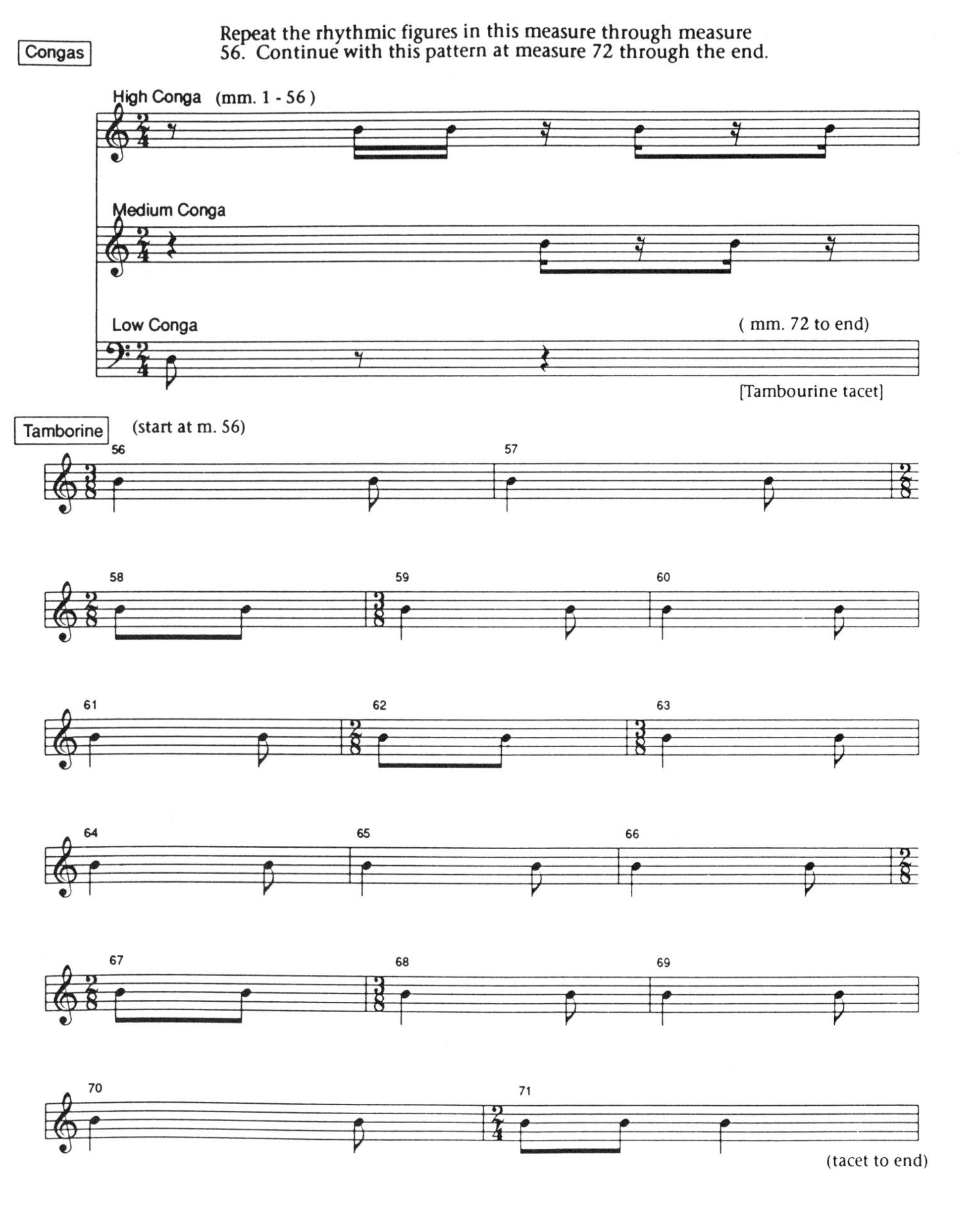
Congas
Repeat the rhythmic figures in this measure through measure 56. Continue with this pattern at measure 72 through the end.
High Conga (mm. 1 - 56)
Medium Conga
Low Conga
(mm. 72 to end)
[Tambourine tacet]
Tamborine
(start at m. 56)
56
57
58
59
60
61
62
63
64
65
66
67
68
69
70
71
(tacet to end)

The Lord Is My Shepherd

Psalm 23, paraphrased
COMPOSER: Allen Pote

Focus

OVERVIEW
Phrasing; upbeat entrances; tuning intervals.

OBJECTIVES
After completing this lesson, students will be able to:

- Identify and sing phrases using correct phrasing techniques.
- Prepare and breathe correctly for upbeat entrances.
- Sight-sing in major tonality.
- Tune unison/octaves, thirds, and sixths.

CHORAL MUSIC TERMS
Define the Choral Music Terms for students, giving pronunciation, and answering any questions that may arise.

Rhythm Drill

This is designed to prepare students to:

- Sight-read rhythm, including syncopation.
- Practice reading rhythms with combinations of sixteenth notes.
- Identify phrases and practice building toward the peak, then releasing to the end.
- Identify upbeat entrances, and determine how to prepare the breath.

Have students:

- Read through the Rhythm Drill directions.
- Perform the drill.

LESSON 9

CHORAL MUSIC TERMS
major tonality
phrase
sight-sing
sixths
thirds
tuning
unison/octaves
upbeat entrance

The Lord Is My Shepherd

Psalm 23, *paraphrased*
COMPOSER: *Allen Pote*

VOICING
SATB

PERFORMANCE STYLE
Calmly
Accompanied by piano

FOCUS

- Identify and sing phrases using correct phrasing techniques.
- Prepare and breathe correctly for upbeat entrances.
- Sight-sing in major tonality.
- Tune unison/octaves, thirds, and sixths.

Warming Up

Rhythm Drill
First read and clap these rhythms. Then add the words. Feel each example as a complete phrase, with a beginning, peak, and ending. Notice which phrases have upbeat entrances, and decide how many beats you need for a full preparatory breath.

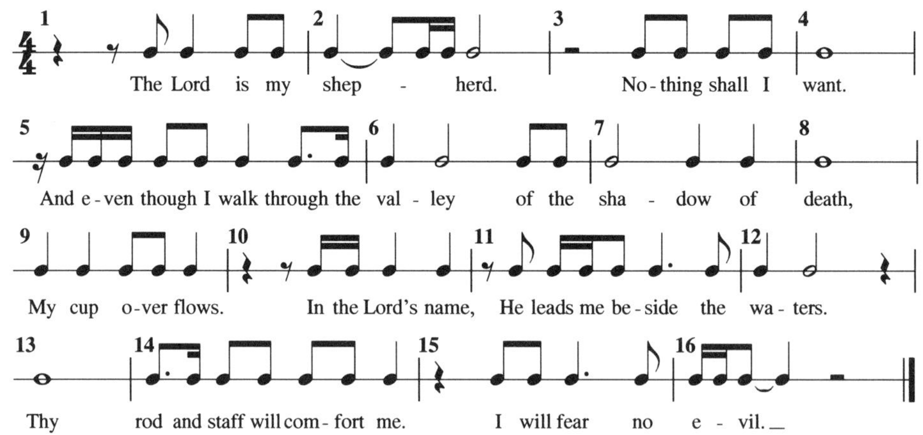

Vocal Warm-Up
Take a breath through the nostrils only, then sing this exercise on *ah*. Move up a half step on each repeat. Feel the soft palate rising as you breathe, and sing with a dropped jaw.

TEACHER'S RESOURCE BINDER
Blackline Master 7, *Sight-Singing in Major Tonality*, page 85

National Standards

1. Singing, alone and with others, a varied repertoire of music. **(a, b, c, e)**
5. Reading and notating music. **(a, b)**
6. Listening to, analyzing, and describing music. **(a, b, c)**
7. Evaluating music and music performances. **(a, b)**
9. Understanding music in relation to history and culture. **(a)**

Sight-Singing

Sight-sing this exercise using solfège and hand signs or numbers. Identify each harmonic interval as a unison, octave, third, fourth, or sixth. Challenge yourself to read accurately the first time through, and be sure to tune as you sing.

Singing: "The Lord Is My Shepherd"

Can you sight-read rhythm and pitch at the same time? If you can, you're an excellent sight-reader! What strategies do you use when you sight-sing? What clues can help you be a successful reader?

Now turn to the music for "The Lord Is My Shepherd" on page 86.

HOW DID YOU DO? ? ?

Once you can read rhythm and pitch, you'll have plenty of time to work on phrasing and interpretation. Think about your preparation and performance of "The Lord Is My Shepherd."

1. What makes the phrases in "The Lord Is My Shepherd" unusual? How did you decide to shape the phrases? Was it successful?

2. Tell how the rests at the beginning of phrases affected your breath preparation for phrases. Sing a phrase with an upbeat entrance to demonstrate your ability.

3. Is your sight-singing ability improving? Describe your ability, and your progress.

4. Sing from measure 55–end of "The Lord Is My Shepherd" in a quartet, showing your ability to sing and tune unison/octaves and intervals.

Arranger Allen Pote

With his training as an organist under the tutelage of Flor Peeters of Belgium, Allen Pote has composed numerous organ pieces, folk anthems, and pieces with religious themes, including two musicals, *He Is Born* and *He Is Risen.* Pote has held the position of Director of Music for Westcliff Methodist Church in Fort Worth, Texas, and, most recently, Minister of Music for the Memorial Drive Presbyterian Church in Houston, Texas. In addition, he arranges music, such as this piece, and leads workshops in music composition.

Warming Up

Vocal Warm-Up

This Vocal Warm-Up is designed to prepare students to:

- Raise the soft palate while singing.
- Drop the jaw while singing.

Have students:

- Read through the Vocal Warm-Up directions.
- Sing, following your demonstration.

Sight-Singing

This Sight-Singing exercise is designed to prepare students to:

- Sight-sing in major tonality.
- Identify harmonic intervals of unison, octave, third, fourth, and sixth.
- Tune intervals while reading.

Have students:

- Read through the Sight-Singing exercise directions.
- Read through each voice part rhythmically, using rhythm syllables.
- Sight-sing through each part separately using solfège and hand signs or numbers.
- Sing all parts together.

Singing: "The Lord Is My Shepherd"

Focus on rhythmic sight-singing. Have students:

- Read the text on page 85.
- Assess individual and group sight-singing abilities.
- Discuss strategies for good sight-singing, including using rhythm and pitch systems, setting a beat internally before beginning, constantly looking ahead for trouble spots, and watching the entire score.
- Sight-sing their voice part of "The Lord Is My Shepherd" from the beginning as far as they are able, in full ensemble.
- Continue this once every day until the entire piece is read.

Suggested Teaching Sequence

1. Review Rhythm Drill.
Sight-read rhythms. Identify phrases. Determine breathing for upbeat entrances.
Have students:

- Review the Rhythm Drill on page 84, first clapping rhythms, then adding words.
- Identify each as a phrase, determining the peak of each, and the problem caused by rests in the middle of phrases. (The intensity of the phrase must be carried through the rest to the peak, which occurs sometime after the rest.)
- Identify the first two examples as having upbeat entrances, and practice taking a full beat of breath in preparation, so there is no "hiccup" entrance.

2. Review Vocal Warm-Up.
Sing with raised soft palate and dropped jaw for a rich sound.
Have students:

- Review the Vocal Warm-Up on page 84.
- Identify the connection between nasal breath and raised soft palate.
- Identify the connection between the *ah* syllable and dropped jaw.
- Discuss the rich, full sound created by the combination of raised soft palate and dropped jaw.

For the San Francisco Bay Area Chapter of Choristers Guild in celebration of their fifth Youth Choir Festival

The Lord Is My Shepherd

Psalm 23, paraphrase A.P.
Allen Pote

(10)

— in fields of green. leads me be-side still wa - ters. —

— in fields of green. leads me be-side still wa - ters. —

(13)

mf The Lord is my shep - herd.

mf The Lord is my

(16)

who re - stores my life.

shep - herd. — who re - stores my

3. Review Sight-Singing.

Sight-sing using solfège and hand signs or numbers. Identify and tune intervals.

Have students:

- Review the Sight-Singing exercise on page 85.
- Analyze each harmonic interval as a unison, octave, third, fourth, or sixth.
- Practice reading once each day, tracking improvement over time.

4. Sight-sing "The Lord Is My Shepherd" using solfège and hand signs or numbers.

Have students:

- Divide into voice sections (SATB) and read each part rhythmically, using rhythm syllables.
- Still in sections, sing with solfège and hand signs or numbers, identifying and working on problem areas.
- Sing the piece through, using solfège and hand signs or numbers, with full ensemble.
- Divide into sections and recite the text rhythmically for each voice part.
- Sing the piece through with text as a full ensemble.

TEACHING STRATEGY

Sight-Singing

Have students:

- Identify strategies they can use to become better sight-singers.

— At first read only the rhythm, then add the pitch, then text.

— Read simple melodies and two parts before trying four.

— Practice a little every day, using new materials.

— Don't worry about making mistakes. When a mistake is disastrous, analyze what happened so it can be addressed, practiced, and improved.

— Challenge each other with support and good humor.

— Remember that sight-singing, like any skill, needs to be practiced to improve.

5. Refine phrasing.

Have students:

- Practice correct breathing technique for upbeat entrances by singing entrances in "The Lord Is My Shepherd" in the following examples: soprano and alto sing measure 14; tenor and bass sing measure 15; all parts sing measure 26; all parts sing measure 30.
- Sing the entire piece on *loo,* making certain phrases are correctly defined, following expression marks.
- Discuss the conversation between treble and tenor/bass voices through overlapping phrases at measures 14–20.
- Sing the piece, attending to upbeat entrances and phrasing, in full ensemble.

25

mf with intensity

And e-ven though I walk through the

And e-ven though I walk through the

27

val - ley ___ of the shad - ow of death.

val - ley ___ of the shad - ow of death.

30

I will fear no e - vil, ___ for you are with me, _ your

I will fear no e - vil, ___ for you are with me, _ your

TEACHING STRATEGY

The Preparatory Breath

Have students:

- Conduct in 4/4, and sing "Twinkle, Twinkle Little Star," making note of which beats they began singing on, and on which ones they took a preparatory breath. (breath on 4, sing on 1)
- Conduct in 2/4, singing the first line of "The Battle Hymn of the Republic," noting which beats they began singing on, and on which ones they took a preparatory breath. (breath on 1/2, sing on $1\frac{1}{2}$)
- Identify the concept that all songs do not begin on the downbeat, but that a preparatory breath should give the singer one full beat in which to inhale.

VOCAL DEVELOPMENT

To encourage vocal development, have students:

- Sing with a firm, articulated tone. Lift the soft palate and stretch the opening of the throat to create large spaces for resonance.
- Use principles of good English by singing with tall, open vowels and clearly articulated consonants with adequate breath support.
- Articulate the rhythm precisely. Speak the text in rhythm while tapping the beat.
- Conduct and speak. Note the triplet rhythms.
- Energize the sustained notes by increasing breath support and dynamic intensity.
- Attack and release consonants with precision.
- Demonstrate the correct singing of the *r* consonant after a vowel in English; it should be almost silent, as in *Lord, shepherd, waters, restores, fear, are, comfort, before, overflows, mercy,* and *forever.*
- Listen for diphthongs, that is, two vowel sounds when one vowel sound is written. Sing the first vowel sound and barely sing the second vowel elided into next syllable. Diphthongs are found in such words as *my, I,* and *life.*
- Balance the voice parts by listening to each voice part. Note where the parts are singing in unison. Adjust the weight or loudness of each part to achieve a balanced blend of the voices.

39

— in fields of green, leads me be - side still

41

wa - ters. ___

43

mf

The Lord is my shep - herd.

mf

The Lord is my

mf

CONNECTING THE ARTS

Phrasing in the Arts

Have students:

- Discuss how the phrase is represented in arts other than music—dance, drama, visual art, or poetry.
- Watch, look at, listen to, or read in language or visual arts to experience how the phrase is managed.
- Discuss with artists how they do or do not use the concept of phrasing.
- Discuss with performers whether and how they consider phrasing in their work.
- Share the information collected and construct a presentation or demonstration based on their findings entitled "Phrasing in the Arts," or a title of their own choosing.

Assessment

Informal Assessment

During this lesson, students showed the ability to:

- Sight-read rhythms, identify phrases, and practice upbeat entrances in the Rhythm Drill.
- Sing with a rich, warm sound in the Vocal Warm-Up exercise.
- Sight-sing using solfège and hand signs or numbers, and identify and tune intervals in the Sight-Singing exercise.
- Sing with correct phrasing and breathing in "The Lord Is My Shepherd."

Student Self-Assessment

Have students:

- Evaluate their performance with the How Did You Do? section on page 85.
- Answer the questions individually. Discuss them in pairs or small groups and/or write their responses on a sheet of paper.

Individual Performance Assessment

To further demonstrate accomplishment, have each student:

- In a quartet, perform "The Lord Is My Shepherd" into a tape recorder in an isolated space, demonstrating correct phrasing and breathing techniques, and in-tune singing of intervals.
- Using Blackline Master 7, *Sight-Singing in Major Tonality,* sight-sing a selection chosen by you.
- Using a taped recording of their performance, write a critique of their own performance of "The Lord Is My Shepherd," discussing phrasing and breathing techniques, and tuning of intervals. Rate their own overall performance, and make any necessary recommendations for improvement.

92 *Choral Connections Level 4 Mixed Voices*

51

strongly

You pre - pare a ta - ble be - fore me. in the

You pre - pare a ta - ble be - fore me. in the

53

pres - ence of my en - e - mies. You a -

pres - ence of my en - e - mies.

55

noint my head with oil. a - noint my head with oil. my

a - noint my head with oil. my

National Standards

The following National Standards are addressed through the Extension and bottom-page activities:

1. Singing, alone and with others, a varied repertoire of music. **(a, b, c, f)**
3. Improvising melodies, variations, and accompaniments. **(a, b, c, d, e)**
4. Composing and arranging music within specified guidelines. **(a, d)**
5. Reading and notating music. **(a, b, c)**
6. Listening to, analyzing, and describing music. **(a, b)**
8. Understanding relationships between music, the other arts, and disciplines outside the arts. **(a, b, c, d, e)**
9. Understanding music in relation to history and culture. **(c)**

Extension

Singing at Parallel Intervals

Students should be familiar with intervals by now, but might enjoy aurally exploring singing parallel lines at different intervals.

Have students:

- Compose a melody line on the board in a key of their choice.
- Sing the melody together.
- In small groups, sing a third above, a sixth below, a fourth below, or an octave below or above the melody sung by the remainder of the ensemble.
- In a group, choose their own interval to sing against the melody.

Improvising Dialogue in Phrases

The dialogue format of phrases, beginning at measure 14 of "The Lord Is My Shepherd," provides an interesting structure for melodic improvisation in pairs. Build this activity slowly over several weeks, so confidence has time to grow along with improvisational skills.

Have students:

- Choose a tone set, meter, phrase length, and harmonic structure over which to work.
- Improvise a few phrases all together to get the feel of this new combination.
- In pairs, improvise dialogue by one singing a phrase, then the other singing a responding phrase, following the harmonic structure, but also using rhythmic or melodic ideas from the partner's previous improvisation.
- Some students may wish to work out a vocal accompaniment that fits the harmonic structure and sets a style for the improvisation.

Sight-Singing with Style

Have students who are good sight-singers:

- Read in small ensembles to build independence.
- Work on sight-singing with interpretive sensitivity, anticipating phrasing, dynamics, tempo changes, and stylistic articulation as they sing.
- Discuss and analyze their reading critically in order to improve.

Composing for Quotable Text

Have students:

- Identify the source of the text for "The Lord Is My Shepherd" as the Book of Psalms.
- Recall any other biblical or quotable texts they have sung during their choral experiences, identifying sources for quotations, including *Bartlett's Familiar Quotations* or similar sources.
- Research the Book of Psalms or other texts for quotes they think would be enhanced by a musical setting. (Consider quotes by historical figures, naturalists, poets, philosophers, and so on, perhaps related to learning taking place in another discipline.)
- Discuss what musical features and elements, or compositional devices and techniques are suggested by the text.
- Compose a piece based on this text for the ensemble, or commission a local composer to work with the ensemble to create a piece for them.

LESSON 10

Forest Cool, Thou Forest Quiet

COMPOSER: Johannes Brahms (1833–1897)
EDITED BY: S. Stephen Barlow

Focus

OVERVIEW
Phrasing; intensity; independent singing.

OBJECTIVES
After completing this lesson, students will be able to:
- Identify and sing phrases using intensity.
- Sing one part independently when four parts are being sung.
- Sing using correct German pronunciation.

CHORAL MUSIC TERMS
Define the Choral Music Terms for students, giving pronunciation, and answering any questions that may arise.

Warming Up

Vocal Warm-Up

This Vocal Warm-Up is designed to prepare students to:
- Sing with controlled intensity, following dynamic markings.

Have students:
- Read through the Vocal Warm-Up directions.
- Sing, following your demonstration.

LESSON 10

CHORAL MUSIC TERMS
dynamics
independent singing
intensity
morendo
phrase

Forest Cool, Thou Forest Quiet

COMPOSER: Johannes Brahms (1833–1897)
EDITED BY: S. Stephen Barlow

VOICING
SATB

PERFORMANCE STYLE
Slowly and sweetly
A cappella

FOCUS
- Identify and sing phrases using intensity.
- Sing one part independently when four parts are being sung.
- Sing using correct German pronunciation.

Warming Up

Vocal Warm-Up

Conduct as you sing this warm-up using solfège and hand signs or numbers. Give special attention to the dynamics. Move up or down by half steps on repeats.

TEACHER'S RESOURCE BINDER

Blackline Master 8, *Translation and Pronunciation Guide for "Forest Cool, Thou Forest Quiet,"* page 87

National Standards

1. Singing, alone and with others, a varied repertoire of music. **(a, b, c, f)**
5. Reading and notating music. **(a, b)**
6. Listening to, analyzing, and describing music. **(a, b, c, f)**
7. Evaluating music and music performances. **(a, b, c)**
8. Understanding relationships between music, the other arts, and disciplines outside the arts. **(c)**
9. Understanding music in relation to history and culture. **(a)**

Sight-Singing

Sight-sing each voice line separately, first without dynamic intensity, then with it. Now sing in full ensemble, with dynamic intensity. Notice that "x" marks the beginning, peak, and release of each phrase.

Singing: "Forest Cool, Thou Forest Quiet"

Imagine that you are holding a soft-drink can that has been shaken. What is going on inside the can? What might happen if you open the can? What happens inside if you don't open it? Think of your breath as the carbonation or energy in the beverage. When the dynamics in a musical performance stir up the "carbonation," an intensification from the beginning of each phrase to the peak, and then release energy to the end of the phrase. Just like the energy inside the can, you must keep the intensity always under control as it is stirred up by the emotion of the music.

Now turn to the music for "Forest Cool, Thou Forest Quiet" on page 98.

HOW DID YOU DO?

This piece was really intense. Think about your preparation and performance of "Forest Cool, Thou Forest Quiet."

1. Describe how you shaped the phrases in "Forest Cool, Thou Forest Quiet." In a quartet, sing a phrase to demonstrate your ability to shape phrases with intensity.

2. Can you hold your part when three other parts are being sung? When is it most easy? When is it most difficult? Do a performance of measures 1–17 in a quartet, demonstrating your skill.

3. How good is your German pronunciation? Read a phrase or two to demonstrate.

4. Why do you suppose "Forest Cool, Thou Forest Quiet" is considered a great piece of music? Do you think it is great? Why or why not? Give specific examples from the piece to support your argument.

5. Do you personally like "Forest Cool, Thou Forest Quiet"? Why or why not?

Composer Johannes Brahms

Johannes Brahms was a late Romantic period composer. His father, a theater orchestra musician, taught him to play dance music on several instruments. He arranged popular waltzes for a local publisher and composed piano music, until the death of his mother. After composing *A German Requiem,* which was well received, he became a more confident composer of larger works. His art songs, many based on folk songs, are among his most popular works.

Brahms embraced the Classical forms, but used the more lyric and expansive harmonic palette of the Romantic period, innovatively exploring new harmonies and settings. Brahms, like Bach, synthesized innovations of the whole period, and both honored the old and altered it forever.

Sight-Singing

This Sight-Singing exercise is designed to prepare students to:

- Sight-sing using solfège and hand signs or numbers.
- Sing one part independently when four parts are being sung.
- Identify beginning, peak, and release of a phrase.
- Shape phrases using dynamic intensity.

Have students:

- Read through the Sight-Singing exercise directions.
- Read through each voice part rhythmically, using rhythm syllables.
- Sight-sing through each part separately using solfège and hand signs or numbers.
- Sing all parts together.

Singing: "Forest Cool, Thou Forest Quiet"

Identify the concept of intensity. Have students:

- Read the text on page 97.
- Answer the questions about the soft drink, identifying the concept of contained intensity.
- Discuss the analogy of the soft drink to a singer's breath, and the use of contained intensity to provide dynamic intensity in shaping musical phrases.
- Preview "Forest Cool, Thou Forest Quiet," finding phrases, identifying the beginning, peak, and release of each, and noting the dynamic markings throughout the piece.

Suggested Teaching Sequence

1. Review Vocal Warm-Up.
Shape phrases with dynamics. Have students:

- Review the Vocal Warm-Up on page 96.
- Discuss the dynamic shaping of the phrase.
- Identify the beginning, peak, and release of the phrase.

2. Review Sight-Singing.
Identify beginning, peak, and release of phrases. Shape phrases with dynamic intensity. Sing independently in four parts. Have students:

- Review the Sight-Singing exercise on page 97.
- Sing lines with and without dynamic intensity to feel the difference.
- Identify the beginning, peak, and release of each phrase, discussing how to use dynamic intensity to increase the dramatic impact of the phrase.
- Sing, then discuss places that present problems, isolating and working them out.

Forest Cool, Thou Forest Quiet

Waldesnacht, du Wunderkühle

SATB Chorus

Johannes Brahms
Edited by S. Stephen Barlow
English Text by S.S.B.
(ASCAP)

Slowly
p dolce

SOPRANO
For - est cool, thou for - est qui - et, Thee a
Wal - des - nacht, du wun - der - küh - le, Die ich

ALTO
For - est cool, thou for - est qui - et, Thee a
Wal - des - nacht, du wun - der - küh - le, Die ich

TENOR
For - est cool, thou for - est qui - et, Thee a
Wal - des - nacht, du wun - der - küh - le, Die ich

BASS
For - est cool, thou for - est qui - et, Thee a
Wal - des - nacht, du wun - der - küh - le, Die ich

PIANO *for rehearsal only*
Slowly
p dolce

thou-sand times I greet; Far a - way from life's con - fu - sion, Oh, thy
tau-send-ma - le grüss, Nach dem lau - te welt - ge - wüh - le, O wie

thou-sand times I greet; Far a - way from life's con - fu - - -
tau-send-ma - le grüss, Nach dem lau - te welt - ge - wüh - - -

thou-sand times I greet; Far a - way from life's con - fu - sion, Oh, thy
tau-send-ma - le grüss, Nach dem lau - te welt - ge - wüh - le, O wie

thou-sand times I greet; Far a - way from life's con - fu - sion, Oh, thy
tau-send-ma - le grüss, Nach dem lau - te welt - ge - wüh - le, O wie

p *cresc.*

"Forest Cool, Thou Forest Quiet"

This song is a lovely example of the Romantic art song. The text refers to a quiet, forest place where one can escape from the confusion and disappointment of life. The chromatic alterations, so typical of the Romantic period, allow each phrase to begin and end with stability, while venturing into unsure harmonies within. This musically represents the turmoil inside this person, even as the person is enclosed in a safe and sweet forest.

The phrase and rhythm match the text, and provide a setting that allows each phrase to swell and retreat like the waves of emotion. The ending of each section is marked by an interweaving of voices, painting the words *troubles, bitterness,* and then *restless heart* with bittersweet harmonies.

3. Sight-sing "Forest Cool, Thou Forest Quiet" using solfège and hand signs or numbers.

Have students:

- Divide into voice sections (SATB) and read each part rhythmically, using rhythm syllables, adding dynamics as marked.
- Still in sections, sing with solfège and hand signs or numbers, identifying and working on problem areas.
- Sing the piece through, using solfège and hand signs or numbers, with full ensemble.

4. Learn German pronunciation.

Have students:

- Using Blackline Master 8, *Translation and Pronunciation Guide for "Forest Cool, Thou Forest Quiet,"* echo the text in short phrases.
- Echo in this order: measures 1–12; measures 12–16; measures 17–25.
- Read through measures 1–25, speaking the German text in rhythm.
- Repeat this same process for the second verse.
- Sing the piece with correct German pronunciation.

CONNECTING THE ARTS

Impressionism in the Arts

Have students:

- Discuss how the musical setting of "Forest Cool, Thou Forest Quiet" creates a musical impression of the meaning of the text.
- Identify Impressionism as a technique where the artist captures the impression of an image or idea without necessarily being literal.
- Research Impressionist paintings of the late 1800s that offer the same impression as "Forest Cool, Thou Forest Quiet."
- Create a painting or poem that uses this concept of Impressionism to give the sensation of both calm, safe escape and underlying emotional turmoil.

VOCAL DEVELOPMENT

To encourage vocal development, have students:

- Sing with a clear and floating resonant tone. Lift the soft palate and stretch the opening of the throat to create large spaces for resonance.
- Use principles of good German or English diction by singing with tall, open vowels and clearly articulated consonants with adequate breath support.
- Tune the chords between the parts. Balance the voice parts by listening to other voice parts. Adjust the weight or loudness of each part to achieve a balanced blend of the voices.
- Analyze the contrapuntal entrances for imitations. Practice the entrances precisely.
- Articulate the rhythm precisely, emphasizing the moving lines.
- Plan the dynamics using full breath support for soft as well as loud singing.
- Demonstrate the correct singing of the *r* consonant after a vowel in English; it should be almost silent, as in *cares, here, pleasures, heart, surrender, depart,* and *bitterness.*
- Listen for diphthongs in English, that is, two vowel sounds when one vowel sound is written. Sing the first vowel sound and barely sing the second vowel with the next syllable. Diphthongs are found in such words as *I, life's, thy, my, bright,* and *night.*

dream: — All is rest and peace; 'Tis as
Glie - der Berg ich weich ins Moos, Und mir

dream: — All is rest and peace; — 'Tis as
Glie - der Berg ich weich ins Moos, — Und mir

— I dream: — All is rest and peace; 'Tis as
- den Glie - der Berg ich weich ins Moos, Und mir

— I dream: — All is rest and peace; 'Tis as
- den Glie - der Berg ich weich ins Moos, Und mir

if, be-neath thy shad - ows, All my cares and trou - bles cease, All my
ist, als würd ich wie - der all der ir - ren Qua - len los, All der

if, be-neath thy shad - ows, All my cares and trou - bles cease,
ist, als würd ich wie - der all der ir - ren Qua - len los,

if, be-neath thy shad - ows, All my cares and trou-bles cease,
ist, als würd ich wie - der all der ir - ren Qua-len los,

if, be - neath thy shad-ows, All my cares and trou-bles cease,
ist, als würd ich wie-der all der ir - ren Qua-len los,

Assessment

Informal Assessment

During this lesson, students showed the ability to:

- Shape phrases with dynamic intensity in the Vocal Warm-Up exercise.
- Shape phrases with dynamic intensity, identifying beginning, peak, and release in the Sight-Singing exercise.
- Sing one part independently when four parts are being sung in the Sight-Singing exercise.
- Sing with correct phrasing and German pronunciation in "Forest Cool, Thou Forest Quiet."

Student Self-Assessment

Have students:

- Evaluate their performance with the How Did You Do? section on page 97.
- Answer the questions individually. Discuss them in pairs or small groups and/or write their responses on a sheet of paper.

Individual Performance Assessment

To further demonstrate accomplishment, have each student:

- In a quartet, perform "Forest Cool, Thou Forest Quiet" while being videotaped, demonstrating correct phrasing, German pronunciation, and independent singing.
- Write a short paragraph describing a phrase, explaining how to shape the phrase using dynamic intensity.
- Videotape and then watch their performance, and write a self-assessment of their ability to shape phrases, use correct German pronunciation, and sing independently. (Develop and use a rubric if you wish. See the Extension activity on page 102.)

Extension

Developing an Assessment Rubric

Have students:

- Identify the three objectives they will be assessing in their own performance: German pronunciation, phrase shaping, and independent singing.
- Determine levels of accomplishment for each of these objectives, listing those characteristics that they would consider (1) needing improvement, (2) adequate, (3) good, (4) very good, and (5) excellent.
- Construct an evaluation grid, and use it to assess their own performance.

Note: If you also assess the performance using the rubric, hold a conference with each student to determine where you agree and disagree, and formulate a plan of action for improvement or enrichment.

The Forest as Metaphor; Music as Impression

Have students:

- Read the text of "Forest Cool, Thou Forest Quiet."
- Paraphrase the text.
- Review the concepts of the symbol and the metaphor. (A symbol is something that stands for or suggests something else, as the heart is a symbol of love. A metaphor is an implied comparison, as in the phrase "Life is a journey.")
- Describe what the symbolism and metaphor in the text suggest.
- Identify musical devices and techniques the composer used to communicate the meaning of this piece: the slow tempo; the ebb and flow of phrases; the alternating consonance and dissonance; tone painting on words of trouble or despair; and return to familiar chords at the end of each phrase.

heart! To the peace of night sur - ren - der, Let the
herz, und ein Frie - de schwebt mit lei - sen Flü - gel -
heart! To the peace of night sur - ren - - -
herz, und ein Frie - de schwebt mit lei - - -
heart! To the peace of night sur - ren - der, Let the
herz, und ein Frie - de schwebt mit lei - sen Flü - gel -
heart! To the peace of night sur - ren - der, Let the
herz, und ein Frie - de schwebt mit lei - sen Flü - gel -

bit - ter - ness de - part, Let the bit - ter -
schlä - gen nie - der - wärts, Frie - de schwe - bet
der, Let the bit - ter - ness de - part, the bit -
sen, schwebt mit lei - sen Flü - gel - schlä - gen nie -
bit - ter - ness de - part, Let the bit - ter - ness
schlä - gen nie - der - wärts, Frie - de schwe - bet nie -
bit - ter - ness de - part, Let the bit - ter -
schlä - gen nie - der - wärts, Frie - de schwe - bet

National Standards

The following National Standards are addressed through the Extension and bottom-page activities:

1. Singing, alone and with others, a varied repertoire of music. **(a, b, c)**
5. Reading and notating music. **(a, b)**
6. Listening to, analyzing, and describing music. **(a, b, c, f)**
7. Evaluating music and music performances. **(a, b)**
8. Understanding relationships between music, the other arts, and disciplines outside the arts. **(a, b, c, e)**
9. Understanding music in relation to history and culture. **(a, c, d)**

pp
ness de - part. Sing, oh sing, ye night - in -
nie - der - wärts. Sin - get hol - de Vo - gel-
pp
- ter - ness de - part. Sing, oh sing, ye night - in -
- - - der - wärts. Sin - get hol - de Vo - gel-
pp
de - part. Sing, oh sing, ye night -
- - der - wärts. Sin - get hol de Vo -
pp
ness de - part. Sing, oh sing ye night -
nie der - wärts. Sin - get hol - de Vo -
pp
p
gale, Sing your song so bright! All my
lie - der, mich in Schlum - mer sacht! Ir - re
p
gale, Sing your song so bright! All my
lie - der, mich in Schlum - mer sacht! Ir - re
p
- - in - gale, Sing your song so bright! All my
- gel - lie - der, mich in Schlum-mer sacht! Ir - re
p
- - in - gale, Sing your song so bright! All my
- gel - lie - der, mich in Schlum-mer sacht! Ir - re
p

Brahms and Wagner: Who Was the Greatest Romantic Composer?

Brahms and Wagner were contemporaries, but had very different roles in the development of music during the Romantic period.

Have students:

- In small groups, research either Wagner or Brahms, developing an argument for their composer as the most reflective of the Romantic spirit.
- Present their arguments as part of a debate team, choosing one person from each team to present their argument in five minutes or less, and someone to rebut the other argument in the same amount of time.
- Discuss the main points of each argument, and, as a whole group, create a press release that represents a compromise position that everyone in class can agree to.

trou - bles are for - got - ten, Rest-less heart, a sweet good - night, Rest - less
Qua - len, löst euch wie - der, wil-des herz, nun gu - te Nacht, wil - des
trou - bles are for - got - ten, Rest-less heart, a sweet good - night,
Qua - len, löst euch wie - der, wil-des herz, nun gu - te Nacht,
trou - bles are for - got - ten, Rest-less heart, a sweet good - night,
Qua - len, löst euch wie - der, wil-des herz, nun gu - te Nacht,
trou-bles are for - got-ten, Rest-less heart, a sweet good - night,
Qua-len, löst euch wie-der, wil-des herz, nu gu - te Nacht,
heart, a sweet good - night.
herz, nun gu - te Nacht.
Rest - less heart, a sweet good - night.
wil - des herz, nun gu - te Nacht.
Rest - less heart, a sweet good - night.
wil - des herz, nun gu - te Nacht.
A sweet good - night.
nun gu - te Nacht.

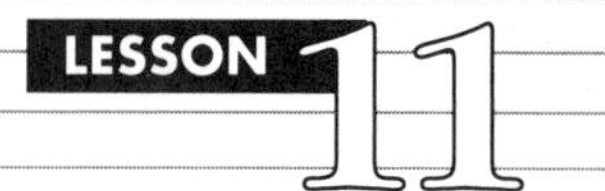

Keep Your Lamps!

Spiritual
ARRANGER: *André J. Thomas*

CHORAL MUSIC TERMS
accent
minor tonality
syncopation

VOICING
SATB

PERFORMANCE STYLE
Moderately
Accompanied by conga drums

FOCUS
- Identify and perform written accents.
- Identify and perform accents created by syncopation.
- Identify and sing in minor tonality.

Warming Up

Body Warm-Up

Do this stepping and clapping exercise until it becomes natural and familiar. Clap each line several times. The claps create a pattern of accents over the steady beat steps.

HANDS:	***Clap***		***Clap***	
FEET:	Step Left	Close Right	Step Left	Close Right
HANDS:		***Clap***		***Clap***
FEET:	Step Right	Close Left	Step Right	Close Left
HANDS:			***Clap***	
FEET:	Step Left	Close Right	Step Left	Close Right
HANDS:				***Clap***
FEET:	Step Right	Close Left	Step Right	Close Left

Vocal Warm-Up

Sing this exercise with great energy on *doot*. Notice the minor and major triads as you sing, and tune the third carefully. Add accents to some pitches—decide before you sing. Move up by half steps on each repeat.

LESSON 11

Keep Your Lamps!

Spiritual
ARRANGER: André Thomas

Focus

OVERVIEW
Written accents; syncopation; minor tonality.

OBJECTIVES
After completing this lesson, students will be able to:
- Identify and perform written accents.
- Identify and perform accents created by syncopation.
- Identify and sing in minor tonality.

CHORAL MUSIC TERMS
Define the Choral Music Terms for students, giving pronunciation, and answering any questions that may arise.

Warming Up

Body Warm-Up

This Body Warm-Up is designed to prepare students to:
- Feel the basic beat of a rhythm pattern.
- Clap accents over the basic beat.

Have students:
- Read through the Body Warm-Up directions.
- Perform the exercise.

TEACHER'S RESOURCE BINDER

National Standards

1. Singing a varied repertoire of music. **(a, b, c, f)**
4. Composing and arranging music within specified guidelines. **(b)**
5. Reading and notating music. **(a, b)**
6. Listening to, analyzing, and describing music. **(a, b, c, f)**
7. Evaluating music and music performances. **(a, b)**
8. Understanding relationships between music and other disciplines. **(c)**
9. Understanding music in relation to history and culture. **(a, b)**

Vocal Warm-Up

The Vocal Warm-Up on page 105 is designed to prepare students to:

- Sing major and minor triads.
- Tune the thirds of triads carefully.
- Sing with good energy, accenting with diaphragmatic control.

Have students:

- Read through the Vocal Warm-Up directions.
- Sing, following your demonstration.

Sight-Singing

This Sight-Singing exercise is designed to prepare students to:

- Sight-sing using solfège and hand signs or numbers in minor.
- Read and sing in cut time.
- Identify and sing accents caused by accent marks and syncopation.
- Read the dotted quarter-eighth rhythm.

Have students:

- Read through the Sight-Singing exercise directions.
- Read through each voice part rhythmically, using rhythm syllables.
- Sight-sing through each part separately using solfège and hand signs or numbers.
- Sing all parts together.

Singing: "Keep Your Lamps!"

Identify and practice accents.
Have students:

- Read the text on page 106.
- Read the sentence out loud, first with no accents, then with the notated accents.
- Notice how the shift in accent alters the meaning of the sentence.
- Try creating syncopation by stretching one of the syllables or saying it off the beat.
- Find the syncopation and accents in the Sight-Singing exercise, and in the notation for "Keep Your Lamps!"

Sight-Singing

Sight-sing each line separately, reading rhythm and pitch together. Focus carefully for accuracy the first time through. Notice the accents marked with accent marks, and find the one created by syncopation. How will you combine these lines? Try different combinations until you have sung each line.

Singing: "Keep Your Lamps!"

An accent indicates a sound that has more stress than the sounds around it. There are two kinds of accents in music—those caused by more stress (>), and those caused by unexpected stress or duration (syncopation).

Read this sentence without any accents:

Jill is our best fan.

Now read it with the accents shown:

> **Jill** *is our best fan.*   > *Jill* **is** *our best fan.*   > *Jill is* **our** *best fan.*

> *Jill is our* **best** *fan.*   > *Jill is our best* **fan**.

To create syncopation, stretch one of the syllables out longer, or say it off the beat.

Now turn to the music for "Keep Your Lamps!" on page 107.

HOW DID YOU DO? ? ?

"Keep Your Lamps!" will be an accent in your program. Think about your preparation and performance of "Keep Your Lamps!"

1. Describe how you recognize written accents, and what they tell you to do.
2. Describe syncopation and tell why it is considered an accent.
3. Sing the natural minor scale, then the harmonic minor scale. Tell which is used in "Keep Your Lamps!" and then sing from measures 8–16 using solfège and hand signs or numbers to show your ability to sing in minor.
4. Describe the ensemble's performance of "Keep Your Lamps!" What was good, and what needs work?
5. Identify what you like about "Keep Your Lamps!" What would you change if you were writing the arrangement?

Keep Your Lamps!

Spiritual
Arranged by André J. Thomas

Mixed Voices, SATB, with Conga Drums

Moderato

Conga Drums

High

Medium

Low

mf

6 S.

A.

T.

B.

mf

Keep your___ lamps trimmed and burn - - - ing, Keep your lamps trimmed and burn - - ing, Keep your___

10

13

lamps trimmed and burn - - ing,___ the time is draw - ing nigh.__

Suggested Teaching Sequence

1. Review Body Warm-Up.
Step the beat. Clap accents.
Have students:

- Review the Body Warm-Up on page 105.
- Identify the stressed sounds caused by the claps as accents.

2. Review Vocal Warm-Up.
Sing major and minor triads. Tune the thirds carefully. Sing accents.
Have students:

- Review the Vocal Warm-Up on page 105.
- Identify the minor and major triads based on the relationship of the third to the tonic.
- Sing slowly, tuning the third.
- Choose several pitches to sing with accents, and accent with diaphragmatic control.

3. Review Sight-Singing.
Sight-sing using solfège and hand signs or numbers. Identify and sing accents with accent marks and syncopation. Sing in four parts.
Have students:

- Review the Sight-Singing exercise on page 106.
- Read and sing each line, trying for accuracy on the first try.
- Identify accent marks.
- Identify the syncopation in the first line, third measure.
- Decide how to combine the lines to create a vocal piece, then sing their plan.

Arranger André Thomas

André J. Thomas is Director of Choral Activities and Associate Professor of Music Education (choral) at the Florida State University School of Music. Previously, he served on the faculty of the University of Texas Department of Music at Austin.

Dr. Thomas is frequently in demand as a choral adjudicator, clinician, and director of honor choirs and all-state choirs throughout the United States, Europe, and Australia. Besides his extensive conducting credits, he has distinguished himself as a composer/arranger. In the 1992–93 academic year, Dr. Thomas was awarded the University Award for Excellence in Teaching. He currently serves as the President-Elect of the Florida American Choral Directors Association.

4. Sight-sing "Keep Your Lamps!" using solfège and hand signs or numbers.

Have students:

- Divide into voice sections (SATB) and read each part rhythmically, using rhythm syllables, carefully noticing and accurately performing syncopations and accents.
- Still in sections, sing with solfège and hand signs or numbers, identifying and working on problem areas.
- Sing the piece through, using solfège and hand signs or numbers, with full ensemble.
- Divide into sections and recite the text rhythmically for each voice part.
- Sing the piece through with text as a full ensemble.

VOCAL DEVELOPMENT

To encourage vocal development, have students:

- Demonstrate exuberant vocal tone by singing with tall, open vowels and clearly articulated consonants, supported by firmly controlled breath.
- Create a full resonant sound by keeping a consistently large space in the mouth and pharynx.
- Energize sustained tones by increasing the breath support and dynamic level.
- Perform the rhythms precisely while conducting and speaking rhythm or speaking the text in rhythm. Emphasize the syncopated and tied rhythms.
- Reflect the excitement of the text and rhythm by building and contrasting the dynamics. Give accented notes extra intensity using diaphragmatic muscle action.
- Balance the chords between the parts by listening to them.

Soprano
Keep your— chil-dren don't get wea - ry, chil - dren
Alto
Wea - ry,
Tenor
Bass

don't get wea - ry, chil - dren don't get
Wea - ry, wea -
Wea ry, Wea - ry, wea -
Wea - ry, chil - dren,

wea - ry 'til your work is— done. Chil - dren
ry, 'til your work is done.

TEACHING STRATEGY

Adding Movement

Have students:

- Add the movement from the Body Warm-Up to their singing of "Keep Your Lamps!" It will keep their singing flexible, and is stylistically appropriate.

Vocal Style

Have students:

- Describe the style of this piece, and the cultural background. (a spiritual)
- Describe the range of their part. (mostly comfortably low)
- Sing with a relaxed, slightly heavier tone, but keep the rhythm accurate and the diction clear.

(40) S. A. T. B.

2. *f*

done. Chris-tian jour - ney soon be ov - er, Chris-tian

(43)

jour - ney soon be ov - - er, Chris-tian jour - ney soon be ov -

(46)

- - er, The time is draw - ing nigh. 1. Chris-tian

(56)

2. *p* (Repeat *f*)

nigh. Keep your lamps trimmed and burn -

Assessment

Informal Assessment

During this lesson, students showed the ability to:

- Identify and clap accents over a steady beat in the Body Warm-Up exercise.
- Sing major and minor triads, and sing accents in the Vocal Warm-Up exercise.
- Read and sing in minor tonality in the Sight-Singing exercise.
- Identify and sing accents and syncopation in the Sight-Singing exercise.
- Sing in minor tonality with accents and syncopation in "Keep Your Lamps!"

Student Self-Assessment

Have students:

- Evaluate their performance with the How Did You Do? section on page 106.
- Answer the questions individually. Discuss them in pairs or small groups and/or write their responses on a sheet of paper.

Individual Performance Assessment

To further demonstrate accomplishment, have each student:

- In each quartet, perform "Keep Your Lamps!" while being videotaped, demonstrating the ability to perform accents and syncopation.
- Write a short melody in F minor, and then share it with a classmate, each singing the other's melody. Assess each other's accuracy.

The Spiritual

The enslaved Africans brought music with the following elements to the New World: syncopation, polyrhythm, pentatonic and gap scales, and the idea of music combined with body movements.

From the suffering of the ocean crossing and a life of subjugation, they created a new genre, the "spiritual," or religious folk song of the slave. It revealed their unhappiness and suffering, taught facts, sent messages, provided a common language, and shared religious rituals and beliefs. In the spiritual, the singer must express a personal connection with the deity or God. The spiritual reflects a true historical picture of the lives of slaves as told by slaves themselves.

Extension

Adding the Conga Drum Part

Have students:

- Clap the rhythm of the part.
- Practice the part on high, middle, and low drums, or with high, middle, and low sounds on one drum. (high with a finger tap on the rim, middle with fingers bouncing off a spot about an inch inside the rim, and low with a cupped hand or flat hand strike in the middle of the drum)
- Try out for the part, with those who perform best accompanying the ensemble during performances.

Improvising with Accents and Syncopation

Have students:

- Improvise or compose echo patterns in a chosen key and meter.
- Add accents and syncopation as they are able, until they feel comfortable with these new elements.
- Continue to have each four patterns combine to create one long melody or rhythm, with the "echoers" first echoing all four patterns, then singing them one after the other. This builds memory as well as phrase-building ability.

58

- - ing, keep your lamps trimmed and burn-

60

- - ing, keep your lamps trimmed and burn - - ing, the

63

time is draw - ing nigh. Keep your - - ing, the

70

rit. a tempo fp pp

time is draw - ing nigh.

National Standards

The following National Standards are addressed through the Extension and bottom-page activities:

1. Singing, alone and with others, a varied repertoire of music. **(a, b, c)**
3. Improvising melodies, variations, and accompaniments. **(b)**
6. Listening to, analyzing, and describing music. **(a, b, c)**
8. Understanding relationships between music, the other arts, and disciplines outside the arts. **(a, c)**
9. Understanding music in relation to history and culture. **(a, b, c, d)**

Blessed Are the Pure of Heart

CHORAL MUSIC TERMS
- homophonic
- mental image of sound
- polyphonic
- Romantic period
- vocal tone color

COMPOSER: *Woldemar Voullaire* (1825–1902)
EDITED BY: K. *Köpe*
TRANSLATOR: R. *Steelman*

VOICING

SATB

PERFORMANCE STYLE

Andante
Accompanied by organ

FOCUS

- Sing using vocal tone colors drawn from mental images of sound.
- Identify and perform a full, rich, Romantic period vocal sound.
- Sing polyphonic and homophonic textures.
- Sing with correct German pronunciation.

Warming Up

Vocal Warm-Up

Sing this warm-up employing the five basic vowels, preceded by a voiced consonant (*m* or *n*). Strive for a warm, full sonority. Conduct in 4/4 while repeating this exercise up or down by half steps. Notice that the parts move together, creating a homophonic texture.

Sight-Singing

Sight-sing this exercise using solfège and hand signs or numbers, and a rich, warm tone color. Read each melody through, trying for accuracy the first time through. Then divide into three parts, each combining the melodies into a different pattern—1, 2, 3; 2, 3, 1; 3, 1, 2. Sing through all the melodies from where you begin. Which part is most difficult? Why?

TEACHER'S RESOURCE BINDER

Blackline Master 9, *Translation and Pronunciation Guide for "Blessed Are the Pure of Heart,"* page 89

National Standards

1. Singing, alone and with others, a varied repertoire of music. **(a, b, c, f)**
5. Reading and notating music. **(a, b)**
6. Listening to, analyzing, and describing music. **(a, b, c, f)**
7. Evaluating music and music performances. **(a, b)**
8. Understanding relationships between music, the other arts, and disciplines outside the arts. **(c)**
9. Understanding music in relation to history and culture. **(a)**

LESSON 12

Blessed Are the Pure of Heart

COMPOSER: Woldemar Voullaire (1825–1902)
EDITED BY: K. Köpe

Focus

OVERVIEW

Vocal tone color; polyphonic and homophonic texture; German pronunciation.

OBJECTIVES

After completing this lesson, students will be able to:
- Sing using vocal tone colors drawn from mental images of sound.
- Identify and perform a full, rich, Romantic period vocal sound.
- Sing polyphonic and homophonic textures.
- Sing with correct German pronunciation.

CHORAL MUSIC TERMS

Define the Choral Music Terms for students, giving pronunciation, and answering any questions that may arise.

Warming Up

Vocal Warm-Up

This Vocal Warm-Up is designed to prepare students to:
- Develop vowel focus.
- Sing with vocal resonance.
- Conduct in 4/4 meter.
- Identify homophonic texture.

Have students:
- Read through the Vocal Warm-Up directions.
- Sing, following your demonstration.

Sight-Singing

This Sight-Singing exercise is designed to prepare students to:

- Sight-sing using solfège and hand signs or numbers in 3/4 meter.
- Sing one part independently when three parts are being sung.

Have students:

- Read through the Sight-Singing exercise directions.
- Read through each voice part rhythmically, using rhythm syllables.
- Sight-sing through each part separately using solfège and hand signs or numbers.
- Sing all parts together.

Singing: "Blessed Are the Pure of Heart"

Explore the idea of the mind's ability to create tone quality before the physical act of producing a tone.

Have students:

- Read the text on page 112.
- Make the sounds of different size dogs, realizing that the sound was imagined before it was produced.
- Sing the Vocal Warm-Up in the suggested ways, again realizing that the sound of each tone color was imagined before it was produced.
- Discuss the characteristics of a Romantic period vocal tone color, including fullness and richness of tone.
- Sing the Vocal Warm-Up using this rich, warm tone color of the Romantic period.

Singing: "Blessed Are the Pure of Heart"

Your voice can reproduce any sound you can hear and any sound your brain can imagine. Make the sound of a small dog, then a medium dog, and finally a large dog.

Sing the Vocal Warm-Up in the following ways:

- a young child singing
- young teenagers singing
- seniors in high school singing
- adults singing

Your mind will tell your voice the tone quality it wants to use, then you will produce that sound.

What will your mind tell your voice to do to create a Romantic period vocal tone?

Now turn to the music for "Blessed Are the Pure of Heart" on page 113.

HOW DID YOU DO?

Using appropriate style is one key to excellent performance. Think about your preparation and performance of "Blessed Are the Pure of Heart."

1. Describe what the mind has to do with vocal tone color. Demonstrate with several different examples of tone colors you can imagine and sing.

2. Describe a Romantic period vocal sound, then demonstrate it using the first phrase of your voice part of "Blessed Are the Pure of Heart."

3. Describe and distinguish between polyphonic and homophonic textures, pointing them out in "Blessed Are the Pure of Heart."

4. How well did you pronounce the German in this piece? What made it easy? What was difficult?

5. Describe the ensemble's performance of "Blessed Are the Pure of Heart." What was good, and what needs work?

Blessed Are the Pure of Heart

(Selig Sind Die Reines Herzens Sind)

Mixed Voices, SATB, with Organ

Woldemar Voullaire (1825–1902)
Edited by K. Köpe
English by R. Steelman

Suggested Teaching Sequence

1. Review Vocal Warm-Up.
Sing using unified vowels. Use a warm vocal tone color. Sing homophonic texture.
Have students:

- Review the Vocal Warm-Up on page 112.
- Use different vowels on the repeats.
- Identify and use a warm, full sound, and remember that this is considered an appropriate sound for the Romantic period.
- Identify the homophonic texture created by chords moving in the same rhythm.

2. Review Sight-Singing.
Sight-sing using solfège and hand signs or numbers in 3/4 meter. Sing independently in three parts.
Have students:

- Review the Sight-Singing exercise on page 112.
- Read and sing each line, trying for accuracy on the first try.
- Sing in three parts, with each part beginning at a different section, and singing twice through.
- Identify the part they find hardest. (probably part 3, because the rhythm is different from the other two parts; it has leaps that need to be carefully tuned, and it moves in contrary motion at some points)

MORE ABOUT Composer Woldemar Voullaire

Henri Marc Hermann Woldemar Voullaire was born in 1825, and died at the turn of the twentieth century (1902). Born in Neuwelke, once part of the Soviet Balkan region, he served the people of German Moravia in his music. Voullaire was both a teacher and pastor, in addition to his composing. For inspiration he drew on the work of Romantic composers, especially Brahms. This musically adept minister—universally unknown compared to his fellow Moravian composer Leos Janacek—would be appreciative of the consideration given to his work today.

3. Sight-sing "Blessed Are the Pure of Heart" using solfège and hand signs or numbers.

Have students:

- Divide into voice sections (SATB) and read each part rhythmically, using rhythm syllables.
- Still in sections, sing with solfège and hand signs or numbers, identifying and working on problem areas.
- Sing the piece through, using solfège and hand signs or numbers, with full ensemble.

4. Learn the German pronunciation.

Have students:

- Using Blackline Master 9, *Translation and Pronunciation Guide for "Blessed Are the Pure of Heart,"* echo the text.
- Read through the piece, speaking the German text in rhythm.
- Sing the piece with correct German pronunciation.

11

p

Bless - ed

se - lig

mf

dim.

p

Ped.

Man.

16

p

Bless - ed are the

se - lig sind die

p

Bless - ed are the pure of

se - lig sind die rei - nes,

are the pure of heart, the pure of heart, the

sind die rei - nes Her - zens sind, die rei - nes

p

Bless - ed are the pure of heart, the pure, the

se - lig sind die rei - nes Her - zens, rei - nes

"Blessed Are the Pure of Heart"

This Romantic period piece was written for the full, rich sound of mature voices. The present anthem was edited from a manuscript copy in the archives of the Moravian Music Foundation. The keyboard part is an idiomatic adaptation of the orchestral accompaniment. All dynamic markings, as well as the tempo indication, are the composer's own.

VOCAL DEVELOPMENT

To encourage vocal development, have students:

- Demonstrate good vocal tone by singing with tall vowels in German and English. Alter (or modify) the vowel sounds in English when necessary, as in *of, shall,* and *Father.*
- Enjoy the resonance of the *oo* vowel sound on words such as *pure.*
- Arch or lift the tone on melodic leaps by increasing the space in the mouth and pharynx.
- Energize sustained tones by increasing the breath support and dynamic level.
- Sustain phrases by staggering the breathing and moving forward through the phrases.
- Increase intensity on repeated notes to feel forward movement of the melodic lines.
- Demonstrate the correct singing of the *r* consonant after a vowel. It should be almost silent, as in *are* and *heart.*
- Analyze the contrapuntal entrances of each voice to identify the thematic phrases and imitations between the voices.
- Feel the arched contour of each musical phrase as it begins, builds, then tapers off. The dynamics should reflect the melodic contour.
- Emphasize the two-note phrases by "leaning into" the first note and tapering off on the second note. Demonstrate this by using the arm with the palm up in a circular motion away from the body, ending with the palm down to sense the feeling of loud to soft. Actually sing the loud-soft motion.

Assessment

Informal Assessment

During this lesson, students showed the ability to:

- Identify and use a warm, rich tone color in the Vocal Warm-Up exercise.
- Sing homophonic texture in Vocal Warm-Up exercise.
- Sight-read and sight-sing in 3/4 meter using solfège and hand signs or numbers in the Sight-Singing exercise.
- Sing one part independently when three parts are being sung in the Sight-Singing exercise.
- Sing with a warm, rich tone color and both polyphonic and homophonic textures, using correct German pronunciation, in "Blessed Are the Pure of Heart."

Student Self-Assessment

Have students:

- Evaluate their performance with the How Did You Do? section on page 112.
- Answer the questions individually. Discuss them in pairs or small groups and/or write their responses on a sheet of paper.

41

Fa - ther.
Gott schau'n.

Fa - ther.
Gott schau'n.

Fa - ther.
Gott schau'n.

Fa - ther.
Gott schau'n.

46

p
Bless - ed are the
Se - lig sind die

p
Bless - ed, bless - ed are the
Se - lig sind - die rei - nes,

p

HMC-974

Individual Performance Assessment

To further demonstrate accomplishment, have each student:

- In a trio, perform the Sight-Singing exercise while being videotaped, demonstrating the ability to sing in two different tone colors indicated by you.
- After listening to a model performance of Romantic period vocal tone color, listen to their taped performance of "Blessed Are the Pure of Heart," and write a comparison of their performance to the model sound.
- In a quartet, perform "Blessed Are the Pure of Heart," signaling with one finger on the right shoulder for polyphonic texture, and two fingers for homophonic texture.
- Into a tape recorder in an isolated space, read the text of their voice part from measures 15–35, demonstrating correct German pronunciation.

MUSIC LITERACY

When Does Polyphonic Texture Work?

To help students expand their music literacy, have them:

- Identify several familiar melodies and sing them as rounds, raising a hand when the melodies stop sounding good.
- Identify several familiar melodies that they know will work as rounds, for example: "Frère Jacques" and "Row, Row, Row Your Boat."
- Discuss the reason some melodies work better than others as rounds. (They are based on one chord, or a repeating chord sequence, that allows the harmony to remain consonant.)

Extension

Polyphony and Homophony

Have students:

- Compose a melody in major or minor tonality that uses a pitch of the tonic chord on every strong beat.
- Decide how to create polyphony using this new melody; for example, sing it as a round, or begin by singing it as a round, then have the parts alter the melody to end together.
- Decide how to create homophony using this new melody; for example, improvise chordal accompaniment for the other three voices, or sing parallel harmonic lines for two or three other parts, adjusting as necessary to accommodate the ear.
- Create a short piece by using the melody alone, the polyphonic section, and the homophonic section.

51

pure of heart,— the pure,— the pure ——— of
rei - nes Her - zens, rei - nes Her - - zens

pure of heart, the pure, the pure ——— of
rei - nes Her - zens, rei - nes Her - - zens

p
Bless - ed— are the pure, the pure——— of
Se - lig— sind die rei - nes Her - - zens

p
Bless - ed— are the pure, the pure of
Se - lig— sind die rei - nes Her - zens

Ped.

56

heart.
sind.

heart.
sind.

heart.
sind.

heart.
sind.

f

p

National Standards

The following National Standards are addressed through the Extension and bottom-page activities:

1. Singing, alone and with others, a varied repertoire of music. **(a, b, c)**
2. Performing on instruments, alone and with others, a varied repertoire of music. **(b, c)**
3. Improvising melodies, variations, and accompaniments. **(a, b, c)**
4. Composing and arranging music within specified guidelines. **(a, c)**
6. Listening to, analyzing, and describing music. **(a, b, c)**
8. Understanding relationships between music, the other arts, and disciplines outside the arts. **(a, b, c)**
9. Understanding music in relation to history and culture. **(a, c, d)**

Listening to Vocal Tone Color of the Romantic Period

Have students:

- Research and listen to at least three different performances of Romantic period pieces that demonstrate vocal tone color.
- Write a paragraph discussing the following statement, using the three listening selections to support or refute the statement: "The three characteristics of the Romantic period were extravagance, exaggeration, and expression."

The Romantic Period

"Blessed Are the Pure of Heart" explores a small amount of text in different ways.

Have students:

- Research characteristics of arts in the Romantic period. (See pages 194–197.)
- Identify the musical characteristics and treatment of the text of "Blessed Are the Pure of Heart."
- Find examples of fine art of the Romantic period that reflect similar characteristics and treatment of the subject.

CURRICULUM CONNECTIONS

Science

This lesson has students imagine a sound, then produce it. The suggestion is that the vocal apparatus can physically produce any vocal sound the mind can imagine, and the mind tells the body what sound to produce. Have students:

- Learn more about the areas of the brain, what specializations there are, and how they control parts of the body.
- Identify the parts of the brain that are involved in both music perception and music production.
- Discuss the many different types of mental activities that can be involved in or involve music, including listening, composing, conducting, performing, recording, and so on.

93
p
are, bless - ed are the
sind, se - lig sind die
are, bless - ed are the
sind, se - lig sind die
are, bless - ed are
sind, se - lig sind
are, bless - ed are
sind, se - lig sind
sempre dim.
98
pp
pure of heart, of heart.
rei - nes Her - - - zens sind.
pure of heart, of heart.
rei - nes Her - - - zens sind.
the pure of heart, of heart.
die rei - nes Her - zens sind.
div.
the pure of heart, of heart.
die rei - nes Her - zens sind.

V'amo di Core

COMPOSER: *Wolfgang Amadeus Mozart* (1756–1791)

CHORAL MUSIC TERMS

canon
independent singing
Italian language
round

VOICING

SATB

PERFORMANCE STYLE

Procession
A cappella, for three four-part choruses

FOCUS

- Sing independently.
- Identify and sing in a round.
- Distinguish between round and canon.
- Sing with correct Italian pronunciation.

Warming Up

Vocal Warm-Up

Sing this warm-up using solfège and hand signs or numbers. Stand on part 1, sit on part 2, sit with crossed legs and arms on part 3. Sing this exercise as a three part canon, with the movements. Decide on a good place to end all together. Notice the pitches of the tonic chord.

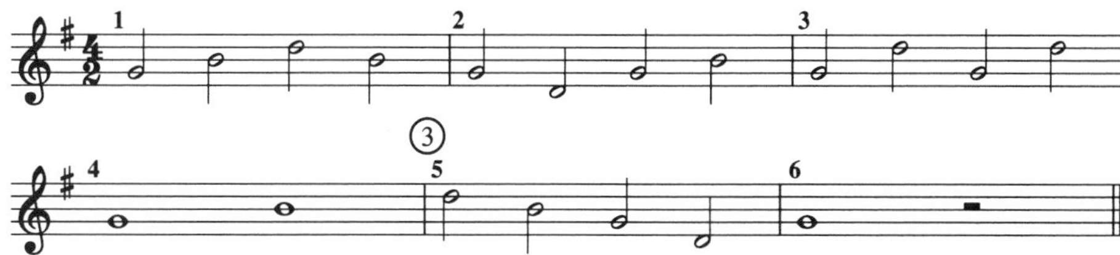

TEACHER'S RESOURCE BINDER

Blackline Master 10, *Rounds and Canons to Read,* page 90

Blackline Master 11, *Pronunciation Guide for "V'amo di Core,"* page 92

National Standards

1. Singing, alone and with others, a varied repertoire of music. **(a, b, c, f)**
5. Reading and notating music. **(a, b)**
6. Listening to, analyzing, and describing music. **(a, b, c, f)**
7. Evaluating music and music performances. **(a, b)**
8. Understanding relationships between music, the other arts, and disciplines outside the arts. **(c)**
9. Understanding music in relation to history and culture. **(a)**

LESSON 13

V'amo di Core

COMPOSER: Wolfgang Amadeus Mozart (1756–1791)

Focus

OVERVIEW

Independent singing; round and canon; Italian language.

OBJECTIVES

After completing this lesson, students will be able to:

- Sing independently.
- Identify and sing in a round.
- Distinguish between round and canon.
- Sing with correct Italian pronunciation.

CHORAL MUSIC TERMS

Define the Choral Music Terms for students, giving pronunciation, and answering any questions that may arise.

Warming Up

Vocal Warm-Up

This Vocal Warm-Up is designed to prepare students to:

- Read and sing tonic chord tones.
- Read in cut time.
- Involve the total body in singing.
- Sing a round.

Have students:

- Read through the Vocal Warm-Up directions.
- Sing, following your demonstration.

Sight-Singing

This Sight-Singing exercise is designed to prepare students to:

- Sight-sing using solfège and hand signs or numbers in cut time.
- Sing one part independently when four parts are being sung.
- Sing a three-part canon in three four-part choirs.

Have students:

- Read through the Sight-Singing exercise directions.
- Read through each voice part rhythmically, using rhythm syllables.
- Sight-sing through each part separately using solfège and hand signs or numbers.
- Sing all parts together.

Singing: "V'amo di Core"

Identify and distinguish between a round and a canon.

Have students:

- Read the text on page 124.
- Describe a round. (a composition in which a perpetual theme begins in one group and is strictly imitated by other groups in an overlapping fashion; the last voice to enter becomes the final voice to complete singing)
- Distinguish between a round and a canon. (A canon is a composition similar to a round. Unlike the round, the canon closes with all voices ending together.)
- Using Blackline Master 10, *Rounds and Canons to Read,* sight-sing the pieces as rounds and canons.

TEACHING STRATEGY

Listen to a Canon

Have students:

- Listen to Pachelbel's Canon in D.
- Tell whether it is a canon. (It is a chaconne.)

Sight-Singing

Sight-sing this exercise using solfège and hand signs or numbers. Can you sight-sing it with all four parts right away? Once the full ensemble is familiar with the piece, divide into three choirs of four parts, and sing the exercise as a canon. Decide on a good place to end all together.

Singing: "V'amo di Core"

In the "good old days" before television and radio, singing was a popular evening activity. Rounds were very popular because everyone could learn the same part together, then make complex-sounding music with comparative ease.

How would you describe a round? Do you know the difference between a round and a canon? (In a round all voice parts end separately; in a canon all voice parts end at the same time.) Rounds and canons can be very complex, if the composer is very clever. Sing a round as part of your warm-ups each day.

Now turn to the music for "V'amo di Core" on page 125.

HOW DID YOU DO?

Mozart was one of the most imaginative composers in history. Think about your preparation and performance of "V'amo di Core."

1. How well could you hold your part independently when the piece was sung in four parts? Did that change when your ensemble became three four-part choruses and sang in a round?

2. Describe a round and a canon, and identify the difference between them.

3. Sing the Vocal Warm-Up, or some other canon of your choice, with at least two other classmates—one person on a part.

4. How well did you pronounce the Italian in this piece? What language, other than English, do you find easiest to sing? Hardest?

Wolfgang Amadeus Mozart (1756–1791)

As a representative composer of the Classical Period, Mozart embodied the spirit of the classical style: crisp harmonies, exuberant melodies, formal balance and symmetry. He composed in virtually all forms of the time, including symphonies, operas, string quartets, art songs, and masses. A household word, due to the immense popularity of the movie, "Amadeus," Mozart died at the early age of 35, cutting short the career of one of the most prolific composers of all times.

V'amo di Core

Kanon für three vierstimmigre Chöre*

Wolfgang Amadeus Mozart

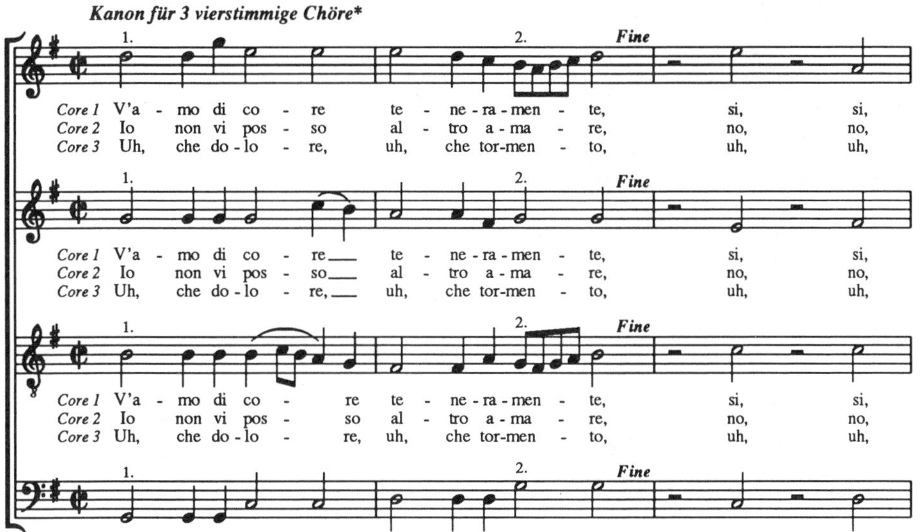

*) Die Chöre, deren jeder seinen eigenen Text singt, schlissen nacheinander beim Fine.– Textunterlegung vom Herausgeber überarbeitet (vgl. Anm. S. 2 unten).

VOCAL DEVELOPMENT

Have students:

- Sing with tall vowels in Italian.
- Lift the tone on melodic leaps by increasing the space in the mouth and pharynx.
- Energize sustained tones by increasing the breath support and dynamic level.
- Sustain phrases by staggering the breathing through the phrases.
- Increase intensity on repeated notes to feel forward movement of the melodic lines.
- Analyze the contrapuntal entrances of each voice to identify the thematic phrases and imitations between voices.
- Feel the contour of musical phrases.
- Note when the voices move from parts to unison singing to adjust the dynamic attack.

Suggested Teaching Sequence

1. Review Vocal Warm-Up.
Have students:

- Review the Vocal Warm-Up on page 123.
- Add the movements.
- Identify the pitches of the tonic chord.
- Sing in canon with movement.

2. Review Sight-Singing.
Have students:

- Review the Sight-Singing exercise on page 124.
- Sight-sing in four parts, aiming for pitch and rhythm accuracy.
- Sing the piece in four parts.
- Sing in three-part canon, with three four-part choirs created by rearranging your ensemble sections.

3. Sight-sing "V'amo di Core" using solfège and hand signs or numbers.
Have students:

- Divide into voice sections (SATB) and read each part using rhythm syllables.
- Still in sections, sing with solfège and hand signs or numbers, identifying and working on problem areas.
- Sing the piece through, using solfège and hand signs or numbers, with full ensemble.

4. Learn the Italian pronunciation.
Have students:

- Using Blackline Master 11, *Pronunciation Guide for "V'amo di Core,"* echo the text.
- Speak the Italian text in rhythm.
- Sing the piece with correct Italian pronunciation.

5. Sing in three-part canon.
Have students:

- Divide into three equal four-part choirs.
- Sing the piece as a three-part canon, with three four-part choirs.

Assessment

Informal Assessment

During this lesson, students showed the ability to:

- Define and distinguish between a round and canon.
- Sing a round.
- Sight-read and sight-sing in cut time using solfège and hand signs or numbers.
- Sing a round in three four-part choirs.
- Sing independently in a round, using correct Italian pronunciation in "V'amo di Core."

Student Self-Assessment

Have students:

- Evaluate their performance with the How Did You Do? section on page 124.
- Answer the questions individually. Discuss them in pairs or small groups and/or write their responses.

Individual Performance Assessment

Have each student:

- In a quartet, sing the Sight-Singing exercise into a tape recorder to show vocal independence.
- Sing from Blackline Master 10, *Rounds and Canons to Read,* in three or four parts, one person on a part, demonstrating ability to sing a round or canon.
- Into a tape recorder in an isolated space, speak the text of their voice part for all three verses in rhythm, demonstrating correct Italian pronunciation.

Extension

Composing a Round or Canon

Have students:

- Identify the characteristics of a round or canon.
- Construct a round or canon.
- Sing their piece as a round and canon.

Deutsche Textübertragung:
Kanon für 3 vierstimmige Chöre

(Deutsche Textübertragung: Gottfried Wolters)
Aus: Mozart Kanons im Urtext, herausgegeben von Gottfried Wolters, Finken - Bücherei, Bd. 1/2, Mössler Verlag, Wolfenbüttel. (Dort mit Anmerkungen und Revisions - Bericht).

National Standards

The following National Standards are addressed through the Extension and bottom-page activities:

1. Singing, alone and with others, a varied repertoire of music. **(a, b, c)**
4. Composing and arranging music within specified guidelines. **(a, c)**
6. Listening to, analyzing, and describing music. **(a, b, c)**
8. Understanding relationships between music, the other arts, and disciplines outside the arts. **(c)**
9. Understanding music in relation to history and culture. **(a, d)**

I Will Lay Me Down in Peace

COMPOSER: *Healey Willan*

CHORAL MUSIC TERMS
independent singing
melodic skips
melodic steps
rhythmic interplay
tone painting

VOICING
SATB

PERFORMANCE STYLE
Slow and soft
A cappella

FOCUS
- Read and sing independently parts with rhythmic interplay.
- Identify and sing melodic steps and skips accurately.
- Identify combination of text and music, or tone painting.

Warming Up

Vocal Warm-Ups

1. Sing this warm-up using *hoo*. Notice the articulation, and use good diaphragmatic action for clear articulation. Be sure to keep the third in tune as you sing. Move up by half steps on each repeat. Change the vowel after *h* (*ha, ho, hi, hee*, etc.) to keep this exercise interesting.

1
Hoo - hoo - hoo - hoo - hoo.
2
Hoo - hoo - hoo - hoo - hoo.
etc.

2. Sing this exercise using solfège and hand signs or numbers, then text. Then sing it in a three part round, at a moderate tempo. Listen to the harmonies that result from the combination of voices. Notice the steps and skips in the melody. Tenors and Basses, sing with a light tone in the upper register to match that of the Sopranos and Altos.

I will lay me down in peace. I will
lay down, lay down in peace.

TEACHER'S RESOURCE BINDER

National Standards

1. Singing, alone and with others, a varied repertoire of music. **(a, b, c, f)**
5. Reading and notating music. **(a, b)**
6. Listening to, analyzing, and describing music. **(a, b, c, f)**
7. Evaluating music and music performances. **(a, b)**
8. Understanding relationships between music, the other arts, and disciplines outside the arts. **(a, c)**
9. Understanding music in relation to history and culture. **(a)**

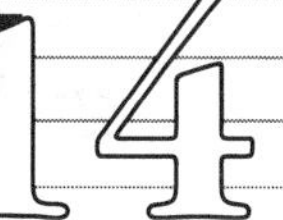

I Will Lay Me Down in Peace

COMPOSER: Healey Willan

Focus

OVERVIEW
Independent singing; rhythmic interplay; melodic steps and skips; tone painting.

OBJECTIVES
After completing this lesson, students will be able to:
- Read and sing independent parts with rhythmic interplay.
- Identify and sing melodic steps and skips accurately.
- Identify the matching of text and music, or tone painting.

CHORAL MUSIC TERMS
Define the Choral Music Terms for students, giving pronunciation, and answering any questions that may arise.

Warming Up

Vocal Warm-Up 1
This Vocal Warm-Up is designed to prepare students to:
- Use staccato and legato articulation.
- Keep diaphragmatic action precise.
- Keep the third of the scale tuned high.
- Sing unified vowels.

Have students:
- Read through the Vocal Warm-Up 1 directions.
- Sing, following your demonstration.

Vocal Warm-Up 2

The second Vocal Warm-Up on page 127 is designed to prepare students to:

- Sing in a round.
- Hear harmonies in 3/4 meter.
- Sing with a light tone. (tenors and basses)

Have students:

- Read through the Vocal Warm-Up 2 directions.
- Sing, following your demonstration.

Sight-Singing

This Sight-Singing exercise is designed to prepare students to:

- Sight-sing using solfège and hand signs or numbers, with rhythmic interplay.
- Sing one part independently when four parts are being sung.
- Sing melodic steps and skips.
- Sing and tune dissonant chords.

Have students:

- Read through the Sight-Singing exercise directions.
- Read through each voice part rhythmically, using rhythm syllables.
- Sight-sing through each part separately using solfège and hand signs or numbers.
- Sing all parts together.

Singing: "I Will Lay Me Down in Peace"

Have students:

- Read the text on page 128.
- Read the text of "I Will Lay Me Down in Peace."
- Listen to the separate lines, identifying the steps and skips, and where the composer used tone painting either by reinforcing a word, or doing the opposite of its meaning.
- Listen to the combined vocal parts, identifying how the composer used harmonic and rhythmic tone painting to enhance the text.

Sight-Singing

Sight-sing this exercise using solfège and hand signs or numbers. Tune carefully to the parts around you, and listen for the rhythmic interplay among the parts.

Singing: "I Will Lay Me Down in Peace"

A jigsaw puzzle is a combination that is greater than the sum of its parts because each of the pieces contributes to completing the whole picture. Text and music unite to create an expressive force. Read the text of "I Will Lay Me Down in Peace." Now sing or listen to each line separately, and describe the leaps and steps. How does each line enhance the text? How does the combination of melodies enhance the text? The composer has made a tone painting in which text and music express more than the text alone.

Now turn to the music for "I Will Lay Me Down in Peace" on page 129.

HOW DID YOU DO?

The combination of text and music is only as powerful as your performance. Think about your preparation and performance of "I Will Lay Me Down in Peace."

1. How well could you hold your part independently when the piece was sung in four parts? What is different about this piece than others you have sung lately?
2. Describe the rhythm of "I Will Lay Me Down in Peace" and explain how it adds to the meaning of the text. Give general and specific examples.
3. Describe the use of melodic steps and skips in "I Will Lay Me Down in Peace" and explain how it adds to the meaning of the text. Give general and specific examples.
4. Sing "I Will Lay Me Down in Peace" in a quartet to show your ability to hold your part, and sing the rhythms and pitches accurately.
5. Describe what it means when a composer tone paints a text. Give examples of when and how this occurs in "I Will Lay Me Down in Peace."

Composer Healey Willan

Healey Willan was born in the late 1800s in England. However, he was a composer and performer of the twentieth century, generating works from the early 1900s until his death in 1968. Healey was made a Fellow of the Royal College of Organists in 1899, where he received his academic training.

From 1903 until 1913 he was musical director for St. John the Baptist Church in London. He then moved to Toronto, Canada, to provide musical direction for St. Paul's Church. Also at this time he taught at the Toronto Conservatory of Music, and later at the University of Toronto. In 1920, the University of Toronto awarded him a Doctorate of Music. Mr. Willen directed music at the Church of St. Mary Magdalene for the next 47 years, until his death.

I Will Lay Me Down in Peace

Healey Willan

Quartet or Chorus

Suggested Teaching Sequence

1. Review Vocal Warm-Up 1.
Have students:

- Review Vocal Warm-Up 1 on page 127.
- Work on the articulation and diaphragmatic control.
- Identify and carefully tune the thirds.

2. Review Vocal Warm-Up 2.
Have students:

- Review Vocal Warm-Up 2 on page 127.
- Sing in a round, identifying and tuning dissonant harmonies.
- Identify the melodic steps and skips.
- Tenor and basses sing with a light tone.
- Describe how the music and text work together.

3. Review Sight-Singing.
Have students:

- Review the Sight-Singing exercise on page 128.
- Identify the harmonic style as dissonant, and the rhythmic style as complex.

4. Sight-sing "I Will Lay Me Down in Peace" using solfège and hand signs or numbers.
Have students:

- Divide into voice sections (SATB) and read each part rhythmically, using rhythm syllables, identifying phrase beginnings and endings.
- Still in sections, sing with solfège and hand signs or numbers, identifying and working on problem areas and practicing altered tones and rhythmic challenges.
- Sing the piece through, using solfège and hand signs or numbers, with full ensemble.
- Divide into sections and recite the text rhythmically for each voice part.
- Sing the piece through with text as a full ensemble.

TEACHING STRATEGY

Suspensions and Altered Tones as Part of a Style

Have students:

- Identify the altered tones in their voice part, and practice them in isolation until they are familiar.
- Discuss how a suspension holds a pitch in one part while the other parts move to a new chord, thereby creating dissonance.
- Find places in their voice part where they have a suspended tone.
- Sing the piece again, listening to the effect of suspensions in keeping the tension of the piece constant, and moving the piece ever forward without rest until a cadence.

5. Identify tone painting in the piece.
Have students:

- Review the meaning of tone painting. (matching of text and music in which the sum effect is more than either by itself)
- Identify the literal meaning of the text alone.
- Identify the musical characteristics of the piece.
- Discuss how the music and text are matched to create a total effect.
- Sing the piece, listening to the effect of the music/text matching as they sing.

Assessment

Informal Assessment

During this lesson, students showed the ability to:

- Sing dissonant harmonies.
- Identify melodic steps and skips and identify how music and text work together.
- Sight-read and sight-sing dissonant harmonies and complex rhythms using solfège and hand signs or numbers.
- Sing independently in "I Will Lay Me Down in Peace."
- Identify examples of text/music matching in "I Will Lay Me Down in Peace."

Student Self-Assessment

Have students:

- Evaluate their performance with the How Did You Do? section on page 128.
- Answer the questions individually. Discuss them in pairs or small groups and/or write their responses.

Individual Performance Assessment

Have each student:

- In a quartet, sing the Sight-Singing exercise into a tape recorder to show vocal independence.
- Sing "I Will Lay Me Down in Peace," signaling with a "thumbs up" each time a melodic leap is sung.
- Point to three melodic steps and three melodic leaps in their own voice part.

VOCAL DEVELOPMENT

Have students:

- Sing tall vowels and clear consonants.
- Lift the tone on melodic leaps by increasing the space in the mouth and pharynx.
- Energize sustained tones by increasing the breath support and dynamic level.
- Sustain phrases by staggering the breathing through the phrases.
- Listen for diphthongs in words such as *I, lay, down,* and *my*.
- Sing the *r* consonant after a vowel almost silently, as in *Lord*.
- Feel the arched contour of each musical phrase. The dynamics should reflect the melodic contour.
- Analyze the linear melodic intervals and tune carefully.

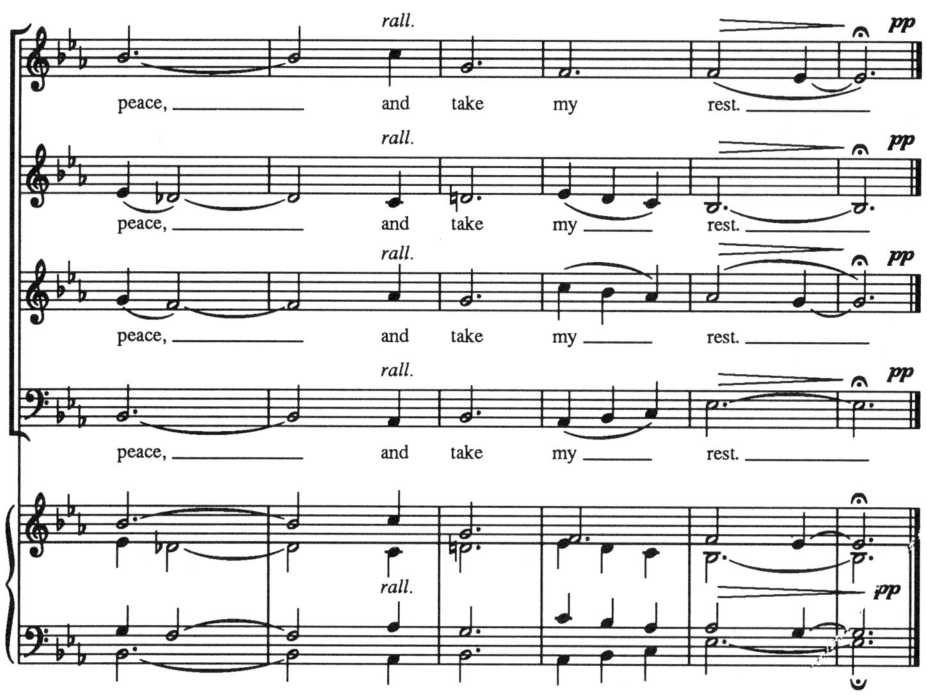

National Standards

The following National Standards are addressed through the Extension and bottom-page activities:

1. Singing, alone and with others, a varied repertoire of music. **(a, b, c)**

6. Listening to, analyzing, and describing music. **(a, b, c, e, f)**

8. Understanding relationships between music, the other arts, and disciplines outside the arts. **(a, b, c, e)**

9. Understanding music in relation to history and culture. **(a, c, d)**

Extension

Tuning Dissonant Intervals and Harmonies

Have students:

- Listen as you assign a pitch to each section of the ensemble, and then sustain that pitch using staggered breathing.
- Listen in each section as you point to one person to change their section's pitch. (The section members must listen to those around them for the new pitch sung by the selected individual, and then change to match their section.)
- Continue to change pitches, trying to choose discordant pitches to challenge their section.

Writing Program Notes

Have students:

- Write program notes for "I Will Lay Me Down in Peace," to be printed on the program for the performance, explaining to the audience what the piece is about and what to listen for.

Finding a Text for Tone Painting

Have students:

- Explore quotation and literature books to find texts that would be appropriate for tone painting.
- Write some sketchy suggestions for a composer, stating what they hear as possibilities, both overall and for specific words.
- Optional: Commission a composer to create a setting for their chosen text, consulting with the composer to give guidelines for range, difficulty, and so on.
- Perform the commissioned piece at an upcoming concert, inviting the composer to the premiere performance.

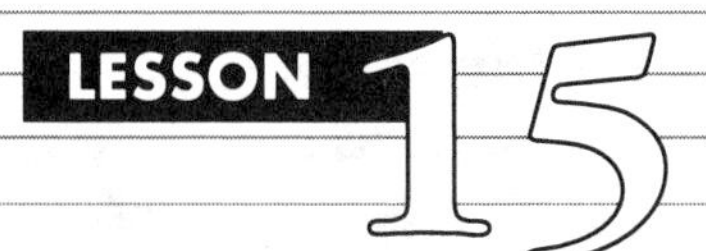

The Cloths of Heaven

COMPOSER: Adolphus Hailstork

TEXT: William Butler Yeats (1865–1939)

Focus

OVERVIEW

Tuning; melodic leaps; altered tones; staggered breathing.

OBJECTIVES

After completing this lesson, students will be able to:

- Tune pitches accurately.
- Read and sing melodic leaps with accuracy.
- Read and sing altered tones using solfège and hand signs or numbers.
- Use staggered breathing.

CHORAL MUSIC TERMS

Define the Choral Music Terms for students, giving pronunciation, and answering any questions that may arise.

Warming Up

Vocal Warm-Up

This Vocal Warm-Up is designed to prepare students to:

- Tune pitches solidly.
- Read and analyze pitch changes.
- Sing as the harmony shifts from major to augmented, to minor second inversion, and back to major.
- Stagger breathing.

Have students:

- Read through the Vocal Warm-Up directions.
- Sing, following your demonstration.

LESSON 15

The Cloths of Heaven

COMPOSER: Adolphus Hailstork

TEXT: William Butler Yeats (1865–1939)

CHORAL MUSIC TERMS

altered tones
melodic leaps
staggered breathing
tuning pitches

VOICING

SATB

PERFORMANCE STYLE

With flexibility, slowly
A cappella

FOCUS

- Tune pitches accurately.
- Read and sing melodic leaps with accuracy.
- Read and sing altered tones using solfège and hand signs or numbers.
- Use staggered breathing.

Warming Up

Vocal Warm-Up

Are you ready for a challenge? This exercise is a serious study in tuning. Sing this warm-up on the text provided. Notice that with each new measure, one voice raises its pitch by a half step. On the fourth measure, the alto and bass move up together. Stagger your breathing so there are no breaks over a bar line. Listen carefully as you sing!

TEACHER'S RESOURCE BINDER

National Standards

1. Singing, alone and with others, a varied repertoire of music. **(a, b, c, f)**
5. Reading and notating music. **(a, b)**
6. Listening to, analyzing, and describing music. **(a, b, c, f)**
7. Evaluating music and music performances. **(a, b)**
8. Understanding relationships between music, the other arts, and disciplines outside the arts. **(a, c)**
9. Understanding music in relation to history and culture. **(a)**

Sight-Singing

Here's another challenge for you! This exercise is written with many uncommon leaps and several altered tones. It will prepare you for the upcoming piece, so take the time to become familiar with the intervals and style. Can you perfect the melody so the pitches are exactly in tune when you sing each one?

Singing: "The Cloths of Heaven"

If the richness and beauty of heaven were represented in an embroidered cloth, what do you imagine it would look like? Read the text of "The Cloths of Heaven," then explain the message in your own words.

Had I the heavens' embroidered cloths,
Enwrought with golden and silver light,
The blue and the dim and the dark cloths
Of night and light and the half-light.
I would spread the cloths under your feet:

But I, being poor, have only my dreams:
I have spread my dreams under your feet,
Tread softly because you tread on my dreams.
—William Butler Yeats

If you were going to compose a setting to enhance this text, in twentieth-century style, what musical characteristics and compositional techniques might you use?

Now turn to the music for "The Cloths of Heaven" on page 134.

HOW DID YOU DO?

You have embroidered your own sound painting. Think about your preparation and performance of "The Cloths of Heaven."

1. Describe the challenge of singing in tune in "The Cloths of Heaven," then tell how well you did.

2. Choose a section of "The Cloths of Heaven" to sing with three classmates, demonstrating your ability to sing melodic leaps and altered tones, and to stagger your breathing.

3. Describe the musical characteristics and compositional techniques the composer used to tone paint the text. Was this treatment effective?

4. Did you predict the compositional techniques that the composer used? What else might you have suggested?

5. If you were going to give advice to an ensemble that was just beginning to learn this piece, what would you tell them in order to guide them to a really effective and convincing performance?

Sight-Singing

This Sight-Singing exercise is designed to prepare students to:

- Sing uncommon leaps and altered tones with accuracy.
- Practice intervals until they become comfortable and familiar.

Have students:

- Read through the Sight-Singing exercise directions.
- Read through each voice part rhythmically, using rhythm syllables.
- Sight-sing through each part separately using solfège and hand signs or numbers.
- Sing all parts together.

Singing: "The Cloths of Heaven"

Predict the musical characteristics and compositional techniques to be used in tone painting the text.

Have students:

- Read the text on page 133.
- Read the text of "The Cloths of Heaven."
- Explain the message in their own words.
- Predict what a twentieth-century composer would do to tone paint this text.

TEACHING STRATEGY

Sight-Singing: A Lifelong Skill

As the reading becomes complex, with altered tones, remind students that sight-singing is a life skill that will be appreciated if mastered. However, like any other skill, it is pretty easy to be good, but hard work to become great.

Composer Adolphus Hailstork

Adolphus Hailstork has received extensive training in music, attending the Manhattan School of Music, the American Institute at Fontainebleau, Howard University, and Michigan State University, where he earned his doctorate in composition. A career marked with numerous awards and recordings has reflected the diversity and depth of his training. In the 1990s alone, five orchestras and a symphony have commissioned works by Hailstork. He has written for chorus, solo voice, various chamber ensembles, band, and orchestra. Dr. Hailstork is currently Professor of Music and Composer-in-Residence at Norfolk State University in Virginia.

Suggested Teaching Sequence

1. Review Vocal Warm-Up.
Have students:

- Review the Vocal Warm-Up on page 132.
- Identify which voice part moves on each measure. (tenor, measure 2; soprano, measure 3; alto and bass, measure 4)
- Notice that the last measure is repeated as the first measure of the repeat.

2. Review Sight-Singing.
Have students:

- Review the Sight-Singing exercise on page 133.
- Identify the altered tones and learn their solfège names. (assuming C is *do:* F♯ = *fi,* E♭ = *me,* B♭ = *te,* A♭ = *le,* C♯ = *di*)
- In sections, preview their part in "The Cloths of Heaven," discussing difficult leaps and altered tones.

3. Sight-sing "The Cloths of Heaven" using solfège and hand signs or numbers.
Have students:

- Divide into voice sections (SATB) and read each part rhythmically, using rhythm syllables, adding dynamics to shape the phrases.
- Still in sections, sing with solfège and hand signs or numbers, identifying and working on problem areas, and identifying and practicing melodic leaps and altered tones.
- Sing the piece through, using solfège and hand signs or numbers, with full ensemble.
- Sing the entire piece on *loo,* standing in a circle, listening across the room for accuracy in tuning.
- Divide into sections and recite the text rhythmically for each voice part.
- Sing the piece through with text as a full ensemble.

The Cloths of Heaven

No. 4 from *Five Short Choral Works*

Adolphus Hailstork
William Butler Yeats (1865–1939)

SATB, A cappella

"The Cloths of Heaven"

This piece is from a cycle of a larger work for choir titled *Five Short Choral Works.* The titles of the four other pieces are "I Will Sing of Life," "Nocturne," "Crucifixion," and "The Lamb."

4. Working on intonation accuracy.

Have students:

- First secure their own voice part.
- Sing problem intervals out of context until accurate. (soprano sing measures 14 and 25; alto I sing measures 31–32 and measure 47; tenor sing measures 34–35; bass I and II sing measure 24–25)
- Sing sections of the piece in two-part ensembles (SA, SB, TB, and so on).

5. Isolate problem chord progressions.

Have students:

- Sing measures 12–13, pickup to 28–32, 34–35, and 49–51. (Stop on beat one of the final measure.)
- Discuss and work out the harmonic difficulty in each of these spots.
- Sing the piece through in full ensemble with the text.

6. Identify tone painting in the piece.

Have students:

- Review the meaning of tone painting. (matching of text and music in which the sum effect is more than either by itself)
- Identify the literal meaning of the text alone.
- Identify the musical characteristics of the piece.
- Discuss how the music and text are matched to create a total effect.
- Sing the piece, listening to the effect of the music/text matching as they sing.

MUSIC LITERACY

To help students expand their music literacy, have them:

- Conduct the mixed meters of "The Cloths of Heaven" while speaking the rhythm or text.

VOCAL DEVELOPMENT

To encourage vocal development, have students:

- Demonstrate good vocal tone by singing tall vowels and clear consonants.
- Energize sustained tones by increasing the breath support and dynamic level.
- Sustain phrases by staggering the breathing and moving forward through the phrases.
- Sing the *piano* dynamics with the same full breath support and intensity as *forte* singing.
- Demonstrate the correct singing of the *r* consonant after a vowel. It should be almost silent, as in *silver, embroidered, dark, under,* and *your.*
- Listen for diphthongs (two vowel sounds when one vowel sound is written) in words such as *I* and *my.* Sing or sustain the first vowel sound and barely sing the second vowel sound with the next syllable.
- Identify intervals and chords between the parts and tune them carefully.

20

S. night and light and the half - light,

A. night and light and the half - light, *pp* I

T. night and light and the half - light, *div.* *pp*

B. night and light and the half - light,

20

pp

S. *div.* *pp* *p* I would spread the cloths / I would spread the cloths *f*

A. would spread the cloths *f* *div.*

T. would spread the / I would spread the cloths *p* *f* *unis.*

B. I would spread the cloths *p* *f* *div.*

f

TEACHING STRATEGY

Interpreting the Text

In this lesson, students are asked to analyze and interpret the text of "The Cloths of Heaven" in their own words. The poem both contrasts the poor person's dreams to the rich embroidered cloths of heaven, and compares them as equally rich in value. Both are imaginary riches of the most sparkling and elegant hues, almost unimaginable, and yet describable. The dreams are offered in reverence by putting them under the listener's feet—a sign of honor and trust—but also come with a caution to tread carefully because they are valuable.

Symbolized in this analogy is the full spectrum of possibilities, from bright to pastel, dark to light, shining to sublime. Like-

wise symbolized is the fragile quality of the heavens. The musical setting suggests the endless expanse of the heavens, and the unbounded richness of hue, created by the combination of so many pitches at once, so many tonalities combined, and the wide intervals between parts. The texture and tonality continue into the section on dreams, continuing the analogy between the cloths of heaven and the author's dreams, which also have great expanse and possibility.

The continually changing meter contributes to the floating feeling of the piece, and the altered tones prevent the listener from "coming down to earth." Encourage students to find more specific word painting in the piece.

Assessment

Informal Assessment

During this lesson, students showed the ability to:

- Sing dissonant harmonies and use staggered breathing in the Vocal Warm-Up exercise.
- Sight-read and sight-sing melodic leaps and altered tones using solfège and hand signs or numbers in the Sight-Singing exercise.
- Sing independently in the Sight-Singing exercise.
- Sing independently, with dissonant harmonies and altered tones in "The Cloths of Heaven."
- Identify specific examples of text/music matching in "The Cloths of Heaven."

Student Self-Assessment

Have students:

- Evaluate their performance with the How Did You Do? section on page 133.
- Answer the questions individually. Discuss them in pairs or small groups and/or write their responses on a sheet of paper.

Individual Performance Assessment

To further demonstrate accomplishment, have each student:

- In a quartet, sing the Sight-Singing exercise into a tape recorder to show vocal independence and the ability to tune pitches accurately when singing melodic leaps and altered tones.
- Sing "The Cloths of Heaven," signaling with a "thumbs up" each time a melodic leap or altered tone is sung.
- Sing the Vocal Warm-Up exercise, raising a hand each time a breath is taken, and putting it down when rejoining the singing.

Extension

Assessing a Piece

There is a great difference between personal preference for a piece or style, and the quality of that piece in the style in which it is written. Have students:

- Discuss whether they like "The Cloths of Heaven," stating the criteria they are using for their judgment.
- Discuss whether they think it is a good example of twentieth-century choral literature, stating the criteria they are using.
- Discuss the distinction between personal preference and exemplary models of a style.

Composing a Tone Painting

Have students:

- Choose another poem by Yeats for tone painting.
- Individually or in groups, create a setting of the text for their choice of instruments and voices.
- After sharing, conferencing, and several revisions, perform their piece for the ensemble or other real audience.
- Assess the success of their piece from their own (composer's) point of view, a strictly musical point of view, and from the audience response point of view.

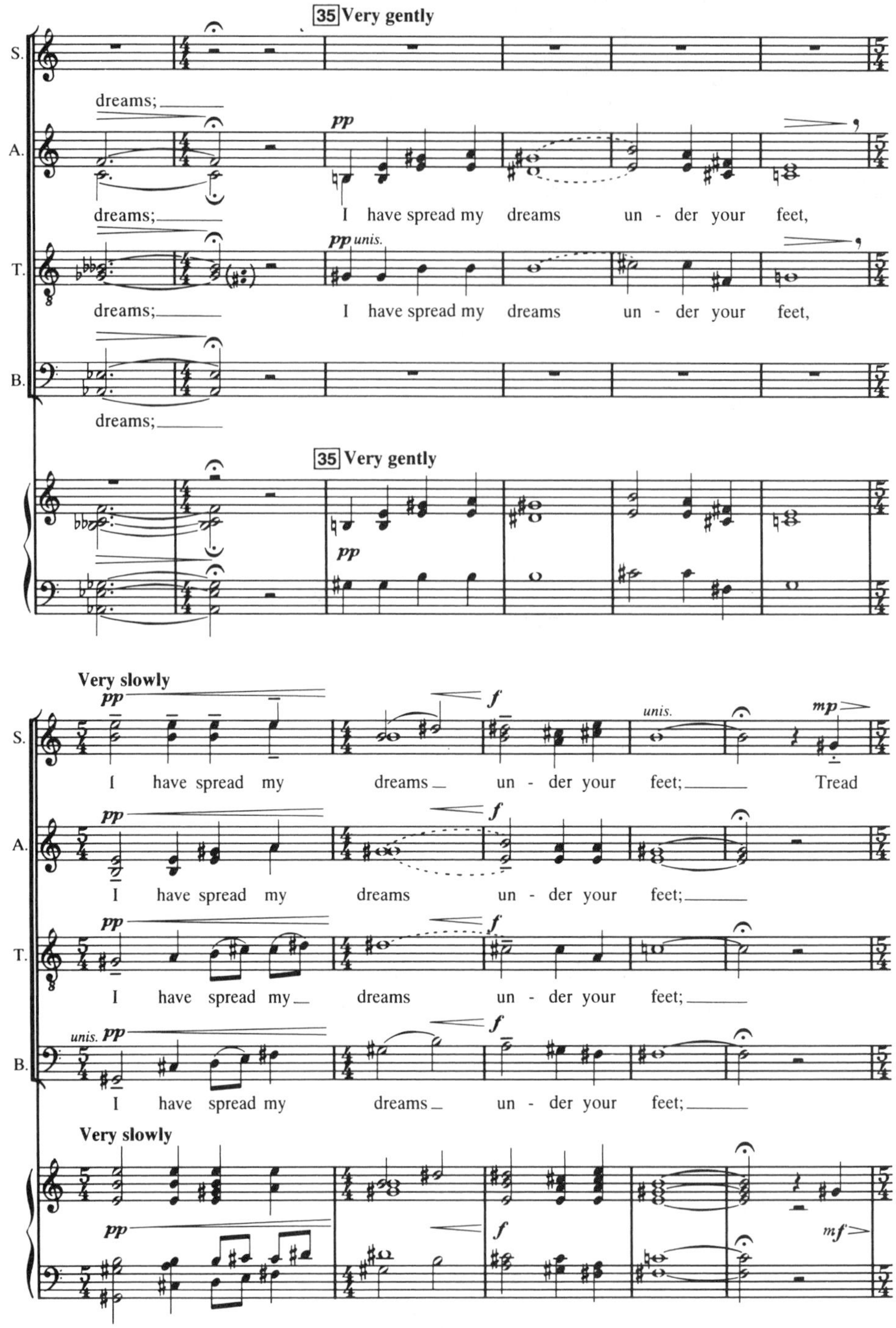

35 Very gently

S. dreams;

A. dreams; I have spread my dreams un - der your feet,

T. dreams; I have spread my dreams un - der your feet,

B. dreams;

Very slowly

S. I have spread my dreams un - der your feet; Tread

A. I have spread my dreams un - der your feet;

T. I have spread my dreams un - der your feet;

B. I have spread my dreams un - der your feet;

National Standards

The following National Standards are addressed through the Extension and bottom-page activities:

1. Singing, alone and with others, a varied repertoire of music. **(a, b, c)**
4. Composing and arranging music within specified guidelines. **(a, b, c, d)**
6. Listening to, analyzing, and describing music. **(a, b, c, e, f)**
7. Evaluating music and music performances. **(c)**
8. Understanding relationships between music, the other arts, and disciplines outside the arts. **(a, b, c, e)**
9. Understanding music in relation to history and culture. **(a, d)**

CONNECTING THE ARTS

Abstract Representation Across the Arts

Have students:

- Explore contemporary fine art, vocal and orchestral music, popular music (including all styles), and dance to discover pieces that represent endless space, richness, or possibility.
- Extend the discussion of tone painting to visual art and movement painting as well, particularly abstract representation of ideas, and find common elements and differences between the arts.
- Consider what earlier artists would have thought of contemporary art, and whether it is a reflection of the world or anticipates characteristics of the future world.

LESSON 16

Ave María

COMPOSER: Franz Biebl

Focus

OVERVIEW
Tuning; dissonant harmonies; role of the conductor; Latin pronunciation.

OBJECTIVES
After completing this lesson, students will be able to:
- Tune pitches accurately.
- Read and sing in dissonant harmonies accurately.
- Follow the conductor.
- Sing using correct Latin pronunciation.

CHORAL MUSIC TERMS
Define the Choral Music Terms for students, giving pronunciation, and answering any questions that may arise.

Warming Up

Vocal Warm-Up
This Vocal Warm-Up is designed to prepare students to:
- Tune pitches solidly.
- Sing with a full, rich sound.
- Use legato articulation.
- Watch the conductor.

Have students:
- Read through the Vocal Warm-Up directions.
- Sing, following your demonstration.

LESSON 16 Ave María

COMPOSER: *Franz Biebl*

CHORAL MUSIC TERMS
conductor
dissonant harmonies
Latin language
tuning pitches

VOICING
SATB

PERFORMANCE STYLE
Quietly flowing
A cappella

FOCUS
- Tune pitches accurately.
- Read and sing in dissonant harmonies accurately.
- Follow the conductor.
- Sing using correct Latin pronunciation.

Warming Up

Vocal Warm-Up
Sing this exercise using the text provided with a full rich sound and legato articulation. Watch and follow your conductor, who may decide to go faster or slower at any time!

Sight-Singing
Sight-sing these two examples using solfège and hand signs or numbers. Identify the musical characteristics of each, and tell if you think they come from the same piece or two different pieces, and what clues there are to support your theory.

TEACHER'S RESOURCE BINDER
Blackline Master 12, *Pronunciation Guide for "Ave Maria,"* page 93

National Standards
1. Singing, alone and with others, a varied repertoire of music. **(a, b, c, d, e, f)**
5. Reading and notating music. **(a, b, e)**
6. Listening to, analyzing, and describing music. **(a, b, c, f)**
7. Evaluating music and music performances. **(a, b)**
8. Understanding relationships between music, the other arts, and disciplines outside the arts. **(c)**
9. Understanding music in relation to history and culture. **(a, c)**

Singing: "Ave Maria"

Imagine you are a conductor of a fine ensemble. They are preparing, with your guidance, to perform a piece that has two separate groups, both performing at the same time. Each group has different music, but the two parts fit together.

What problems might occur in this conducting situation? What might the conductor do to minimize this situation? What can the singers do to help?

Now turn to the music for "Ave Maria" on page 142.

HOW DID YOU DO? ? ? ?

You have embroidered your own sound painting. Think about your preparation and performance of "Ave Maria."

1. Describe the challenge of singing in tune in "Ave Maria," then tell how well you did.

2. Choose a section of "Ave Maria" which you found difficult to learn, and sing it showing how accurately you have learned the pitches.

3. Discuss the role of the conductor, and why it is especially important in the performance of "Ave Maria." What is the performer's responsibility regarding the conductor?

4. How well did you pronounce the text in Latin? What was easy? What needs work?

5. If you were going to conduct an ensemble in learning and performing this piece, how would you go about introducing it, practicing it, and performing it?

"Ave Maria"

This piece was originally written for TTBB, and has been used by many glee clubs in Ivy League schools in the Northeast. It requires a larger-than-average ensemble for best success, and should be performed in a space where the trio (or small ensemble) is placed away from the main ensemble to create spatial and acoustic interplay. The piece is full of very challenging dissonances, and requires careful performance of dynamics. It should provide a fine challenge for an excellent choir.

Sight-Singing

These Sight-Singing exercises are designed to prepare students to:

- Sight-sing using solfège and hand signs or numbers.
- Sing consonant and dissonant harmonies.
- Identify musical characteristics.
- Compare and contrast musical segments.

Have students:

- Read through the Sight-Singing exercise directions.
- Read through each voice part rhythmically, using rhythm syllables.
- Sight-sing through each part separately using solfège and hand signs or numbers.
- Sing all parts together.

Singing: "Ave Maria"

Have students:

- Read the text on page 141.
- Discuss the problems that might occur when conducting two groups. (keeping them together, assuring balance between the groups)
- Discuss what conductors can do to minimize the situation. (work on constant eye contact, rehearse groups separately at first, position himself/herself to be seen and see both groups, use a video monitor, and so on)
- Discuss what the responsibility of the singer will be. (to watch and listen carefully, and follow closely)
- Look at the notation of "Ave Maria," identifying the two braces for two different groups.
- Follow the manuscript through, finding the solos, repeat signs, and the first, second, and third endings. Identify the order for singing the piece. (bass solo—*Ave Maria* to 1st ending; tenor solo—*Ave Maria* to second ending; tenor solo—*Ave Maria* to 3rd ending, *Sancta Maria* section to end)

Suggested Teaching Sequence

1. Review Vocal Warm-Up.
Have students:
- Review the Vocal Warm-Up on page 140.
- Use a full, rich sound, focusing on the vowels and using a dropped jaw.

2. Review Sight-Singing.
Have students:
- Review the Sight-Singing exercises on page 140.
- Tune the harmonies, and discuss problems.
- Identify the musical characteristics of each exercise.
- Decide if they think these two come from the same or from different pieces.
- Look at the first page of "Ave Maria," identifying both Sight-Singing exercises, and how they fit together. (They are parts for two different groups to sing.)

3. Sight-sing the mixed chorus part of "Ave Maria" using solfège and hand signs or numbers.
Have students:
- Divide into voice sections (SATB) and read each part rhythmically, using rhythm syllables, adding dynamics to shape the phrases.
- Still in sections, sing the chorus part with solfège and hand signs or numbers, identifying and working on problem areas, identifying and practicing melodic leaps and altered tones.
- Sing the chorus part through, using solfège and hand signs or numbers, with full ensemble.
- Sing on *loo,* standing in a circle, listening across the room for accuracy in tuning.

(Angelus Domini)

Franz Biebl

Trio*, SATB, Mixed Chorus, SATB, A cappella

* A small ensemble may be used.

As recorded by Chanticleer on the album "Our Heart's Joy, A Chanticleer Christmas." Available on CD or Cassette from the publisher.

142 *Choral Connections Level 4 Mixed Voices*

"Ave Maria" Through History

Have students:
- Explore settings of "Ave Maria," including at least one from each historical period, and identifying those of well-known and respected composers of the period. (A knowledgeable record shop would be a good resource, where there is a catalog of recorded music.)
- Listen to the pieces, comparing and contrasting styles and compositional techniques of each piece.
- Identify the musical elements and compositional devices used by Biebl in "Ave Maria" that would have been used in prior periods.
- Write a detailed essay, identifying the treatment of the "Ave Maria" text in Western art music.

11
mu - li - e - ris - bus et be - ne - dic - tus
- e - ri - bus et be - ne - dic - tus fruc-tus ven-tris

16
1., 2.
fruc-tus ven-tris tu - i, Je - sus, Je - sus.
tu - i, Je - sus, Je - sus.

1.
Tenor Solo
mp
Ma - ri - a di - xit: Ec - ce an - cil - la Do - mi - ni,
fi - at mi - hi se - com - dom ver - bum tu - um.
Return to measure 1

TEACHING STRATEGY

Gregorian Chant Style

The solo sections of this piece are in Gregorian chant style, the style which emerged in medieval churches to sing the liturgy of the Catholic mass. It was unmetered, and flowed with the rhythm of the text.

Have students:

- Listen to some Gregorian chants to get the feeling of the style.
- Sing the parts in the same style.
- Optional: Sing in very small groups, in unison, rather than solos.

4. Learn the Latin pronunciation.

Have students:

- Use Blackline Master 12, *Pronunciation Guide for "Ave Maria,"* to practice round vowel sounds.
- Listen for the unification of each vowel sound. Identify problem areas.
- Speak the Latin text in rhythm.
- Sing the piece with correct Latin pronunciation.

5. Sight-sing solos and trio parts of "Ave Maria" using solfège and hand signs or numbers.

Have students:

- Divide into voice sections (SATB) and read each part rhythmically, using rhythm syllables, adding dynamics to shape the phrases. (Basses work on the solo at the beginning.)
- Still in sections, sing with solfège and hand signs or numbers, identifying and working on problem areas, identifying and practicing melodic leaps and altered tones.
- Sing the piece through, using solfège and hand signs or numbers, with full ensemble.
- All practice the solo lines, which should be sung in Gregorian chant style—freely and unmetered.

6. Put the piece together.

Have students:

- Discuss with you the location of soloists and the trio (or smaller ensemble).
- Try out several arrangements until you find one that feels comfortable.
- Work out how soloists will leave and reenter the ensemble.
- Perform the piece as a full ensemble, smaller ensemble, and soloists, in tune, following the conductor, and using correct Latin pronunciation.

Assessment

Informal Assessment

During this lesson, students showed the ability to:

- Sing in Latin, following the conductor in the Vocal Warm-Up exercise.
- Sight-read and sight-sing consonant and dissonant harmonies using solfège and hand signs or numbers in the Sight-Singing examples.
- Compare and contrast styles in the Sight-Singing examples.
- Sing independently, with dissonant harmonies, following the conductor and using correct Latin pronunciation in "Ave Maria."

Student Self-Assessment

Have students:

- Evaluate their performance with the How Did You Do? section on page 141.
- Answer the questions individually. Discuss them in pairs or small groups and/or write their responses on a sheet of paper.

Individual Performance Assessment

To further demonstrate accomplishment, have each student:

- In a quartet, sing the first example in the Sight-Singing exercise into a tape recorder to show vocal independence and the ability to tune pitches accurately when singing dissonant harmonies.
- Into a tape recorder, read their voice part in "Ave Maria" from the beginning to the repeat, demonstrating correct Latin pronunciation.
- Watch a videotape of their ensemble's performance of "Ave Maria," with a wide angle shot that gets both performing groups and the conductor. Each write a critique of her or his own performance, including a detailed account of how well he or she watched and followed the conductor.

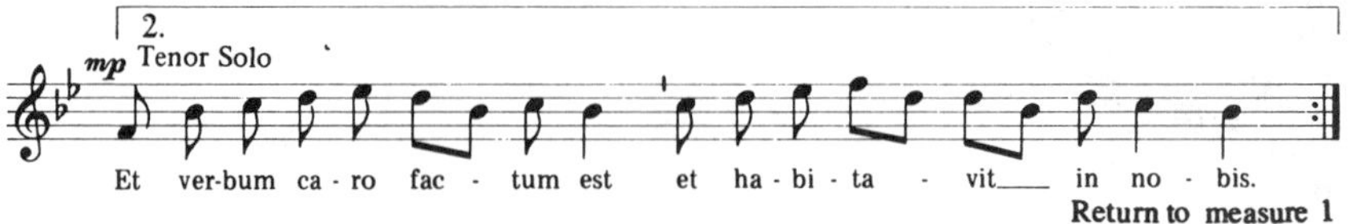
2.
mp Tenor Solo
Et ver-bum ca - ro fac - tum est et ha - bi - ta - vit___ in no - bis.
Return to measure 1

22
3.
mp
- sus. Sanc - ta Ma - ri - a, ma - ter De - i,
mp
p
- sus. Sanc-ta Ma - ri - a, ma - ter De - i, o - ra pro
p

27
o - ra pro no - bis pec - ca - tò - ri - bus. Sanc - ta Ma -
no - bis pec - ca - to - ri - bus. Sanc - ta Ma - ri - a,

MUSIC LITERACY

To help students expand their music literacy, have them:

- Review the notation for all dynamic, tempo, and phrase markings.
- Practice these in sections first.
- Sing the piece in full ensemble, paying particular attention to the phrasing.

32

ri - a, o - ra pro no - bis nunc et in

o - ra pro no - bis nunc et in ho - ra

37

mp cresc.

ho - ra mor - tis no - strae. A -

mp cresc.

A - men,

p cresc.

mor - tis no - strae. A - - men, A -

p cresc.

43

più cresc.

- men, A - - men, A - - men.

A - - men,

più cresc.

men, A - - men, A - - men.

A - - men,

A - - men, A - men, A - - men.

Extension

Assessing a Performance—Why Wait?

Many times students do not have the opportunity to see their own performance until it is videotaped during a concert. However, an earlier taping will help them focus on the audience perspective, and work on essential corrections before a performance.

Have students:

- Perform and videotape before the actual performance, and then watch the tape.
- Critique the videotaped performance, identifying those places where improvement is needed.
- Work on the areas identified.

Comparing "Ave Maria" to "The Cloths of Heaven"

Have students:

- In two groups, each describe one of the above pieces in as much detail as possible, considering the period, style, voicing, use of musical elements, compositional techniques, tone painting, difficulty level, and so on.
- Make a general statement that both compares and contrasts the two pieces.

Using an Old Source for a New Piece

Have the students:

- Choose a text from any of the teaching or historical pieces in this book.
- Choose a style in which to write a new setting for the text.
- Review the characteristics of the chosen style.
- Compose a setting for the text, conferencing with peers and teacher, revising, and finally having the ensemble perform it.

Optional: In a team, some students could compose the piece; others do a fine art project such as a painting, slide show, or video; and others create a dance, all using the style of the period and collaborating to create a multimedia, multiart production.

National Standards

The following National Standards are addressed through the Extension and bottom-page activities:

1. Singing, alone and with others, a varied repertoire of music. **(a, b, c, d, e, f)**
4. Composing and arranging music within specified guidelines. **(a, b, c, d)**
6. Listening to, analyzing, and describing music. **(a, b, c, e, f)**
7. Evaluating music and music performances. **(a, b)**
8. Understanding relationships between music, the other arts, and disciplines outside the arts. **(a, b, c, d)**
9. Understanding music in relation to history and culture. **(a, c, d, e)**

Making Historical Connections

c. 1430–1600

Renaissance Period

Focus

OVERVIEW

Understanding the development of choral music during the Renaissance period.

OBJECTIVES

After completing this lesson, students will be able to:

- Identify musical forms, figures, and developments of the Renaissance period.
- Identify specific performance characteristics to be used in Renaissance choral music.
- Describe the relationship between music and the prevailing social, cultural, and historical events and ideas occurring in Europe during the Renaissance period.
- Describe characteristics of Renaissance art and music.
- Identify the ideas and figures that foreshadowed the Baroque period.

CHORAL MUSIC TERMS

Define the Choral Music Terms for students, giving pronunciation, and answering any questions that may arise.

Introducing the Lesson

Introduce the Renaissance period through visual art.

Analyze the painting by da Vinci on page 148 and Michelangelo's architecture on page 150.

Have students:

- Study the painting and dome.
- Discuss the information at the bottom of pages 149 and 150 in your Teacher's Wraparound Edition.

The perfection of Leonardo da Vinci's (1452–1519) *Ginevra de' Benci* is achieved by exacting attention to detail, including the study of human anatomy. Attention to a balanced distribution of voice parts progressing in a calm, smooth momentum expresses Renaissance musical style.

c. 1474. *Ginevra de' Benci.* Leonardo da Vinci. Oil on panel. 38.8 x 36.7 cm (15 1/4 x 14 1/2"). National Gallery of Art, Washington, D.C. Ailsa Mellon Bruce Fund.

TEACHER'S RESOURCE BINDER

Fine Art Transparency 1, *Ginevra de' Benci,* by Leonardo da Vinci

Optional Listening Selections:

Music: An Appreciation, 6th edition

"Ave Maria": CD 1, Track 71

"The Most Sacred Queene Elizabeth, Her Galliard": CD 1, Track 83

National Standards

6. Listening to, analyzing, and describing music. **(a, b, c, e, f)**
7. Evaluating music and music performances. **(a)**
8. Understanding relationships between music, the other arts, and disciplines outside the arts. **(a, b, c, d, e)**
9. Understanding music in relation to history and culture. **(a, c, d, e)**

Renaissance Period

c. 1430–1600

After completing this lesson, you will be able to:

- *Discuss some of the major changes that took place in Europe during the Renaissance.*
- *Describe the most important characteristics of Renaissance music.*
- *Identify the major forms of sacred and secular music during the Renaissance.*
- *Discuss the most important characteristics of Renaissance choral music.*

Early in the fifteenth century, a "rebirth" began in Europe—a renewal of creative activity, of intellectual curiosity, and of artistic development. This was the beginning of the Renaissance, a period that takes its name from the old French word *renaistre*, meaning "to be born again."

Changes During the Renaissance

The Renaissance was a time of growth, experimentation, and discovery in many fields. Scholars retreated from an acceptance of what they read; instead, they began using observation and experimentation to draw new conclusions about the world around them. The results of this new approach were a series of important advances in science, mathematics, and technology.

The Renaissance also saw important advances in exploration and trade. For the first time, European sailing ships reached the southern coast of Africa, the Americas, and India, and even succeeded in sailing around the world. These journeys brought a new expanding sense of the world, an influx of new ideas, and new opportunities for trade to the people of Renaissance Europe.

A particularly significant development of the Renaissance was the invention of a printing press with movable type, usually credited to Johann Gutenberg. This press meant that books no longer had to be copied by hand. Books—including books about music and books of music—became much less expensive and much more widely available; reading words and reading music were no longer pursuits restricted to the wealthy, privileged few.

Changes in religious practice and belief were also important during the Renaissance. The Catholic church, which had been a center of learning, a formidable political power, and an important force in the daily lives of nearly all Europeans, gradually lost some of its influence. The foremost Renaissance scholars embraced humanism, a belief in the dignity and value of individual human beings. In addition, the Protestant Reformation resulted in the establishment of new Christian churches not under the rule of the Catholic hierarchy.

The visual arts of the Renaissance reflect the era's growing awareness of the natural world. The human figures depicted by painters and sculptors became more realistic and more individualized.

COMPOSERS

John Dunstable (c. 1390–1453)
Guillaume Dufay (1400–1474)
Josquin Desprez (c. 1440–1521)
Heinrich Isaac (c. 1450–1517)
Clement Janequin (c. 1485–1560)
Adrian Willaert (1490–1562)
Christopher Tye (c. 1500–c. 1572)
Thomas Tallis (1505–1585)
Andrea Gabrieli (c. 1520–1586)
Giovanni Pierluigi da Palestrina (c. 1525–1594)
Orlande de Lassus (1532–1594)
William Byrd (1543–1623)
Thomas Morley (c. 1557–c. 1603)
John Dowland (1563–1626)
Michael Praetorius (c. 1571–1621)
Thomas Weelkes (1575–1623)

ARTISTS

Donatello (1386–1466)
Fra Filippo Lippi (c. 1406–1469)
Sandro Botticelli (1445–1510)
Leonardo da Vinci (1452–1519)
Albrecht Dürer (1471–1528)
Michelangelo (1475–1564)
Raphael (1483–1520)
Titian (c. 1488–1576)

AUTHORS

Thomas More (1478–1536)
Martin Luther (1483–1546)
Miguel de Cervantes (1547–1616)
Sir Walter Raleigh (c. 1552–1618)
Sir Philip Sidney (1554–1586)
William Shakespeare (1564–1616)

CHORAL MUSIC TERMS

a cappella
Gregorian chant
madrigal
mass
motet
motive imitation
polyphony
sacred music
secular music

Suggested Teaching Sequence

1. Examine the Renaissance period.

Have students:

- Read the text on pages 149–153.
- Share what they know about the composers, artists, and authors listed on this page.
- Read, discuss, and answer the review questions on page 153 individually, in pairs, or in small groups.
- Discuss their answers with the whole group, clarifying any misunderstandings.

2. Examine the Renaissance in historical perspective.

Have students:

- Turn to the time line on pages 150–153 and read the citations.
- Discuss why these people and events are significant to the Renaissance period.
- Compare each of these events to what they know occurred before and after the Renaissance.
- Discuss both how these events and people affected music and the other arts, and how music and the other arts may have led to new ideas.
- Identify any factors that may have led to new ideas and signaled the beginning of the Baroque period.

Ginevra de' Benci

Painted by Leonardo da Vinci in 1474, *Ginevra de' Benci* is typical of Renaissance art in several ways. Da Vinci was the first painter to use shadow, and his scientific interest in light is evident in the single light source and beginnings of perspective, rather than representation of a flat, two-dimensional plane. His treatment of the subject, Ginevra, reflects a mood, using classic simplicity of line and design. The representation of one person, at one place in time, was also new in the Renaissance; it replaced the tendency during the Middle Ages to represent one character in several situations within the same canvas.

Leonardo da Vinci was a painter, a musician, scientist, inventor, and architect. He was a true "Renaissance man"!

3. Define the musical aspects of the Renaissance period.

Have students:

- Review the changes in music during the Renaissance period.
- Identify the musical styles and forms that dominated the period.
- Review the characteristics of vocal music during the period.
- Identify well-known musical figures of the period.
- Listen to music from the period, analyzing and pointing out characteristics of Renaissance music as they hear them.

Gutenberg press; beginning of modern printing
c. 1435

Ottoman Turks capture Constantinople, marking end of Byzantine Empire
1453

First printed music appears
1465

Every aspect of the dome of St. Peter's by Michelangelo Buonarroti (1475–1564) contributes to the impression of an upward thrust of energy. The ribs, buttresses, and supports of the dome bear a relationship to the borrowed plainsong melodies that support religious music composed during the Renaissance.

1546–64. Dome of St. Peter's Basilica, view from the southwest. Michelangelo Buonarroti. (Completed by Giacomo della Porta in 1590.) Vatican State, Rome, Italy.

Dome of St. Peter's Basilica

Michelangelo's dome of St. Peter's Basilica is an example of the interest in classic design and symmetry characteristic of the Renaissance period. Notice the Roman columns and the high arching dome, both taken from ancient Roman architecture. The symmetry of the dome is enhanced by the equal symmetry of the lower connecting structures. St. Peter's is built in the shape of a cross, with the dome at the center. This dome was designed from 1546 to 1564, and completed by Giacomo della Porta in 1590.

Da Vinci sketches an early helicopter design — 1483

Columbus lands in West Indies/Americas — 1492

1473-1480 — Sistine Chapel built

1488 — Diaz sails around the Cape of Good Hope

1498 — Da Gama sails around Africa and lands in India

Although many paintings and sculptures depicted religious subjects, nonreligious subjects, especially those taken from Greek and Roman mythology, became increasingly acceptable. Artists also created individual portraits, such as the famous *Mona Lisa* by Leonardo da Vinci. New materials and new techniques enhanced the artists' ability to create lifelike works.

Renaissance Music

Throughout the Renaissance, the Catholic church continued to exert a strong influence on the arts. Much of the important music composed during this period was **sacred music,** *music used in religious services.*

In the centuries preceding the Renaissance—the Middle Ages—the most important musical form was the **Gregorian chant,** *a melody sung in unison by male voices.* All these chants were sung **a cappella,** *without instrumental accompaniment.* The earliest Gregorian chants consisted of a single melodic line; later, a second melodic line was added. This addition was the beginning of **polyphony,** *the simultaneous performance of two or more melodic lines.* In polyphonic music, each part begins at a different place, and each part is independent and important. The sacred music of the Renaissance grew from the medieval Gregorian chants. The use of polyphony was extended and developed by Renaissance composers; and although instrumentation was added to many sacred works, the Renaissance is often called the golden age of a cappella choral music.

The two major forms of sacred Renaissance music were the **mass,** *a long musical composition that includes the five major sections of the Catholic worship service,* and the **motet,** *a shorter choral work set to Latin texts and used in religious services, but not part of the regular mass.*

John Dunstable was one of the foremost composers of Renaissance masses and motets. His works show new developments in the harmonic structure of polyphony. Later, Josquin Desprez introduced homophonic harmonies, produced by chords that support a melody. He was also one of the first to compose works with **motive imitation,** *short repeating melodies between voice parts.*

Although many sacred works of the period were sung a cappella, instruments were added in other compositions to accompany and echo the voice parts. Composers such as Adrian Willaert combined voices, pipe organs, and other instruments in sacred music.

Sacred music for Protestant services was also written during the Renaissance. Martin Luther, one of the most important leaders of the Protestant Reformation, wrote hymns that are still sung in Protestant churches today.

There were also changes in **secular music,** *any music that is not sacred.* As secular music gained in importance and popularity, the center of musical activity began to shift from churches to castles and towns.

Assessment

Informal Assessment

In this lesson, students showed the ability to:

- Share what they know about the Renaissance period.
- Describe musical characteristics, styles, forms, and personalities of the Renaissance period.
- Describe specific performance characteristics of Renaissance choral music.
- Describe and compare characteristics of Renaissance art.
- Describe the social, historical, and cultural environment of the Renaissance period.
- Identify ideas, people, and events that foreshadowed the Baroque period.

Student Self-Assessment

Have students:

- Review the questions in Check Your Understanding on page 153.
- Write a paragraph describing how much they understand about the development of music during the Renaissance period.

Individual Performance Assessment

To further demonstrate accomplishment, have each student:

- Select a Renaissance vocal composition.
- Review the piece, identifying the characteristics of the Renaissance period that appear in the piece.
- Prepare a performance guide, discussing the performance style appropriate for the piece, based on characteristics of Renaissance vocal music performance.
- Optional: Rehearse and prepare an ensemble to perform the piece, and conduct it during the concert.

Extension

Notation

Musical notation began in sacred music during the Middle Ages, and notation developed throughout the Renaissance, spurred by the invention of the printing press.

Have students:

- Research the development of musical notation from the Middle Ages through the Renaissance period, including how and when each of the following came into use: one-line staff, five-line staff, *do* clef, treble clef, bass clef, key signatures, rhythmic stem notation, note heads (diamond, triangle, circular), meter signatures, bar lines, dynamics, and tempo markings.
- Share their findings with the class.

Compare Renaissance Music to the Other Arts of the Period

Have students:

- Define characteristics of Renaissance art and architecture.
- Compare the characteristics of music and one or more other art form from the Renaissance period, comparing uses of characteristic elements, artistic processes, and organizational principles.

Sistine Chapel ceiling painted by Michelangelo
1508

Cortez conquers Mexico
1519

1517
Protestant Reformation begins in Germany with Luther's 95 Theses

Magellan begins voyage around the world

The **madrigal,** *a secular form written in several imitative parts,* became the most popular kind of nonsacred composition during the Renaissance. Composers including Clement Janequin, Heinrich Isaac, Thomas Tallis, William Byrd, Thomas Morley, and Thomas Weelkes wrote madrigals to be sung by everyday people; singing madrigals together was an important entertainment during this period.

Characteristics of Choral Music During the Renaissance

Most of the music of the Renaissance was choral; instruments were used primarily as accompaniment. The choral music of the time can be considered in terms of its meter and stress, tempo, dynamics, texture, expressive aspects, and tone quality.

Meter and stress as we know them were not introduced into choral music until after the Renaissance period. Renaissance works lacked a clearly defined beat. Instead, choral works had a gently flowing rhythm. This rhythm often varied among the melodic lines, creating a special challenge for singers of Renaissance compositions. Renaissance works were generally sung at a moderate tempo, without any unusual shifts from one tempo to another.

The dynamics of most Renaissance choral compositions were moderate and steady; there were typically no major shifts from loud to soft or soft to loud.

The texture of Renaissance choral music was primarily polyphonic. The separate voices within a work—as many as six voice parts—usually conveyed equal melodic interest. In general, the music of the period had a fuller, richer sound than did compositions from the Middle Ages.

The expressive aspects of choral music reflected the attitudes of the Renaissance: rational, balanced, and emotionally restrained. Many of the sacred works were intended not only to enhance religious worship but also to strengthen the influence of the Church.

Sacred choral works were performed with men and boys singing all the voice parts, although women participated in singing many madrigals. The tone quality was generally restrained, with little or no vibrato.

Elizabeth I crowned Queen of England (died 1603)
1558

William Shakespeare begins play writing
c. 1590

1584
Sir Walter Raleigh discovers Virginia

1599
Globe Theatre built in London

Check Your Understanding

Recall

1. Why was the invention of a printing press with movable type such an important development during the Renaissance?
2. What is the difference between sacred music and secular music?
3. What is a Gregorian chant?
4. What is polyphony?
5. What is the difference between a mass and a motet?
6. What is a madrigal? How is it different from a motet?
7. What kind of tempo is typical of Renaissance choral music?
8. What kind of texture do most Renaissance choral works have?

Thinking It Through

1. Identify and describe a Renaissance choral work you have heard. In what ways is that work characteristic of the period?
2. What relationships can you identify between Renaissance music and music that is being composed and performed now? Explain your ideas.

The Renaissance in Depth

The Renaissance is an exciting theme for a unit of study. Have students identify areas of interest individually, in pairs, or in groups. Have them write a contract or proposal with you, describing the topic to be researched, a time line describing methodology, stages, and completion dates, and the nature of the final product to be presented (paper, performance, lecture, and so on).

One popular and exciting all-school event is the creation of a Renaissance fair, including food preparation, costumes, music, games (chess, log wrestling), performance of a Shakespearean reading or play, and so on. Students should also be aware of all other projects going on, and link ideas together whenever possible.

ANSWERS TO RECALL QUESTIONS

1. Books became less expensive and more available to everyone.
2. Sacred music is music used in religious services; secular music is all music that is not sacred.
3. A melody sung in unison by male voices.
4. The simultaneous performance of two or more melodic lines.
5. A mass is a long musical composition that includes the five major sections of the Catholic worship service; a motet is a shorter choral work set to Latin text, used in religious services, but not part of the mass.
6. A secular form written in several imitative parts. It is secular, not sacred.
7. A moderate tempo, without unusual shifts.
8. Polyphonic.

RENAISSANCE CONNECTIONS

Listening to... Renaissance Music

This feature is designed to expand students' appreciation of choral and instrumental music of the Renaissance period.

CHORAL SELECTION: "Ave Maria" by Desprez

Have students:

- Read the information on this page to learn more about "Ave Maria."
- Watch as you follow a transparency of Blackline Master, Listening Map 1.

Using the Listening Map

Study the organization of the map: Column 1 (far left) shows the voices heard. Column 2 (middle) shows the Latin text. Column 3 (right) describes the musical events. Examine the key at the bottom.

Have students:

- Examine the key on the map.
- Listen as you explain the types of imitation they will hear in this piece. (Polyphonic imitation of the Renaissance was a technique with several variations. A short melodic phrase was presented by the soprano and then imitated in turn by the alto, tenor, and bass.)
- Notice the interpretation of the text at box 3 (increase the rhythmic movement to show joy) and at box 9 (sustained chords to express Josquin's personal plea to the Virgin).
- Learn the characteristics of the motet.
- Listen to "Ave Maria" as you point to the transparency. Have students signal as they hear single-voice and multi-voice imitation. Reveal the answers on each section after they have signaled their responses.

Listening to... Renaissance Music

CHORAL SELECTION

Desprez — "Ave Maria"

Josquin Desprez was a Flemish Renaissance composer. He was born about the year 1440 and died 1521. He enjoyed an international career and spent much of his time in Italy. His music strongly influenced later composers.

The motet "Ave Maria" is an a cappella choral work set to a sacred Latin text that is not part of the main mass of the Catholic church. It was often used at vesper services at sunset. "Ave Maria" is a four-voice setting of a Latin prayer to the Virgin Mary.

INSTRUMENTAL SELECTION

Dowland — "The Most Sacred Queen Elizabeth, Her Galliard"

John Dowland (1563–1626) was a well-known English Renaissance composer and lutenist. He published eight books of music during his lifetime. As a court musician to the minor aristocracy and to the King of Denmark, he wrote many secular works—both songs and instrumental—as well as sacred pieces. Although his compositions were very popular with the middle class, it was not until five years before his death that he was recognized by the English Court and appointed as one of the King's Lutes to the Court of England.

A *galliard* is a composition written for social dancing. Galliards from the period 1590 to 1625 were plentiful and have a musical substance and interest far beyond the needs of functional dance music. Those written for keyboard and lute often display considerable brilliance. Each strain is followed by a variation enlivened by scales, runs, and other kinds of figuration, instead of a customary repetition of the strain. The use of *hemiola* is one consistent feature of the galliard throughout most of its history.

TEACHER'S RESOURCE BINDER

Blackline Master, Listening Map 1
Blackline Master, Listening Map 2

Optional Listening Selections:

Music: An Appreciation, 6th edition
"Ave Maria": CD 1, Track 71
"The Most Sacred Queene Elizabeth, Her Galliard": CD 1, Track 83

National Standards

This lesson addresses the following National Standard:

6. Listening to, analyzing, and describing music. **(a)**

Introducing . . .

"Ave Regina Coelorum"

Orlande de Lassus

Setting the Stage

"Row, Row, Row Your Boat" is a round song that children learn to sing at an early age. Did you know that a performance of this type of song results in music characteristics that go back over 500 years? We say that a round has linear texture. In other words, the different voice parts move independently in order to form the chordal structure of the song. The selection you will sing, "Ave Regina Coelorum," has this same linear texture, although it is not a round. As you listen to the selection, you will notice that the other voice parts all have rhythms and melodies that move at different times, yet the overall sound is pleasing to the ear. This sacred piece is very typical of Renaissance music. You will find the syllables and words that are very connected to the phrases, or musical thoughts and sentences. Once you have mastered the notes, see how well you and your fellow choir members can define the phrase and bring out the different voice parts—similarly to singing "Row, Row, Row, Your Boat."

Meeting the Composer

Orlande de Lassus

Orlande de Lassus (1532–1594), also known as Orlando di Lasso, was the last of the composers from the Netherlands who dominated European music for more than a hundred years. At a young age, he began to sing in church choirs. At the age of 12, he went to Italy, where he sang in and directed choirs for more than 10 years. De Lassus wrote sacred motets, masses, and hundreds of shorter sacred works for voices. He also wrote French chansons, Italian madrigals, and German part songs. He composed more than two thousand works!

INSTRUMENTAL SELECTION: "The Most Sacred Queene Elizabeth, Her Galliard" by Dowland

Have students:

- Read the information on page 154 to learn more about "The Most Sacred Queene Elizabeth, Her Galliard."
- Watch as you follow a transparency of Blackline Master, Listening Map 2.

Using the Listening Map

Follow the directions provided on your Blackline Master.

Have students:

- Listen to "The Most Sacred Queene Elizabeth, Her Galliard" as you point to the transparency.

INTRODUCING. . . "Ave Regina Coelorum"

This feature is designed to introduce students to the Renaissance Lesson on the following pages.

Have students:

- Read Setting the Stage on this page to learn more about "Ave Regina Coelorum."
- Read Meeting the Composer to learn more about Orlande de Lassus.
- Turn the page and begin the Renaissance Lesson.

ASSESSMENT

Individual Performance Assessment

To further demonstrate understanding of Renaissance music, have each student:

- Identify the musical events heard in "Ave Maria" on individual copies of the listening map.

RENAISSANCE LESSON

Ave Regina Coelorum

COMPOSER: Orlande de Lassus (1532–1594)
EDITED BY: Clifford Richter

Focus

OVERVIEW
Posture and breathing; rhythm; syncopation; vocal independence; Latin pronunciation.

OBJECTIVES
After completing this lesson, students will be able to:

- Sing with correct posture and good breath support.
- Read and perform rhythms including syncopation, eighth-sixteenth combinations, and dotted quarter-eighth note patterns.
- Read and sing one part independently when four parts are sung in polyphonic texture.
- Sing using correct Latin pronunciation.

CHORAL MUSIC TERMS
Define the Choral Music Terms for students, giving pronunciation, and answering any questions that may arise.

Warming Up

Vocal Warm-Up

This Vocal Warm-Up is designed to prepare students to:

- Inhale and exhale properly.
- Use good diaphragmatic control.
- Sing in unison.

Have students:

- Read through the Vocal Warm-Up directions.
- Sing, following your demonstration.

RENAISSANCE LESSON

Ave Regina Coelorum

COMPOSER: *Orlande de Lassus (Orlando di Lasso)* (1532–1594)
TRANSLATOR: *John Colman*
EDITED BY: *Clifford Richter*

CHORAL MUSIC TERMS
breathing
part independence
polyphony
posture
Renaissance
rhythm
syncopation

VOICING
SATB

PERFORMANCE STYLE
Moderate tempo
A cappella

FOCUS

- Sing with correct posture and good breath support.
- Read and perform rhythms including syncopation, eighth-sixteenth combinations, and dotted quarter-eighth note patterns.
- Read and sing one part independently when four parts are sung in polyphonic texture.
- Sing using correct Latin pronunciation.

Warming Up

Vocal Warm-Up

To inhale, imagine being astonished, and feel your whole body suddenly opening, as the air literally falls into your lungs. To exhale, pretend that you are quieting a group by saying "psst" at varying lengths. Now sing the following exercise on *ho* to strengthen the diaphragm. Move up by half steps on each repeat.

Sight-Singing

Read and clap the following rhythm in four parts. Can you clap all parts accurately the first time through? Notice the syncopated rhythms created by ties. Sing your voice part rhythm, using chord tones from one of the following chords: G major, G minor, D major, D VII, or C major. Repeat the activity using a different chord, or assign different chords to each measure of rhythm.

TEACHER'S RESOURCE BINDER

Blackline Master 13, *Translation and Pronunciation Guide for "Ave Regina Coelorum,"* page 94

Blackline Master 14, *Checklist for Correct Posture*, page 95

National Standards

1. Singing a varied repertoire of music. **(a, b, c, f)**
3. Improvising melodies, variations, and accompaniments. **(c)**
5. Reading and notating music. **(a, b)**
6. Listening to, analyzing, and describing music. **(a, b, c)**
7. Evaluating music and performances. **(a)**
8. Understanding relationships between music, the other arts, and disciplines outside the arts. **(c)**
9. Understanding music in relation to history and culture. **(a, c, d)**

Singing: "Ave Regina Coelorum"

"Row, Row, Row Your Boat" is a round you probably learned as a child. A round has linear texture, with different voice parts moving independently to create the chordal structure of the song. Rounds, canons, and polyphony began more than 500 years ago, during the Renaissance period. Each voice part has melody and rhythm that move at different times, yet the overall sound is pleasing to the ear. Repeatedly a voice part imitates the rhythm or melody of the one before it, weaving vocal lines into polyphonic texture.

Now turn to the music for "Ave Regina Coelorum" on page 158.

HOW DID YOU DO? ? ?

Your good technique will help to bring out the best in Renaissance style. Think about your preparation and performance of "Ave Regina Coelorum."

1. Did you use correct posture and breathing? How would the observer know? What would they see? What do you feel?

2. Could you read the rhythms and pitches of the piece? What was easy? What needed practice?

3. Was your Latin pronunciation correct? What was good? What could be better?

4. Describe the characteristics of this piece that indicate its origins in the Renaissance period, and tell how you enhanced these characteristics through your performance.

Sight-Singing

This Sight-Singing exercise is designed to prepare students to:

- Speak and clap rhythms including syncopation, eighth-sixteenth combinations, and dotted quarter-eighth patterns.
- Improvise, using chord tones on a given rhythm.

Have students:

- Read through the Sight-Singing exercise directions.
- Read each voice part rhythmically, clapping the rhythm in four parts.
- Sight-sing through each part separately using solfège and hand signs or numbers.
- Sing all parts together.

Singing: "Ave Regina Coelorum"

Identify polyphonic texture.

Have students:

- Read the text on page 157.
- Sing "Row, Row, Row Your Boat," or another round, to recall the experience of exact vocal imitation.
- Identify polyphony as independent vocal lines that have elements of imitation as they are woven to create harmony.

Suggested Teaching Sequence

1. Review Vocal Warm-Up.
Review correct posture and breathing. Strengthen diaphragmatic control.
Have students:

- Review the Vocal Warm-Up on page 156.
- Review posture and breathing techniques.
- Discuss diaphragmatic control, and hold a hand on the stomach to check as the exercise is repeated.
- Exhale on "s" and stop with the tongue when you raise a hand, continuing when the hand goes down.
- Look at "Ave Regina Coelorum," hissing the rhythm of their voice part, pulsing at each note. Breathe at logical points in the rhythm.

2. Review Sight-Singing.
Speak and clap rhythms in four parts. Improvise chord tone melodies on the rhythms.
Have students:

- Review the Sight-Singing exercise on page 156.
- Identify syncopation, eighth-sixteenth combinations, and dotted quarter-eighth patterns, practicing as needed.
- Sing chord tones to any one chord suggested.
- Repeat with any other chord, or chord progression.

3. Sight-sing "Ave Regina Coelorum" using solfège and hand signs or numbers.
Have students:

- Divide into voice sections (SATB) and read each part rhythmically, using rhythm syllables.
- Still in sections, sing with solfège and hand signs or numbers, identifying and working on problem areas.
- Sing the piece through, using solfège and hand signs or numbers, with full ensemble.

Ave Regina Coelorum

Thou Art the Queen of All Heaven

Four-part Chorus of Mixed Voices
A cappella

Orlande de Lassus (Orlando di Lasso) (1532–1594)
Edited by Clifford Richter
English version by John Colman

(♩ = about 80)
Soprano
Alto
Tenor
Bass
(for rehearsal only)
A - ve Re - gi - na coe - lo - rum, A - ve Do - mi -
Thou art the Queen of all heav - en, and the high - est
A - ve Re - gi - na coe - lo - rum, A - ve Do - mi -
Thou art the Queen of all heav - en, and the high - est
S.
A.
T.
B.
All tempo, dynamic, and expression marks are editorial additions, as are the bar lines and time signature. Editorial accidentals have been placed in square brackets, cautionary accidentals in parentheses.
© Copyright 1963 by Associated Music Publishers, Inc., New York

158 *Choral Connections Level 4 Mixed Voices*

Breathing

Both deep breaths and the control of the breath allow students to interpret music appropriately. There are several images that may work for students to achieve a deep breath.
Have students:

- Take a "cool sip" of air through an imaginary straw, feeling the lungs fill deeply.
- Hold hands around the waist gently, fingertips pointed toward the backbone, and then push them out as the breath is taken. Expand back, sides, and front to achieve the maximum breath support.
- Imagine a "belt of noses" around the waist, and breathe in through the noses to achieve a deep breath.

4. Learn the Latin pronunciation.

Have students:

- Using Blackline Master 13, *Pronunciation Guide for "Ave Regina Coelorum,"* echo or read the words slowly.
- Speak the Latin text in rhythm.
- Sing the piece in Latin, using correct pronunciation.
- Sing the piece through in full ensemble, using English and Latin text.

5. Learning phrasing and dynamics.

Have students:

- Review the notation for phrasing and dynamic markings.
- Define the phrases, determining the correct places to breathe.
- Discuss ways to bring out the different voice parts, and when each is most or least important.
- Identify the ideal Renaissance sound as legato with forward motion, achieved by good posture and breath support.
- Perform the piece in full ensemble, using good posture and breath support, singing parts independently, and using correct Latin pronunciation.

Posture

There are several approaches to achieving correct posture, which is a prerequisite and the most important aspect of breath support. Have students:

- Spread the fingers of their right hand out over the abdomen, the little finger on the navel and the thumb on the breast bone.
- Stretch both hands over the head and reach slowly upward as if touching the ceiling. Gradually lower the hands and arms, leaving the chest high and the body tall.
- Use Blackline Master 14, *Checklist for Correct Posture.*

VOCAL DEVELOPMENT

To encourage vocal development, have students:

- Demonstrate good vocal tone by singing pure Latin vowels and clear consonants.
- Create a rich resonant sound with pure vowels and large spaces in the mouth and pharynx. Drop the jaw and feel the stretch of the throat as when starting a yawn.
- Energize sustained tones by increasing the breath support and dynamic level.
- Sustain phrases by staggering the breathing and moving forward through the phrases.
- Perform the rhythms precisely while conducting and speaking rhythm or speaking the text in rhythm.
- Demonstrate the correct singing of the *r* consonant after a vowel when singing in English. It should be almost silent, as in *art, over,* and *Lord.*
- Emphasize the contrapuntal lines that move in quicker rhythms, contrasting with the energized longer rhythmic values.
- Listen for diphthongs (two vowel sounds when one vowel sound is written) in such English words as *high, light,* and *thy.* Sing or sustain the first vowel sound and barely sing the second vowel sound with the next syllable.

TEACHING STRATEGY

Sight-Singing

Have students:

- Practice sight-reading rhythms and sight-singing pitches every day. Daily practice will build increasing confidence and skill.
- Read the piece through in four parts as far as they are able before breaking into sections and isolating the rhythm and pitch elements.

Assessment

Informal Assessment

During this lesson, students showed the ability to:

- Identify good posture and breathing techniques in the Vocal Warm-Up.
- Read and perform rhythms in the Vocal Warm-Up.
- Sight-sing rhythms in four parts with syncopation, eighth-sixteenth combinations, and dotted quarter-eighth patterns in the Sight-Singing exercise.
- Improvise on chord tones and chord progressions in the Sight-Singing exercise.
- Read and sing independently using good posture and breath support in "Ave Regina Coelorum."
- Sing with correct Latin pronunciation in "Ave Regina Coelorum."

Student Self-Assessment

Have students:

- Evaluate their performance with the How Did You Do? section on page 157.
- Answer the questions individually. Discuss them in pairs or small groups and/or write their responses on a sheet of paper.

Individual Performance Assessment

To further demonstrate accomplishment, have each student:

- In a quartet or double quartet, sing from measures 1–20 of "Ave Regina Coelorum" while being videotaped, demonstrating correct posture and breathing and independent singing.
- Into a tape recorder, individually speak measures 1–20 in rhythm, in Latin, demonstrating correct pronunciation.
- Write a self-evaluation of their own performance, assessing their ability to use correct breathing and posture, sing independently, and use correct Latin pronunciation.

Extension

Renaissance Characteristics

Have students:

- Describe the musical characteristics of "Ave Regina Coelorum."
- Recall the many types of musical characteristics possible in Renaissance music.
- Construct a Venn diagram, demonstrating the overlapping characteristics of the two that define the piece as an example of Renaissance music.
- Identify the characteristics of music of the Middle Ages that have been used by de Lassus in this piece.

Improvising Harmonically on a Rhythm

Daily practice is the key to improvisational comfort and success.

Have students:

- Quickly construct an 8-measure rhythm in 2/4, 3/4, 4/4, 6/8, or 5/4 meter. (a different one each day, and in a different style)
- Choose a chord, and write the chord tones on the board.
- Sing the rhythm on each of the chord tones all the way through, maintaining the predetermined style.
- Sing the rhythm, first using two of the three chord tones, then two others, then the last combination of two.
- Sing the rhythm, improvising and using all three chord tones.
- When this exercise is becoming "old hat," begin constructing chord progressions, with each chord lasting two measures or more.

162 *Choral Connections Level 4 Mixed Voices*

National Standards

The following National Standards are addressed through the Extension and bottom-page activities:

1. Singing, alone and with others, a varied repertoire of music. **(a, b, c)**
3. Improvising melodies, variations, and accompaniments. **(a, c, d, e)**
4. Composing and arranging music within specified guidelines. **(a, b)**
5. Reading and notating music. **(a, b)**
6. Listening to, analyzing, and describing music. **(a, b, c, e, f)**
7. Evaluating music and music performances. **(a, b, c)**
8. Understanding relationships between music, the other arts, and disciplines outside the arts. **(c)**
9. Understanding music in relation to history and culture. **(a, c, d, e)**

Recognizing an Exemplary Renaissance Piece

Have students:

- Discuss the characteristics that make a piece of music great or exemplary, as opposed to ordinary. (demonstrates characteristics of the period, imagination, technical skill, and evokes an aesthetic response through unique, interesting, or expressive elements)
- Identify elements of "Ave Regina Coelorum" that they think may make it exemplary or great.
- Identify aspects of their performance that explored these elements of the piece.

Preparing a Performance of "Ave Regina Coelorum"

Have students:

- Sight-sing through the piece once.
- Individually or in groups, review the stylistic characteristics of Renaissance choral music, described on page 152.
- Review the piece, determining how it should be interpreted to provide a convincing and authentic Renaissance performance.
- Write their ideas as recommendations to the conductor.
- Optional: Have five groups of students each prepare one of the pieces from the historical section of the text, Making Historical Connections. Students should introduce, rehearse, and prepare the ensemble with your guidance, and then conduct the piece in concert.

1600–1750

Baroque Period

Focus

OVERVIEW

Understanding the development of choral music during the Baroque period.

OBJECTIVES

After completing this lesson, students will be able to:

- Identify musical forms, figures, and developments of the Baroque period.
- Identify specific performance characteristics to be used in Baroque choral music.
- Describe the relationship between music and the prevailing social, cultural, and historical events and ideas occurring in Europe during the Baroque period.
- Describe and compare characteristics of Baroque art and music.
- Identify the ideas and figures that foreshadowed the Classical period.

CHORAL MUSIC TERMS

Define the Choral Music Terms for students, giving pronunciation, and answering any questions that may arise.

Introducing the Lesson

Introduce the Baroque period through visual art.

Analyze Murillo's painting on page 164 and Neumann's architecture on page 166.

Have students:

- Study the painting and nave.
- Discuss the information provided at the bottom of pages 165 and 166 in your Teacher's Wraparound Edition.

In *The Return of the Prodigal Son,* Bartolomé Esteban Murillo (1617–1682) expresses the attitude of the Catholic church during the Counter-Reformation, hoping to welcome back the followers of Martin Luther (1483–1546). To the contrary, a significant body of religious music was created to serve the new form of worship in the Protestant churches.

1667–70. *The Return of the Prodigal Son.* (Detail.) Bartolomé Esteban Murillo. Oil on canvas. 236.3 x 261.0 cm (93 x 102 ¾"). National Gallery of Art, Washington, D.C. Gift of the Avalon Foundation.

TEACHER'S RESOURCE BINDER

Fine Art Transparency 2, *The Return of the Prodigal Son,* by Bartolomé Esteban Murillo

Optional Listening Selections:

Music: An Appreciation, 6th edition

Cantata No. 140, Fourth Movement: CD 2, Track 31

La Primavera, First Movement: CD 2, Track 17

National Standards

6. Listening to, analyzing, and describing music. **(a, b, c, e, f)**
7. Evaluating music and music performances. **(a)**
8. Understanding relationships between music, the other arts, and disciplines outside the arts. **(a, b, c, d, e)**
9. Understanding music in relation to history and culture. **(a, c, d, e)**

Baroque Period

1600–1750

After completing this lesson, you will be able to:

- *Discuss some of the major changes that took place in Europe during the Baroque period.*
- *Describe the most important characteristics of Baroque music.*
- *Identify at least three musical forms that developed during the Baroque period.*
- *Discuss the most important characteristics of Baroque choral music.*

The balance and restraint of the Renaissance period were followed by an era in which all the arts, including music, became more emotional, dramatic, and decorative: the Baroque period.

Changes During the Baroque Period

The explorations and developments undertaken during the Renaissance period continued and expanded during the Baroque period. European navigators, explorers, traders, and settlers traveled to other parts of the world, and the first colonies were established in the Americas. Science and mathematics also expanded; scholars used new instruments and new insights to develop specialized fields of study.

The paintings, sculpture, and architecture of the Baroque period reflect society's interests in flamboyance and dramatic detail. Many were created as displays of the wealth and splendor of European emperors, kings, and other power aristocrats. Elaborate palaces, surrounded by vast formal gardens and decorated with large-scale and dramatic paintings and sculpture, typified the artistic intentions of the Baroque period. Baroque painters, including Caravaggio, Rubens, Rembrandt, and Velázquez, brought dramatic new effects to their works. The sculptors of the period, especially Bernini and Borromini, created pieces with a new sense of movement. Drama and emotional effects—and eventually flamboyance—were emphasized in the visual artworks of the Baroque period.

Baroque Music

Like the visual artworks of the time, Baroque music was characterized by complex details and new emotional content. Many works were composed with a strong sense of movement and a highly ornamental melody. One important musical feature developed during this period was the **continuo,** *a continually moving bass line*. Another was the use of improvisation; musicians often improvised additional melodic ornamentations during performances.

Instrumental music gained in importance during the Baroque period. Two major instrumental forms developed. The **concerto grosso** *is a composition for a small chamber orchestra consisting of several movements and featuring a bass line and an elaborate melody*. The Baroque concerto grosso

COMPOSERS

Claudio Monteverdi (1567–1643)
Arcangelo Corelli (1643–1713)
Henry Purcell (1659–1695)
Antonio Vivaldi (1678–1741)
Johann Sebastian Bach (1685–1750)
George Frideric Handel (1685–1759)
Giovanni Battista Pergolesi (1710–1736)

ARTISTS

El Greco (1541–1614)
Michelangelo da Caravaggio (c. 1565–1609)
Peter Paul Rubens (1577–1640)
Frans Hals (1580–1666)
Artemisia Gentileschi (1593–1653)
Gianlorenzo Bernini (1598–1680)
Francesco Borromini (1599–1667)
Rembrandt van Rijn (1606–1669)
Judith Leyser (1609–1660)
Bartolomé Esteban Murillo (1617–1682)

AUTHORS

John Donne (c. 1573–1631)
René Descartes (1596–1650)
John Milton (1608–1674)
Molière (1622–1673)

CHORAL MUSIC TERMS

cantata
chorale
concerto grosso
continuo
opera
oratorio
recitative
suite
terraced dynamics

The Return of the Prodigal Son

The Return of the Prodigal Son, painted in 1667–70 by Bartolomé Esteban Murillo, was created as one of a set of six paintings for a church in Seville. Notice the continued use of shadow, as was common in the Renaissance, but a more pronounced use of three-dimensional perspective. The eye is drawn to the central figures of the painting in several ways. The lighting focuses attention on them, and all the secondary figures face them. They are in the center of the canvas and form a central triangle. The background does not distract from the figures. The characters in the painting are involved with one another, and the canvas tells the viewer a story with a specific mood.

Suggested Teaching Sequence

1. Examine the Baroque period.

Have students:

- Read the text on pages 165–167.
- Share what they know about the composers, artists, and authors listed on this page.
- Read, discuss, and answer the review questions on page 167 individually, in pairs, or in small groups.
- Discuss their answers with the whole group, clarifying misunderstandings.

2. Examine the Baroque period in historical perspective.

Have students:

- Turn to the time line on pages 166 and 167 and read the citations.
- Discuss why these events and people are significant to the Baroque period.
- Compare each of these events to what they know occurred before and after the Baroque period.
- Discuss both how these events and people affected music and the other arts, and how music and the other arts may have led to new ideas.
- Identify any factors that may have led to new ideas and signaled the beginning of the Classical period.

3. Define the musical aspects of the Baroque period.

Have students:

- Review the changes in music from the Renaissance to the Baroque period.
- Identify the musical styles and forms of the period.
- Review the characteristics of vocal music during the period.
- Identify well-known musical figures of the period.
- Listen to music from the period, pointing out characteristics of Baroque music.

Assessment

Informal Assessment

During this lesson, students showed the ability to:

- Share what they know about the Baroque period.
- Describe musical characteristics, styles, forms, and personalities of the Baroque period.
- Describe specific performance characteristics of Baroque choral music.
- Describe and compare characteristics of Baroque art.
- Describe the social, historical, and cultural environment of the Baroque period.
- Identify ideas, people, and events that foreshadowed the Classical period.

Student Self-Assessment

Have students:

- Review the questions in Check Your Understanding on page 167.
- Write a paragraph describing how much they understand about the development of music during the Baroque period.

Individual Performance Assessment

To further demonstrate accomplishment, have each student:

- Select a Baroque vocal composition.
- Review the piece, identifying the characteristics of the Baroque period that appear in the piece.
- Prepare a performance guide, discussing the performance style appropriate for the piece, based on characteristics of Baroque vocal music performance.
- Optional: Rehearse and prepare an ensemble to perform the piece, and conduct it during the concert.

Galileo **1564–1642**

1607 Jamestown, Virginia, established settlement

1608 Telescope invented

Henry Hudson explores the Hudson River **1609**

1618–1648 Thirty Years' War

Pilgrims land in America **1620**

1636 Harvard College founded

Isaac Newton **1642–1727**

1643–1715 Reign of Louis XIV, as King of France

Quakers arrive in Massachusetts **1656**

features interplay between a small group of soloists and the larger group of players. The contrast between the small and large groups, between the soft and loud sounds, is one of the key features of Baroque music.

Another important new instrumental form was the **suite,** *a set of musical movements, usually inspired by dances, of contrasting tempos and styles.* Suites were written for solo instruments, for small instrumental groups, and for complete orchestras.

One of the most characteristic developments of the Baroque period was the **opera,** *a combination of singing, instrumental music, dancing, and drama that tells a story.* Claudio Monteverdi composed *Orfeo*, the first important opera, in 1607. The most famous English composer of the period, Henry Purcell, wrote the opera *Dido and Aeneas* in 1689.

In replacing symmetry and balance with the ornate and intricate, Balthazar Neumann, in the Nave of Vierzehnheiligen Pilgrim Church, expressed the distinction between Renaissance and Baroque style in both art and music. Complexity and ornamentation are prevalent characteristics of music in the Baroque period, in contrast to the calm, smooth style of the Renaissance.

1743–72. The Nave of Vierzehnheiligen Pilgrim Church. Balthazar Neumann. Vierzehnheiligen Pilgrim Church, near Bamberg, West Germany.

Although the Baroque period is noted for its rise in the importance of instrumental music, there were also significant developments in vocal music. The **cantata** was *a collection of compositions with instrumental accompaniment consisting of several movements based on related secular or sacred text segments.* The fact that this form could be composed either as a sacred or as a secular work was, in itself, an innovation.The **chorale** was a hymn tune, generally composed for Protestant worship services with German texts. Chorales were intended to be easy to sing and to remember so that all members of a church congregation could join in.

The third major vocal development was closely related to opera, but without the acting, costumes, and scenery. The **oratorio** was *a composition for solo voices, chorus, and orchestra that was an extended dramatic work on a literary or religious theme presented without theatrical action.* An oratorio was typically performed by a small chorus, an orchestra, and four solo voices. Though most oratorios recount religious stories, they were not intended to be part of a religious service.

The Nave of Vierzehnheiligen Pilgrim Church

The Nave of Vierzehnheiligen Pilgrim Church, by Balthazar Neumann, was built from 1743 to 1772, and provides a worthy example of Baroque opulence. Notice the ornamentation and extravagant detail throughout the nave. Layer upon layer greet the eye until it is almost too ornate to take in. Yet each set of details has its own symmetry and pattern.

Johann Sebastian Bach **1685–1750**

First American newspaper established, *Boston News Letter* **1704**

Handel comes to England **1710**

1682 LaSalle explores the Mississippi

1685–1759 George Frideric Handel

1687 Publication of Newton's *Mathematical Principles*

1706–1790 Benjamin Franklin

Characteristics of Choral Music During the Baroque Period

Like all forms of Baroque music, the choral works of the period were more dramatic and emotional than the vocal music of the Renaissance. The developments of the period can be considered in terms of the meter and stress, tempo, dynamics, texture, and expressive aspects of Baroque choral music.

The Baroque period saw the introduction of metered music; music was organized and notated in regular groups of beats. The accents within these groups came at regular intervals. Typically, weak beats led into stronger beats, and short notes led into longer notes in choral works of the time. The **recitative,** *a vocal line in an oratorio or a cantata (or opera) that imitates the rhythm of speech*, moved the focus to textual declamation.

The tempo of Baroque choral music was generally moderate. A steady, unflagging rhythm is considered a major characteristic in choral works of the time. In many works, the tempo is held back slightly as one melodic phrase concludes and before the next section begins. Such variations and pauses were often used to heighten the emotional quality of a work. By the end of the seventeenth century, the Italian words used to indicate tempo at the beginning of a piece (*largo*, *allegro*, and *presto*, for example) had come into general use.

Within the dynamics of choral music, extremes were generally avoided during the Baroque period. **Terraced dynamics**—*a rather abrupt alteration between loud and soft*—were most common; crescendo and decrescendo were not frequently used. Instrumentation became more important in choral works; rather than simply doubling the voices, instruments began to "accompany" the singers.

Check Your Understanding

Recall

1. How were the visual artworks of the Baroque period different from those of the Renaissance period?
2. How did Baroque musicians use improvisation?
3. What is a suite?
4. What is a cantata? On what kinds of text were Baroque cantatas based?
5. What is an oratorio? How is it similar to and different from an opera?
6. What kind of tempo did most Baroque choral works have?

Thinking It Through

1. Based on what you have read and what you have heard, which do you prefer—Renaissance choral music or Baroque choral music? Why?
2. Choose any form of popular music you enjoy listening to. Explain the similarities and differences between that music and the choral music of the Baroque Period.

ANSWERS TO RECALL QUESTIONS

1. More flamboyant, dramatic, and embellished.
2. To provide melodic ornamentation.
3. A set of musical movements of contrasting tempos and styles.
4. A collection of compositions with instrumental accompaniment consisting of several movements. Secular or sacred texts.
5. A composition for solo voices, chorus, and orchestra that was an extended dramatic work on a literary or religious theme presented without theatrical action. Like the opera, it was composed for many voices, but had no acting, costumes, and scenery.
6. An abrupt alteration between loud and soft. They took the place of the crescendo and decrescendo.

Extension

Networking with Your Community

Baroque music is performed today by small chamber choirs or orchestras. Large symphony orchestras often have a smaller Baroque ensemble within the larger group, and this ensemble plays part of the concert. Check with your local performing ensembles, churches, arts councils, and universities to discover when Baroque music will be performed in the community.

Non-European Cultures and Music During the Baroque Period

Have students:

- Identify the dates of the Baroque period in Europe.
- Research events in at least one non-European culture during those years.
- Research what non-European music was being performed and created at the time of the Baroque period, and where European music was being introduced as a result of military conquest, colonization, or trade.

The Baroque in Depth

The Baroque is an exciting theme for a unit of study. Have students identify areas of interest individually, in pairs, or in groups. Have them write a contract or proposal with you, describing the topic to be researched, a time line describing methodology, stages, and completion dates, and the nature of the final product to be presented. (paper, performance, lecture, and so on) Students should also be aware of all other projects going on, and link ideas together whenever possible.

Listening to...

Baroque Music

This feature is designed to expand students' appreciation of choral and instrumental music of the Baroque period.

CHORAL SELECTION: "Zion hort die Wachter singen" from Bach's Cantata No. 140
Have students:

- Read the information on this page to learn more about "Zion hort die Wachter singen."
- Watch as you follow a transparency of Blackline Master, Listening Map 3.

Using the Listening Map
Start at top left corner and move down the page. The different "lines" denote the four different phrases in the melody (violins). The rhythmic notation under the lines is the rhythm of the basso continuo (low strings). The bass clef staff shows the vocal part, sung by the men in the chorus.
Have students:

- Understand that Bach's cantatas were sacred choral works with multiple sections, including a chorale.
- Listen as you introduce similarities of stylistic characteristics in Baroque music, as illustrated in the cantata and concerto forms. (very structured form; an alternation between passages of different timbre—solo vs. tutti; basso continuo, emoting the quality of the music; repetitive motives—ritornello; varying lengths of phrases; cantus firmus; etc.)
- Listen to the recording as you point to the transparency.

BAROQUE CONNECTIONS

Listening to . . .

Baroque Music

CHORAL SELECTION

Bach — *Cantata No. 140,* Fourth Movement, Chorale

Johann Sebastian Bach (1685–1750) was a German composer and organist, the youngest son of a town musician. He wrote music of all genres including vocal, instrumental, and keyboard/organ. He wrote over 200 church cantatas, one of the most famous being *Cantata No.* 140 (1731). In the fourth movement, "Zion hort die Wachter singen," Bach utilizes a chorale as the "cantus firmus," using a free ritornello to separate the phrases of the chorale melody.

INSTRUMENTAL SELECTION

Vivaldi — *La Primavera,* First Movement

Antonio Vivaldi(1678–1741) was an Italian composer. He is best known as the master of concertos, having written over 500, half of them for solo violin and orchestra. His most well-known work is *The Four Seasons*. It is a set of four solo concertos for violin, string orchestra, and basso continuo. As programmatic music, each portrays one of the seasons of the year, corresponding with sonnets that preface each concerto.

TEACHER'S RESOURCE BINDER
Blackline Master, Listening Map 3
Blackline Master, Listening Map 4

Optional Listening Selections:
Music: An Appreciation, 6th edition
Cantata No. 140, Fourth Movement: CD 2, Track 31
La Primavera, First Movement: CD 2, Track 17

National Standards
This lesson addresses the following National Standard:

9. Understanding music in relation to history and culture. **(a)**

Introducing . . .

"Alleluia"

Giovanni Battista Pergolesi

Setting the Stage

While not specified in this edition of "Alleluia," this piece by Pergolesi is most likely a larger part of a larger work, perhaps from a setting of the mass. The piece is very reflective of the mature Baroque style in the use of sequences as a compositional technique and as an example of the now clearly defined major-minor harmonic system.

Meeting the Composer

Giovanni Battista Pergolesi

Giovanni Battista Pergolesi (1710–1736) was one of the northern Italian composers known as the "Neapolitans." His style reflected an attempt to offer the audience music that was clear, simple, and pleasant to hear. From these ideals came the beginnings of what we now call the Classical period. The Neapolitans also used more chromaticism (moving in half steps) in their music, affecting both the melodies and harmonies. Pergolesi wrote a musical setting of the *Stabat Mater* (a liturgical text from the thirteenth century, "By the Cross the Mother Standing" referring to Mary, the Mother of Jesus), which shows the delicate texture, the very balanced phrasing, and the lyrical tone of Italian sacred music of this time period. He also composed instrumental pieces and serious operas. His opera buffa (comic opera), *La serva padrona* (The Maid Mistress, 1733), established Pergolesi as the first master of this new style.

ASSESSMENT

Individual Performance Assessment

Have each student:

- Listen to an unfamiliar Baroque selection. In small groups, discuss how this new piece is characteristic of the Baroque period and identify its similarities to "Zion hort die Wachter singen."
- List at least two characteristics of Baroque programmatic concerto music in Vivaldi's *La Primavera.* (solo instrument and orchestra; repetition of ritornello; basso continuo; terraced dynamics; instrumentation; ornamentation) Identify sounds and events Vivaldi chose to "illustrate" through music.

INSTRUMENTAL SELECTION: *La Primavera*, First Movement, by Vivaldi

Have students:

- Read the information on page 168 to learn more about *La Primavera.*
- Watch as you follow a transparency of Blackline Master, Listening Map 4.

Using the Listening Map

Follow the picture frames, left to right, and down the page. This is a tapping map; use the eraser end of a pencil to keep beat with the music. Tap twice on each picture throughout. In the fifth frame, tap twice on each pair of violins and the daisies. Then rest the pencil during the violin solo. Resume tapping at the closing phrase of the ritornello (tulips).

Have students:

- Listen as you give background information on Vivaldi and the programmatic concerto form.
- Study the listening map as a class and answer the following questions:
—Where and how often is the closing phrase of the ritornello (tulip patch) repeated? (seven times, at the end of each section)
—What terraced dynamics does Vivaldi use? (*forte* and *piano*) Do they appear in a pattern? (several distinct changes from *forte* to *piano* in each section)
—What elements of "Spring" has Vivaldi chosen to portray with his music? (bird song, water moving, lightning, and so on)
- Listen to the recording as you point to the transparency.

INTRODUCING. . . "Alleluia"

This feature is designed to introduce students to the Baroque Lesson on the following pages.

Have students:

- Read Setting the Stage on this page to learn more about "Alleluia."
- Read Meeting the Composer to learn more about Giovanni Battista Pergolesi.
- Turn the page and begin the Baroque Lesson.

BAROQUE LESSON

Alleluía

COMPOSER: Giovanni Battista Pergolesi (1710–1736)
EDITED BY: Hubert Bird

Focus

OVERVIEW
Vocal independence; polyphony; melodic imitation; melodic sequences.

OBJECTIVES
After completing this lesson, students will be able to:
- Read and sing one part when five parts are sung in polyphony.
- Identify and sing melodic imitation.
- Identify and perform melodic sequences.

CHORAL MUSIC TERMS
Define the Choral Music Terms for students, giving pronunciation, and answering any questions that may arise.

Warming Up

Vocal Warm-Up

This Vocal Warm-Up is designed to prepare students to:
- Sing with a warmed-up voice.
- Sing the single-word text of the piece.
- Close the vowels of the first two syllables quickly on quarter and eighth-note values.
- Identify melodic sequences.

Have students:
- Read through the Vocal Warm-Up directions.
- Sing, following your demonstration.

BAROQUE LESSON

Alleluía

COMPOSER: *Giovanni Battista Pergolesi* (1710–1736)
EDITED BY: *Hubert Bird*

CHORAL MUSIC TERMS
Baroque
melodic imitation
melodic sequences
part independence
polyphony

VOICING
SSATB

PERFORMANCE STYLE
Strongly, boldly
A cappella

FOCUS
- Read and sing one part when five parts are sung in polyphony.
- Identify and sing melodic imitation.
- Identify and perform melodic sequences.

Warming Up

Vocal Warm-Up

Read and sing this exercise with good energy, closing quickly to the "l" on the first two syllables. Move upward in scalewise steps on each repeat. When you sing the same melodic pattern beginning on different pitches each time, it is called a sequence.

Sight-Singing

Sight-sing this exercise using solfège and hand signs or numbers. Try a variety of voicings, for example: S/A sing part I, T/B sing part II, S/T sing part I, A/B sing part II. Support the higher pitches with plenty of breath. Notice the sequences in each part line and the imitative rhythms between parts.

TEACHER'S RESOURCE BINDER

National Standards

1. Singing, alone and with others, a varied repertoire of music. **(a, b, c, e, f)**
5. Reading and notating music. **(a, b, c)**
6. Listening to, analyzing, and describing music. **(a, b, c, d, f)**
7. Evaluating music and music performances. **(a)**
9. Understanding music in relation to history and culture. **(a, d)**

Singing: "Alleluia"

Imagine a Slinky© toy descending down stairs, step by step. Each motion has the same pattern, but begins one step lower than the one before. A melodic sequence resembles the toy. Once a pattern is established, it is repeated, beginning either higher or lower than the previous pattern.

Echo some melodic patterns. Now, instead of echoing, create a melodic sequence by singing the pattern two more times, one step higher or lower on each repeat, keeping the same pitch relationships intact.

Now turn to the music for "Alleluia" on page 172.

HOW DID YOU DO?

? ?

By now, you know the sequence for learning and preparing a piece of music for performance. Think about your preparation and performance of "Alleluia."

1. Can you read and sing your voice part when four other parts are being sung? What makes it easy or difficult in this particular piece?

2. Describe melodic imitation between voices, and point out where it occurs in "Alleluia."

3. Describe melodic sequences, point them out in the Sight-Singing exercise, then sing the exercise with one or three classmates, to demonstrate how they sound.

4. Describe the characteristics of this piece that indicate its origins in the Baroque period, and tell how you enhanced these characteristics through your performance.

Sight-Singing

This Sight-singing exercise is designed to prepare students to:

- Sight-sing using solfège and hand signs or numbers.
- Identify and sing melodic sequences.
- Identify and sing imitative rhythms between parts.
- Support higher pitches with adequate breath support.

Have students:

- Read through the Sight-Singing exercise directions.
- Read each voice part rhythmically, using rhythm syllables.
- Sight-sing through each part separately using solfège and hand signs or numbers.
- Sing all parts together.

Singing: "Alleluia"

Identify concept of melodic sequence.

Have students:

- Read the text on page 171.
- Identify melodic sequence as a series of melodic intervals repeated three times at successive pitches upward or downward.
- First echo short melodic patterns, then create a sequence by singing the patterns twice more, up or down a step on each repeat.

Suggested Teaching Sequence

1. Review Vocal Warm-Up.
Sing with energy. Close "l" quickly. Identify melodic sequence.
Have students:
- Review the Vocal Warm-Up on page 170 with energy.
- Close quickly to the "l," cutting the vowel short on the first two syllables, for a crisp rhythmic effect.
- Discuss how this quick close only occurs on quarter and eighth-note values. On half and tied quarter notes, the syllables are sung with sustained vowels.
- Preview their voice part of "Alleluia" to find places where they will close quickly, and where they will sustain the vowels, based on note values.
- Identify the Vocal Warm-Up pattern of moving up or down a step on each repeat as a melodic sequence.

2. Review Sight-Singing.
Sight-sing using solfège and hand signs or numbers. Sing melodic sequences and rhythmic imitation between parts.
Have students:
- Review the Sight-Singing exercise on page 170.
- Try a variety of voicings as suggested.
- Support the higher pitches with good breath.
- Identify the melodic sequences in each line, as well as the imitative rhythm between parts.
- Preview the whole score of "Alleluia" to visually identify imitation between parts, and melodic sequences.

3. Sight-sing "Alleluia" using solfège and hand signs or numbers.
Have students:
- Divide into voice sections (SSATB) and read each part rhythmically, clapping and speaking the rhythm of each voice part, adding dynamics to shape the phrases.

To Al Thrasher

Alleluia

Giovanni Battista Pergolesi (1710–1736)
Edited by Hubert Bird

Five-part Chorus of Mixed Voices,
(SSATB) A cappella

*The original is a whole tone lower and *alle breve*.

MUSIC LITERACY

Harmonic Sequences

To help students expand their music literacy, have them:
- Use what they know about melodic sequences to predict the definition of harmonic sequence.
- Identify harmonic sequence as a harmonic progression repeated at least twice in sequence.
- Find places in "Alleluia" where there are harmonic sequences, for example, measures 15–18.
- Discuss any musical characteristics helpful in identifying harmonic sequences, such as similar melodic shapes, and the presence of accidentals.

- Still in sections, sing with solfège and hand signs or numbers, identifying and working on problem areas.
- Sing the piece through, using solfège and hand signs or numbers, with full ensemble, using appropriate dynamics and phrasing.
- Divide into sections and recite the text rhythmically for each voice part.
- Sing the piece through with text as a full ensemble.

4. Finding the imitation between voice parts in "Alleluia."

Have students:

- Identify places on page 172 (first octavo page) where there is imitation between voice parts, for example: soprano I in measure 1 and bass in measure 4; alto in measure 1 and soprano I in measure 4; soprano II in measure 2 and alto in measure 5, and so on.
- Continue to identify the imitation throughout the piece, noticing that some imitation is exact, and some just begins, but doesn't develop into full imitation.
- Sing the piece, raising a hand each time their voice part is imitating some already stated motif.

5. Finding melodic sequences in "Alleluia."

Have students:

- Sing the piece on staccato *doot* from the beginning to the first beat of measure 19.
- Identify the melodic sequences in the music, for example: bass measure 8, soprano I measure 15, alto measure 16, and tenor measure 11.
- Sing through the piece, attending to the melodic imitation and sequences that occur between parts.

CURRICULUM CONNECTIONS

Natural Science

Have students:

- Identify repetition of patterns in nature, such as the rings of a tree trunk, ripples in a pond, cloud formations, seasons of the year, and so on.
- Make an analogy between these repetitions in nature and repetition that occurs in music.
- Discuss the function of repetition in nature and music. (Accept any reasonable idea. There is a theory that repetition sets up expectations that are both satisfying when they are met, and surprisingly pleasing when they are not met. It is the balance between the meeting of expectation and the surprise that keeps people on an even keel, and provides aesthetic experiences.)

VOCAL DEVELOPMENT

To encourage vocal development, have students:

- Demonstrate good vocal tone by singing pure Latin vowels and clear consonants on the single word text *Alleluia.*
- Create a rich resonant sound by keeping a consistently large space in the mouth and pharynx and articulating *Alleluia* with the lips, tongue, and slight movement of the jaw.
- Energize sustained tones by increasing the breath support and dynamic level.
- Sustain phrases by staggering the breathing and moving forward through the phrases.
- Perform the rhythms precisely while conducting and speaking rhythm or speaking the text in rhythm.
- Emphasize the contrapuntal lines which move in quicker rhythms, contrasting with the energized longer rhythmic values.
- Emphasize the two-note phrases by "leaning into" the first note and tapering off on the second note. Demonstrate this by using the arm with the palm up in a circular motion away from the body, ending with the palm down to sense the feeling of loud to soft. Actually sing the loud-soft motion.

TEACHING STRATEGY

Rhythmic Imitation

To practice rhythmic imitation, and increase listening and thinking skills, have students:

- Echo clap in four- or eight-beat patterns, as you clap one pattern to your right, then one to your left, and alternate every pattern thereafter.
- Echo at four or eight beats after you as you clap the patterns in succession, one pattern on each side, with no rests between patterns. (They will be performing in canon with you, and be clapping one pattern after you while listening to and watching the next pattern. Keep every second pattern easy at first.)

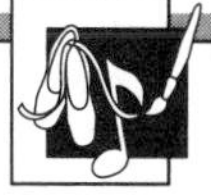

CONNECTING THE ARTS

Visual Art

Have students:

- Find examples of repetition, imitation, and sequence in visual art and architecture of the Baroque period, beginning with the examples included on pages 164 and 166 of this text.
- Identify examples of these same characteristics in the music and art of other periods, looking back to the Renaissance with its polyphonic texture and columns, and forward to the Classical, Romantic, and Contemporary periods.

Assessment

Informal Assessment

During this lesson, students showed the ability to:

- Identify and sing melodic sequence in the Vocal Warm-Up.
- Perform melodic sequences in single parts and rhythmic imitation between parts in the Sight-Singing exercise.
- Identify and perform melodic sequences and rhythmic imitation between parts in "Alleluia."
- Sing one part independently when four other parts are being sung in "Alleluia."

Student Self-Assessment

Have students:

- Evaluate their performance with the How Did You Do? section on page 171.
- Answer the questions individually. Discuss them in pairs or small groups and/or write their responses on a sheet of paper.

Individual Performance Assessment

To further demonstrate accomplishment, have each student:

- In a quintet, sing measures 1–19 of "Alleluia" while being videotaped or audiotaped, demonstrating independent singing.
- Write an evaluation of their own performance, assessing their ability to sing independently in ensemble and with one on each voice part.
- Sing "Alleluia" in full ensemble, signaling to identify melodic imitation of other parts by their own voice part.
- Sing "Alleluia" in full ensemble, signaling when their voice part performs melodic sequences.

Extension

Composing Melodies with Sequence

Have students:

- Compose a very short melodic motif (not more than four beats) in any key they choose.
- Expand that motif by creating a melodic sequence upward or downward.
- Try the same motif upside down, backward, or inside out.
- Using these fragments, compose a two-part exercise to use for a vocal warm-up. (If any are especially appealing or inventive, encourage students to expand the warm-up into a composition.)

Recognizing an Exemplary Baroque Piece

Have students:

- Discuss the musical characteristics that make a piece of music great or exemplary, as opposed to ordinary. (demonstrates characteristics of the period, imagination, technical skill, and evokes an aesthetic response through unique, interesting, or expressive elements)
- Identify elements of "Alleluia" that they think may make it exemplary or great.
- Identify aspects of their performance that explored these elements of the piece.

Al - le - lu - ia, Al - le - lu - ia.
Al - le - lu - ia, Al - le - lu - ia.
le - lu - ia, Al - le - lu - ia.
le - lu - ia, Al - le - lu - ia.
Al - le - lu - ia.

Al-le-lu - ia, Al-le-lu - ia, Al - le - lu - ia. Al - le - lu - ia.
Al-le-lu - ia, Al-le-lu - ia, Al - le - lu - ia. Al - le - lu - ia.
Al-le-lu - ia, Al-le-lu - ia, Al - le - lu - ia. Al - le - lu - ia.
Al-le-lu - ia, Al-le-lu - ia, Al - le - lu - ia. Al - le - lu - ia.
Al-le-lu - ia, Al-le-lu - ia, Al - le - lu - ia. Al - le - lu - ia.

National Standards

The following National Standards are addressed through the Extension and page-bottom activities:

1. Singing, alone and with others, a varied repertoire of music. **(a, b, c, e)**
4. Composing and arranging music within specified guidelines. **(a, b)**
5. Reading and notating music. **(a, b)**
6. Listening to, analyzing, and describing music. **(a, b, c, e, f)**
7. Evaluating music and music performances. **(a, b, c)**
8. Understanding relationships between music, the other arts, and disciplines outside the arts. **(a, b, c, d)**
9. Understanding music in relation to history and culture. **(a, c, d, e)**

Preparing a Performance of "Alleluia"

Have students:

- Sight-sing through the piece once.
- Individually or in groups, review the stylistic characteristics of Baroque choral music discussed in the narrative lesson on page 167.
- Review the piece, determining how it should be interpreted to provide a convincing and authentic Baroque performance.
- Write their ideas as recommendations to the conductor.
- Optional: Have five groups of students each prepare one of the pieces from this section of the text, Making Historical Connections. Students will introduce, rehearse, and prepare the ensemble with your guidance, then conduct the piece in concert.

Baroque Characteristics

Have students:

- Describe the musical characteristics of "Alleluia."
- Recall the musical characteristics that are typical of Baroque music.
- Construct a Venn diagram, demonstrating the overlapping characteristics of the two that define the piece as an example of Baroque music.
- Identify the characteristics of Baroque music that have been used by Pergolesi.

Repetition in Non-European Music

Have students:

- Listen to music of non-European cultures to discover imitation, repetition, and sequence. (Begin with Balinese Gamelan music and African drumming, both of which are based on patterns that repeat and imitate over and over. Native American music and many spirituals have imitative sections in the form of solo and group parts.)

1750–1820

Classical Period

Focus

OVERVIEW

Understanding the development of choral music during the Classical period.

OBJECTIVES

After completing this lesson, students will be able to:

- Identify musical forms, figures, and developments of the Classical period.
- Identify specific performance characteristics to be used in Classical choral music.
- Describe the relationship between music and the prevailing social, cultural, and historical events and ideas occurring in Europe during the Classical period.
- Describe characteristics of Classical art and music.
- Identify the ideas and figures that foreshadowed the Romantic period.

CHORAL MUSIC TERMS

Define the Choral Music Terms for students, giving pronunciation, and answering any questions that may arise.

Introducing the Lesson

Introduce the Classical period through visual art.

Analyze Kauffmann's painting on page 178 and Jefferson's architecture on page 181.

Have students:

- Study the painting and capitol building.
- Discuss the information provided at the bottom of pages 179 and 180 in your Teacher's Wraparound Edition.

***Cornelia Pointing to Her Children as Her Treasures*, by Angelica Kauffmann (1741–1807), focuses on one subject, avoiding details that might distract from the simple statement. Haydn and Mozart, as composers of the Classical period, also focused on the importance of a composition's musical theme and its clarity, avoiding distracting details.**

1785. *Cornelia Pointing to Her Children as Her Treasures.* Angelica Kauffmann. Oil on canvas. 101.6 x 127.0 cm (40 x 50"). Virginia Museum of Fine Arts, Richmond, Virginia. The Adolph D. and Wilkins C. Williams Fund, 1975.

TEACHER'S RESOURCE BINDER

Fine Art Transparency 3, *Cornelia Pointing to Her Children as Her Treasures,* by Angelica Kauffmann

Optional Listening Selections:

Music: An Appreciation, 6th edition

"Dies Irae": CD 3, Track 65

Piano Concerto No. 23 in A Major: CD 4, Track 1

National Standards

6. Listening to, analyzing, and describing music. **(a, b, c, d, e, f)**
7. Evaluating music and music performances. **(a, b)**
8. Understanding relationships between music, the other arts, and disciplines outside the arts. **(a, b, c, d, e)**
9. Understanding music in relation to history and culture. **(a, c, d, e)**

Classical Period

1750–1820

After completing this lesson, you will be able to:

- *Discuss some of the major changes that took place in Europe and the Americas during the Classical period.*
- *Describe the most important characteristics of Classical music.*
- *Identify the most important composers of the Classical period.*
- *Discuss the most important characteristics of Classical choral music.*

The Baroque period, characterized by the emotion, drama, and opulence of its artworks, was followed by the Classical period, in which the arts focused on standards of balance, clarity, and simplicity. Scholars and artists of the period looked back to the works and attitudes of ancient Greece and Rome and adopted as new the ideals they saw reflected in ancient times.

Changes During the Classical Period

The Classical period is often called the Age of Enlightenment. The people of this era put their faith in reason and thought, not in tradition and emotion. This focus on reason resulted in political upheaval and in a return to more restrained, less emotional artistic expression.

The most important political events of the Classical period brought major changes to specific countries and affected the attitudes and ideas of people in other parts of Europe and the Americas. The American colonists revolted against their British rulers and succeeded in founding an independent nation, the United States of America. Several years later, the French Revolution began; this uprising established a new government and confirmed a new societal structure in France.

The visual artists of the Classical period emulated the balance and grandeur they saw in the surviving works from ancient Greece and Rome. This influence can be seen directly in the subjects chosen by painters such as Jacques Louis David, in the heroic yet individualized works by sculptors such as Jean Antoine Houdon, and in the clear Roman elements of structures such as the Brandenburg Gate in Berlin and Monticello, Thomas Jefferson's home in Virginia.

Classical Music

The music of the Classical period left behind the extreme drama and emotion of Baroque compositions, with their exaggerated embellishments and improvisations. Instead, Classical compositions emphasized precision and balance. An essential characteristic of the period was a careful balance between the content of the music and the form in which the music was expressed.

COMPOSERS

Franz Joseph Haydn (1732–1809)
Wolfgang Amadeus Mozart (1756–1791)
Ludwig van Beethoven (1770–1827)
Vincento Bellini (1801–1835)

ARTISTS

Francois Boucher (1703–1770)
Jean-Honoré Fragonard (1732–1806)
Angelica Kauffmann (1741–1807)
Jean Antoine Houdon (1741–1828)
Francisco Gôya (1746–1828)
Jacques Louis David (1748–1825)

AUTHORS

Jonathan Swift (1667–1745)
Samuel Richardson (1689–1761)
Voltaire (1694–1778)
Henry Fielding (1707–1754)
Wolfgang Goethe (1749–1832)
Friedrich von Schiller (1759–1805)
Jane Austen (1775–1817)

CHORAL MUSIC TERMS

chamber music
sonata-allegro form
string quartets
symphony

Cornelia Pointing to Her Children as Her Treasures

Angelica Kauffmann's artwork, painted in 1785, reflects the emphasis on the everyday person, a frequent subject during the Classical period. Common themes included the weak against the strong and an equalizing of wealth. During this time, art was intended to represent the virtuous, and it emulated the style of the ancient Romans and Greeks, as had previously occurred in the Renaissance. Although maintaining the perspective developed during the Baroque period, art became less decorous and frivolous, with clean lines and symmetry.

Suggested Teaching Sequence

1. Examine the Classical period.

Have students:

- Read the text on pages 179–181.
- Share what they know about the composers, artists, and authors listed on this page.
- Read, discuss, and answer the review questions on page 181.
- Discuss their answers with the whole group, clarifying misunderstandings.

2. Examine the Classical period in historical perspective.

Have students:

- Turn to the time line on pages 180 and 181 and read the citations.
- Discuss why these events and people are significant to the Classical period.
- Compare each of these events to what they know occurred before and after the Romantic period.
- Discuss both how these events and people affected music and the other arts, and how music and the other arts may have led to new ideas.
- Identify any factors that may have led to new ideas and signaled the beginning of the Romantic period.

3. Define the musical aspects of the Classical period.

Have students:

- Review the changes in music from the Baroque to the Classical period.
- Identify the musical styles and forms that dominated the period.
- Review the characteristics of vocal music during the period.
- Identify well-known musical figures of the period.
- Listen to music from the period, analyzing, and pointing out characteristics of Classical music.

Assessment

Informal Assessment

During this lesson, students showed the ability to:

- Share what they know about the Classical period.
- Describe musical characteristics, styles, forms, and personalities of the Classical period.
- Describe specific performance characteristics of Classical choral music.
- Describe and compare characteristics of Classical art.
- Describe the social, historical, and cultural environment of the Classical period.
- Identify ideas, people, and events that foreshadowed the Romantic period.

Student Self-Assessment

Have students:

- Review the questions in Check Your Understanding on page 181.
- Write a paragraph describing how much they understand about the development of music during the Classical period.

Individual Performance Assessment

To further demonstrate accomplishment, have each student:

- Select a Classical vocal composition.
- Review the piece, identifying the characteristics of the Classical period that appear in the piece.
- Prepare a performance guide, discussing the performance style appropriate for the piece, based on characteristics of Classical vocal music performance.
- Optional: Rehearse and prepare an ensemble to perform the piece, and conduct it during the concert.

Swift's *Gulliver's Travels* published — 1726

George Washington — 1732–1799

1732–1757 — Franklin writes *Poor Richard's Almanac*

Thomas Jefferson — 1743–1826

American Revolutionary War fought — 1775–1783

1775 — James Watt invents the steam engine

The state capitol of Virginia demonstrates the interest of eighteenth-century artists in the simplicity of Greco-Roman design. Attention to clean, simple forms dominate the music of the late eighteenth century as well.

1785–96. State Capitol of Virginia. Thomas Jefferson. Richmond, Virginia.

Two composers dominated the period: Wolfgang Amadeus Mozart and Franz Joseph Haydn. A third major composer of the time, Ludwig van Beethoven, belongs both to the Classical period and to the next era, the Romantic period. Beethoven's compositions began in the Classical style, but the texture, emotion, and new forms of his later music belong more to the Romantic period.

The most important Classical developments came in instrumental music, which continued to gain in importance. Probably the greatest contribution of this period was the **symphony,** *a large-scale piece for orchestra in three or more movements*. A Classical symphony usually consisted of four movements in the following order: 1) A dramatic, fast movement; 2) A slow movement, often in sonata form; 3) A dance-style movement; 4) An exciting, fast movement.

The Classical period also saw a rise in the popularity of **chamber music,** *music composed for a small group of instruments and designed to be played in a room (or chamber) rather than in a concert hall*. These works are generally light and entertaining, both for the performers and for the listeners. The most popular Classical chamber music compositions were **string quartets,** *pieces composed for two violins, a viola, and a cello*.

Another important instrumental development was the **sonata-allegro form,** *a movement written in AA'BA form*. The sonata-allegro form opens with a single theme (A). Then that theme is repeated with elaboration (A') and followed by a contrasting development (B). The sonata-allegro form closes with a return to the original theme (A).

In general, the vocal and mixed forms of the Baroque period were continued in the Classical period, but with new interpretations that emphasized on balance and elegance.

Characteristics of Choral Music During the Classical Period

Like other compositions of the time, the choral works of the Classical period upheld the standards of simplicity and clarity. These standards were reflected in the meter and stress, tempo, dynamics, texture, and expressive aspects of Classical choral music.

An important characteristic of Classical choral compositions was a definite sense of meter. These works generally had a clear pulsation, but it was more delicate than

State Capitol of Virginia

The State Capitol of Virginia, designed by Thomas Jefferson, and built from 1785 to 1796, echoes the return to Roman structure, stark simplicity of line, and symmetry. Like the sonata-allegro (ABA) form, this building, if cut in half, could be re-formed by placing the center of one half against a mirror.

American Declaration of Independence signed
1776

Federal Government established in America
1789

1789
French Revolution begins

1808
Roman excavations begin at Pompeii, Italy

that heard in Baroque choral works. Choral works of the period usually exhibited a moderate tempo, free from any extremes. Composers became more likely to mark their scores with tempo indications, providing a clear direction for performers. The metronome was invented early in the nineteenth century and helped stabilize the tempo of choral performances. After about 1816, composers were able to mark the specific metronome numbers, showing the exact number of beats per minute, for each section of a composition.

The terraced dynamics of the Baroque period were generally replaced by gradual crescendo and decrescendo in Classical choral works. Audiences considered these gradual changes from loud to soft and from soft to loud an exciting innovation.

Among the expressive aspects of Classical choral music were a clearly defined structure and characteristic emphasis on symmetry, balance, clarity, and restraint. Music ornamentation continued to be featured in choral music, although it was more refined and restrained than in works of the late Baroque period. Although many choral works included emotional content, the emotion was expressed less dramatically and with greater detachment than in Baroque works.

Check Your Understanding

Recall

1. What were the two most important political events of the Classical period?
2. Who were the two most important composers of the Classical period?
3. What is a symphony? What four movements did a Classical symphony usually include?
4. What is chamber music? What was the main characteristic of most Classical chamber works?
5. What is a sonata-allegro form?
6. What kind of tempo was typical of Classical choral works?
7. What were the major features of Classical choral dynamics?
8. How was the tone quality of Classical choral music different from that of Baroque choral music?

Thinking It Through

1. How is Classical choral music similar to Renaissance choral music? What are the major differences?
2. Identify a Classical choral work you have heard. Discuss the meter and stress, the tempo, the dynamics, the texture, the expressive aspects, and the tone quality of the work.

ANSWERS TO RECALL QUESTIONS

1. The American and French Revolutions.
2. Mozart and Haydn.
3. A large-scale piece for orchestra in three or more movements. A dramatic, fast movement; a slow movement, often a sonata; a dance-style movement; a fast movement.
4. Music composed for a small group of instruments and designed to be played in a room or chamber, rather than a concert hall. Most chamber works were light and entertaining.
5. A movement written in AA'BA form.
6. Moderate and free of any extremes.
7. Gradual crescendo and decrescendo.
8. Marked by restraint, without exaggerated vibrato.

Extension

Compare Classical Music to Other Arts of the Baroque

Have students:

- Define the characteristics of art and architecture during the Classical period.
- Compare the characteristics of music to one or more other art forms of the Classical period, comparing uses of characteristic elements, artistic processes, and organizing principles.

Networking with Your Community

Classical music takes many forms. Mozart, Haydn, and Beethoven are favorites in the repertoires of most performing groups. Making a few phone calls and reviewing the events in the local newspaper might help you locate a group that would come and perform for your students, giving them a live performance of Classical music.

Listening to... Classical Music

This feature is designed to expand students' appreciation of choral and instrumental music of the Classical period.

CHORAL SELECTION: "Dies Irae" by Mozart
Have students:

- Read the information on this page to learn more about "Dies Irae."
- Watch as you follow a transparency of Blackline Master, Listening Map 5.

Using the Listening Map
Point to the rhythms under the words as you move from top to bottom of the map.
Have students:

- Read and clap the rhythms on the map.
- Listen as you explain the broad meaning of the Latin text. ("Day of wrath, Day of Woe, Be fearful of your future. We all must die. Judgment is coming.")
- Listen to the recording as you point to the transparency.

Listening to . . . Classical Music

CHORAL SELECTION

Mozart — "Dies Irae" from *Requiem*

Mozart was born in Salzburg, Austria, in 1756. He died at the early age of 35 in the year 1791. Mozart was gifted as both a performer and a composer. His father began taking him on performance tours when Mozart was just six years old, and by the time he was 12, Mozart had composed his first symphony, oratorio, and opera. Although he died just before his thirty-sixth birthday, Mozart composed more than 600 works, including symphonies, concertos, sonatas, and operas. The *Requiem* is one of the last pieces written by Mozart. It was left unfinished at his death.

A *requiem* is a service in the Catholic church that honors the dead. A requiem such as this would only be performed at the funeral of very important people because of the length and the skill required. Sometimes it is now performed on All Saints Day (First Sunday in November) in remembrance of those who have died.

INSTRUMENTAL SELECTION

Mozart — Piano Concerto No. 23 in A Major: First Movement

Wolfgang Amadeus Mozart (1756–1791) was an Austrian composer and child prodigy. He wrote a number of compositions in his short lifespan for all genres—symphonies, operas, masses, and keyboard and solo instruments, both secular and sacred. *Piano Concerto in A Major* was composed during one of Mozart's more productive and successful times in his life. It is in three movements and follows the traditional sonata concerto form.

TEACHER'S RESOURCE BINDER
Blackline Master, Listening Map 5
Blackline Master, Listening Map 6

Optional Listening Selections:
Music: An Appreciation, 6th edition
"Dies Irae": CD 3, Track 65
Piano Concerto No. 23 in A Major: CD 4, Track 1

National Standards
This lesson addresses the following National Standard:

6. Listening to, analyzing, and describing music. **(a)**

Introducing . . . "Come, Lovely Spring"

Franz Joseph Haydn

Setting the Stage

Do you like to dance? How often have you heard a popular song whose beat just impelled you to dance? Just like many of our current songs today, this one will capture your intrinsic desire to move and sway to the music. It lilts in a steady unflagging tempo from beginning to end with lightness and simplicity. The number is typically classical, but fresh as a springtime morning. In fact, have you ever sung an arrangement of the song "Morning Has Broken"? What a wonderful piece this would be preceding a performance of "Come, Lovely Spring." Perhaps you can think of other more current songs that would even fit better. Enjoy!

Meeting the Composer

Franz Joseph Haydn (1732–1809)

Franz Joseph Haydn, Mozart's friend and one of the greatest composers of the Classical period, was born on March 31, 1732, in Ruhr, Austria. Haydn showed an early love of music but did not receive any formal training in composition until his late teens. His works gradually gained recognition, and when he was 29 years old Haydn entered the service of the aristocratic Hungarian Esterhazy family. This patronage provided a steady income and required Haydn to compose work requested by the family and to conduct the court orchestra. Haydn thrived under this system, and he worked diligently. He composed more than 100 symphonies and 68 string quartets, as well as sonatas, operas, oratorios, masses, and other works.

Haydn is well known for taking the already established forms of the symphony and the string quartet and shaping them into the powerful media for musical expression that were recognized by all composers in both the past and the present. Both his masses and his choral works continue as standards in the concert repertory. His operas are also of great musical worth.

Haydn lived from the end of the Baroque period to the beginning of the Romantic period. He led the musical transitions between the two.

ASSESSMENT

Individual Performance Assessment

To further demonstrate understanding of Classical music, have each student:

- Divide into two groups (boys/girls if practical). Group 1 will practice clapping the rhythms under the *Dies Irae, Dies Illa*. Group 2 will practice clapping the rhythms under *Quantus tremor est futurus.* Both groups should practice the last *quantus tremor est futurus* rhythm and the *cunta stricte* rhythm. Perform with the recording.
- Describe to a partner how the rhythm of "Dies Irae" heightens and supports the meaning and emotion of the text.
- With a partner, discuss the form Mozart used to compose the Piano Concerto. (Write a "scrambled" list of terms on the board for students to use.)

INSTRUMENTAL SELECTION: Piano Concerto No. 23 in A Major by Mozart

Have students:

- Read the information on page 182 to learn more about Mozart's Piano Concerto No. 23 in A Major.
- Watch as you follow a transparency of Blackline Master, Listening Map 6.

Using the Listening Map

This map has two pages. Start at the top left-hand corner of each page and move down the page, left to right. Each keyboard picture represents those times when the piano is heard.

Have students:

- Understand the characteristics of the concerto. (a composition for soloist and an orchestra, usually with three movements)
- Review the following terms:

exposition—the first section of the music where the main theme is heard

development—"reshaping" of thematic material

recapitulation—restatement of the exposition theme

cadenza—vivid passage at the end of a concerto movement that shows off the soloist's talent

coda—the "tail," or last section of the piece.

- Study the listening map and together read aloud the headings of each section.
- Listen to the recording as you point to the transparency.

INTRODUCING. . . "Come, Lovely Spring"

This feature is designed to introduce students to the Classical Lesson on the following pages.

Have students:

- Read Setting the Stage on this page to learn more about "Come, Lovely Spring."
- Read Meeting the Composer to learn more about Franz Joseph Haydn.
- Turn the page and begin the Classical Lesson.

CLASSICAL LESSON

Come, Lovely Spring

COMPOSER: Franz Joseph Haydn (1732–1809)
TRANSLATION: Alice Parker and Thomas Pyle
EDITED BY: Robert Shaw

Focus

OVERVIEW
Steady tempo; 6/8 meter; vocal independence; dynamics and tempo.

OBJECTIVES
After completing this lesson, students will be able to:

- Maintain a steady tempo.
- Read and sing accurately in 6/8 meter.
- Sing one part independently when four parts are being sung.
- Identify and interpret Classical dynamic and tempo markings.

CHORAL MUSIC TERMS
Define the Choral Music Terms for students, giving pronunciation, and answering any questions that may arise.

Warming Up

Vocal Warm-Up
This Vocal Warm-Up is designed to prepare students to:

- Sing with a warmed-up, relaxed voice.
- Sing in 6/8 meter, with a lilting feeling.
- Sing with a steady tempo.

Have students:

- Read through the Vocal Warm-Up directions.
- Sing, following your demonstration.

Come, Lovely Spring

COMPOSER: *Franz Joseph Haydn* (1732–1809)
TRANSLATORS: *Alice Parker and Thomas Pyle*
EDITED BY: *Robert Shaw*

CHORAL MUSIC TERMS
Classical period
dynamic markings
independent singing
6/8 meter
tempo markings
tempo

VOICING
Four-part chorus

PERFORMANCE STYLE
Allegretto
Accompanied by piano

FOCUS

- Maintain a steady tempo.
- Read and sing accurately in 6/8 meter.
- Sing one part independently when four parts are being sung.
- Identify and interpret Classical dynamic and tempo markings.

Warming Up

Vocal Warm-Up
Read and sing this exercise first using solfège and hand signs or numbers, then on *doo, loo,* or *la*. Move up or down by half steps on each repeat, and maintain a steady beat. As you sing, gently sway from the waist while relaxing arm and neck muscles. This will give you the lilting feeling of 6/8 meter. Repeat this exercise at the end of your Warm-Up session, just before practicing "Come, Lovely Spring."

Sight-Singing
Sight-sing this exercise using solfège and hand signs or numbers. Then sing it in a round, four measures apart, with women beginning, and men adding the second part. This round is not designed for harmonic consonance, but rather to build your vocal independence.

Write the exercise on the board, and then write different tempo and dynamic markings, interpreting them in the Classical style.

TEACHER'S RESOURCE BINDER
Blackline Master 15, *Rhythms and Melodies in 6/8 Meter,* page 96

National Standards

1. Singing a varied repertoire of music. **(a, b, c, f)**
4. Composing and arranging music within specified guidelines. **(a)**
5. Reading and notating music. **(a, b, c, e)**
6. Listening to, analyzing, and describing music. **(a, b, c, e, f)**
7. Evaluating music and music performances. **(a)**
9. Understanding music in relation to history and culture. **(a, d)**

Singing: "Come, Lovely Spring"

How do you know what a composer was thinking, especially if he lived from 1732 to 1809? Some of the clues are written down. The notation tells you the rhythms and pitches, and the tempo marking tells you how fast to go.

Dynamic markings are not quite so simple, unless you understand the conventions of the period. In the Classical period, a dynamic marking either indicates a sudden dynamic change, or marks the average dynamic level of each phrase. If this is the case, it is your job to shape the phrase with a crescendo to the peak, and then a release to the end of the phrase. Find the tempo and dynamic markings in "Come, Lovely Spring" so you will be prepared when you sing.

Now turn to the music for "Come, Lovely Spring" on page 186.

HOW DID YOU DO?

When you perform, you are the vehicle that brings the music from the composer to the audience. Think about your preparation and performance of "Come, Lovely Spring."

1. Are you able to maintain a steady tempo as you read or perform? Demonstrate by singing the Sight-Singing exercise without any accompaniment.

2. The 6/8 meter should be familiar by now. Are there any rhythms that gave you problems?

3. Are you able to hold your part independently when other parts are being sung? Sing measures 5–30 of "Come, Lovely Spring" with three classmates to demonstrate your ability.

4. Describe the tempo and dynamic markings in "Come, Lovely Spring," and discuss how to interpret them in the style of the Classical period.

5. If Franz Joseph Haydn attended your performance of this piece, what do you suppose he would think of it? What would he like? What might he tell you would improve the performance?

Sight-Singing

This Sight-Singing exercise is designed to prepare students to:

- Sight-sing using solfège and hand signs or numbers.
- Read and sing in 6/8 meter.
- Sing with vocal independence.

Have students:

- Read through the Sight-Singing exercise directions.
- Read each voice part rhythmically, using rhythm syllables.
- Sight-sing through each part separately using solfège and hand signs or numbers.
- Sing all parts together.

Singing: "Come, Lovely Spring"

Interpreting the composer's intentions.

Have students:

- Read the text on page 185.
- Identify the clues to the composer's musical intentions provided in the notation. (rhythm, pitch, dynamics, tempo)
- Identify the two possible meanings of dynamic markings provided during the Classical period. (sudden change, average dynamics for a phrase)
- Review the notation for "Come, Lovely Spring," identifying phrase dynamic markings, as seen in measure 5, and sudden dynamic markings, such as the upbeats to measures 21 and 27.

Suggested Teaching Sequence

1. Review Vocal Warm-Up.
Read and sing in 6/8 meter with lilting feeling.
Have students:

- Review the Vocal Warm-Up on page 184, maintaining a steady tempo.
- Use the suggested movement to feel the lilt and relax the body and vocal mechanism.
- Identify the meter of "Come, Lovely Spring," and "sizzle" the rhythm of their voice part on *tsss,* sight-singing the rhythm as far as they can go without stopping.

2. Review Sight-Singing.
Sight-sing using solfège and hand signs or numbers. Sing in a round to develop vocal independence, interpret tempo, and dynamic markings.
Have students:

- Review the Sight-Singing exercise on page 184.
- Sing in a round as suggested.
- Write the exercise on the board, and explore tempo and dynamic markings by trying out different combinations, using a metronome to set the tempo, and discussing dynamics together.

Come, Lovely Spring

(From "The Seasons")

Franz Joseph Haydn (1732–1809)
Edited by Robert Shaw
English Text by
Alice Parker and Thomas Pyle

Four-part Chorus of Mixed Voices
with Piano Accompaniment

TEACHING STRATEGY

Maintaining a Steady Tempo

This may seem an obvious requirement for advanced ensembles, but is sometimes overlooked as more sophisticated concepts are addressed.
Have students:

- Pat the beat almost inaudibly as they sing.
- Sing with a metronome on occasion.
- Listen to recorded performances when they are inclined to rush, describe the problem, and suggest solutions.
- Understand that students who are struggling with tempo cannot hold back the group alone; they will only split the ensemble. It must be something the group feels together.

10

come, and from her win - t'ry grave a - wak - en slum - b'ring earth.

come, and from her win - t'ry grave a - wak - en slum - b'ring earth.

grave, and from her win - t'ry grave a - wak - en slum - b'ring earth.

from her win - t'ry grave, and from her grave a - wak - en slum - b'ring earth.

Ob. Fl.

16

Come! come, love - ly Spring! a - wak - en slum - b'ring earth, and

Come! come, love - ly Spring! a - wak - en slum - b'ring earth, and

Come, love - ly Spring! a - wak - en slum - b'ring, earth. and

Come! come, love - ly Spring! a - wak - en slum - b'ring earth, and

Str. - Orch.

21

from her win - t'ry grave

from her win - t'ry grave, and from her win - t'ry grave a - wak - en slum - b'ring

from her win - t'ry grave, and from her win - t'ry grave a - wak - en slum - b'ring

from her win - t'ry grave, and from her win - t'ry grave a - wak - en slum - b'ring

Fl.

3. Sight-sing "Come, Lovely Spring" using solfège and hand signs or numbers.

Have students:

- Sight-sing the piece in full ensemble, at a slow tempo, as far as possible without stopping.
- Divide into voice sections and read each part rhythmically, using rhythm syllables, then the rhythm and pitch together, using solfège and hand signs or numbers.
- Still in sections, sing with solfège and hand signs or numbers, identifying and working on problem areas.
- Sing the piece through, using solfège and hand signs or numbers, with full ensemble.
- Sing the piece through with text as a full ensemble, using appropriate dynamics and phrasing.

TEACHING STRATEGY

Tempo Help

Have students:

- Learn to use a metronome to check the tempo markings on pieces.
- Also use a metronome to check their tempo at the end of the piece.
- Understand that the metronome is a machine that gives a mechanical beat, and that a performer sometimes intentionally stretches or diminishes the beat for effect.

VOCAL DEVELOPMENT

To encourage vocal development, have students:

- Sing with tall, open vowels and clearly articulated consonants.
- Create a light, but resonant sound by keeping a consistently large space in the mouth and pharynx.
- Modify vowel sounds for greater resonant tone on such words as *come, lovely, from,* and *touch,* using an *awh* rather than *uh* vowel sound.
- Energize sustained tones by increasing the breath support and dynamic level.
- Sustain phrases by staggering the breathing and moving forward through the phrases.
- Perform the rhythms precisely while conducting and speaking the text in rhythm.
- Emphasize the two-note phrases by "leaning into" the first note and tapering off on the second note.
- Listen for diphthongs in *now, may, thy, joyful, tiny,* and *revive.* Sing or sustain the first vowel sound and barely sing the second vowel sound with the next syllable.
- Demonstrate how the *r* consonant should be almost silent, as in *earth, nearer,* and *winter.*
- Feel the arched contour of each musical phrase as it begins, builds, then tapers off. The dynamics should reflect the melodic contour.
- Balance the chords between the parts by listening to them.

76 B

—— O come, love - ly Spring! O boun-teous God - dess, come. Come, love - ly
earth. O come, love - ly, love - ly Spring! O boun-teous God - dess, come. Come, love - ly
earth. O come, love - ly. love - ly Spring! O boun-teous God - dess, come.
earth. O come, come, love - ly Spring! O boun-teous God - dess, come.

Fl. Fag. Hörn.

82

Spring, — O boun-teous God - dess, come! Come, love - ly Spring! Come, love - ly
Spring, — O boun-teous God - dess, come! Come, love - ly Spring! Come, love - ly
Come, love - ly Spring, — O come! Come, love - ly Spring! Come, love - ly
Come, love - ly Spring, Come, love - ly Spring! love - ly

Fl. Ob. Fag.

88

Spring! — O God - dess, O boun - teous God - dess, come!
Spring! — O God - dess, O boun - teous God - dess, come!
Spring! — O God - dess, O boun - teous God - dess, come!
Spring! — O God - dess, O boun - teous God - dess, come!

Str.-Orch.

MUSIC LITERACY

Dynamics and Shaping Phrases

To help students expand their music literacy, have them:

- Review the parts of a phrase—beginning, peak, and end.
- Discuss how to shape phrases using dynamics, with a crescendo from the beginning to the peak, and then a release to the end.
- Recall that the dynamic marking at the beginning of a phrase may indicate the overall average dynamic for the entire phrase.

48 Sopr. I — C Women's Voices
Come near - er now, O love - ly Spring,
Sopr. II
Come near - er now, O love - ly Spring,
Alt I
Come near - er now, O love - ly Spring,
Alt II
Come near - er now, O love - ly Spring,
Fl. Holzbl. Vcello.

51747

48
that all may feel thy quick - 'ning touch, that ev - 'ry - thing may live a - gain.
that all may feel thy quick - 'ning touch, that ev - 'ry - thing may live a - gain.
that all may feel thy quick - 'ning touch, that ev - 'ry - thing may live a - gain.
that all may feel thy quick - 'ning touch, that ev - 'ry - thing may live a - gain.
Tutti.

58
Come near - er now, come near - er now, O love - ly
Come near - er now, come near - er now, O love - ly
Come near - er now, come near - er now, O love - ly
Come near - er now, come near - er now, O love - ly
Str.-Orch. Fl.

CURRICULUM CONNECTIONS

History

When Haydn was born, Bach was composing his most intricate Baroque music.
Have students:

- Research the historical, cultural, and social developments that occurred during Haydn's life.
- Research Haydn's experiences within the context of the historical events.
- Identify the changes in Haydn's music as a result of his personal contacts, experiences, employment situations, and the popular ideas of his time.
- Compare and contrast Haydn's music and life with that of his contemporaries.
- Summarize the impact of Haydn on the Classical period, and the impact of the Classical period on Haydn.

Assessment

Informal Assessment

During this lesson, students showed the ability to:

- Identify and sing in lilting 6/8 meter in the Vocal Warm-Up.
- Perform with vocal independence in the Sight-Singing exercise.
- Experiment with tempo and dynamic markings in the Sight-Singing exercise.
- Sing in 6/8 meter with steady tempo, using stylistically correct interpretation of tempo and dynamic markings in "Come, Lovely Spring."
- Sing one part independently when three other parts are being sung in "Come, Lovely Spring."

Student Self-Assessment

Have students:

- Evaluate their performance with the How Did You Do? section on page 185.
- Answer the questions individually. Discuss them in pairs or small groups and/or write their responses on a sheet of paper.

Individual Performance Assessment

To further demonstrate accomplishment, have each student:

- Into a tape recorder in an isolated space, clap or sing an assigned example from Blackline Master 15, *Rhythms and Melodies in 6/8 Meter,* demonstrating the ability to sing in 6/8 meter while maintaining a steady tempo.
- In a quartet, sing measures 5–30 of "Come, Lovely Spring" while being videotaped or audiotaped, demonstrating independent singing.
- Write an essay discussing the Classical composer's use of tempo and dynamic markings and how they were interpreted in "Come, Lovely Spring."

Extension

Classical Characteristics

Have students:

- Describe the musical characteristics of "Come, Lovely Spring."
- Recall the musical characteristics possible in Classical music.
- Construct a Venn diagram, demonstrating the overlapping characteristics of the two that define the piece as an example of Classical music.
- Identify the characteristics of music of the Baroque period that have been used by Haydn in this piece.

The Oratorio

"Come, Lovely Spring" is just one of many choruses from Haydn's oratorio *The Seasons.*

Have students:

- Research what an oratorio is.
- Listen to a recording of a portion or the complete performance of *The Seasons.*

58

Men's Voices D

Ten. I Ten. II Baß I Baß II

Spring, Come near - er now, O love - ly Spring! Be

Spring, Come near - er now, O love - ly Spring! Be

Spring, Come near - er now, O love - ly Spring! Be

Spring, Come near - er now, O love - ly Spring! Be

63

joy - ful, yet re - mem - ber still; be joy - ful, yet re - mem - ber still that

joy - ful, yet re - mem - ber still; be joy - ful, yet re - mem - ber still that

joy - ful, yet re - mem - ber still; be joy - ful, yet re - mem - ber still that

joy - ful, yet re - mem - ber still; be joy - ful, yet re - mem - ber still that

67

deep, that deep in mist and fog con - ceal'd, the win - ter walks the

deep, that deep in mist and fog con - ceal'd, the win - ter walks the

deep, that deep in mist and fog con - ceal'd, the win - ter walks the

deep, that deep in mist and fog con - ceal'd, the win - ter walks the

National Standards

The following National Standards are addressed through the Extension and bottom-page activities:

1. Singing, alone and with others, a varied repertoire of music. **(a, b, c, e)**
4. Composing and arranging music within specified guidelines. **(a, b)**
5. Reading and notating music. **(a, b, c, e)**
6. Listening to, analyzing, and describing music. **(a, b, c, e, f)**
7. Evaluating music and music performances. **(a, b, c)**
8. Understanding relationships between music, the other arts, and disciplines outside the arts. **(a, c, d)**
9. Understanding music in relation to history and culture. **(a, c, d, e)**

Haydn's Dynamic Surprise

Haydn was a master at using dynamics for effect, and his most famous use of dynamics is the *Surprise* Symphony.

Have students:

- Recall, or hear the story of Haydn's frustration with the audiences falling asleep during his symphonies, which were often performed after enormous dinners had been served.
- Listen to the first movement of his *Surprise* Symphony to hear the dynamic surprise Haydn wrote for the nappers.

Composing Using Dynamics

Have students:

- In quartets, compose short (8-measure) four-part pieces in 6/8 meter, in the key of G, using I, IV, and V harmonies.
- Share and combine these pieces with another group, creating an ABA form.
- Together, determine a tempo marking and dynamic markings for the piece, using Haydn's Classical style as a model.
- Practice and perform their piece, using the planned dynamics and tempo, and performing in Classical style.

Recognizing an Exemplary Classical Piece

Have students:

- Discuss the characteristics that make a piece of music great or exemplary, as opposed to ordinary. (demonstrates characteristics of the period, imagination, technical skill, and evokes an aesthetic response through unique, interesting or expressive elements)
- Identify elements of "Come, Lovely Spring" that they think may make it exemplary or great.
- Identify aspects of their performance that explored these elements of the piece.

99
come___ and bless the wait - ing world,___ and bless,___ and bless_the wait - ing
come___ O come and bless_the wait - ing, wait - ing world,___ and bless the wait - ing
come,___ O come and bless_the wait - ing, wait - ing world,___ and bless_the wait - ing
come___ and bless the wait - ing world,___ and bless___ the wait - ing
Volles Orch.
L.G. Co. 51747

104
world. O come, come, come!
world. O come, come, come!
world. O come, come, come!
world. O come, come, come!

Preparing a Performance of "Come, Lovely Spring"

Have students:

- Sight-sing and sing through the piece once.
- Individually or in groups, review the stylistic characteristics of Classical choral music, as discussed on pages 180 and 181.
- Review the piece, determining how it should be interpreted to provide a convincing and authentic Classical performance.
- Write their ideas as recommendations to the conductor.
- Optional: Have five groups of students each prepare one of the pieces from this section of the text, Making Historical Connections. Students should introduce, rehearse, and prepare the ensemble with your guidance, then conduct the piece in concert.

1820–1900

Romantic Period

Focus

OVERVIEW

Understanding the development of choral music during the Romantic period.

OBJECTIVES

After completing this lesson, students will be able to:

- Identify musical forms, figures, and developments of the Romantic period.
- Identify specific performance characteristics to be used in Romantic choral music.
- Describe the relationship between music and the prevailing social, cultural, and historical events and ideas occurring in Europe during the Romantic period.
- Describe characteristics of Romantic art and music.
- Identify the ideas and figures that foreshadowed the Contemporary period.

CHORAL MUSIC TERMS

Define the Choral Music Terms for students, giving pronunciation, and answering any questions that may arise.

Introducing the Lesson

Introduce the Romantic period through visual art.

Analyze Constable's painting on page 194 and Bunnell's architecture on page 196.

Have students:

- Study the painting and mansion.
- Discuss the information provided at the bottom of pages 195 and 196 in your Teacher's Wraparound Edition.

***Hay Wain* by John Constable (1776–1837) focuses on the natural effect of the sky, including the ever-changing sun, clouds, and wind. These features correlate to an interest in orchestral color, with the symphony orchestra serving as a magnificent palette.**

1821. *Hay Wain.* John Constable. Oil on canvas. 1.28 x 1.85 m (4′ 2 1/2″ x 6′ 1″). National Gallery, London, England.

TEACHER'S RESOURCE BINDER

Fine Art Transparency 4, *Hay Wain,* by John Constable

Optional Listening Selections:

Music: An Appreciation, 6th edition

A German Requiem, Fourth Movement: CD 6, Track 19

"The Moldau": CD 6, Track 1

National Standards

6. Listening to, analyzing, and describing music. **(a, b, c, e, f)**
7. Evaluating music and music performances. **(a, b)**
8. Understanding relationships between music, the other arts, and disciplines outside the arts. **(a, b, c, d, e)**
9. Understanding music in relation to history and culture. **(a, c, d, e)**

Romantic Period

1820–1900

After completing this lesson, you will be able to:

- *Explain the impact of the Industrial Revolution on other developments of the Romantic period.*
- *Describe the most important characteristics of Romantic music.*
- *Identify at least four important composers of the Romantic period.*
- *Discuss the most important characteristics of Romantic choral music.*

The restraint of the Renaissance was followed by the more extravagant and emotional Baroque period. After the Baroque period came another time of restraint and balance, the Classical period. Not surprisingly, the Classical period was, in turn, followed by a time of greater emotion and exaggeration: the Romantic period.

Changes During the Romantic Period

One of the most important developments of the Romantic period was the Industrial Revolution. This radical change in manufacturing resulted in many new nonagricultural jobs and contributed to the rapid growth of cities. It also contributed to the growth of the middle class and to a rise in middle-class confidence and influence.

The Industrial Revolution also had a direct impact on changes in music. New techniques resulted in greatly improved musical instruments that could be mass produced. This meant that more musicians were available to perform with better instruments. These changes encouraged composers to exercise their creativity and to take new and more challenging approaches to their work.

The visual artists of the period reflected the era's attitudes with bolder, more colorful works. Landscapes by such Romantic painters as William Turner and John Constable conveyed the movements and feelings of nature. Later, Impressionist painters such as Edouard Manet, Claude Monet, and Pierre Auguste Renoir employed revolutionary techniques to bring the sense of the natural world alive.

Romantic Music

Although Romantic composers continued, in large part, to work with musical forms developed in the past, they used original treatments to create new musical statements. Romantic compositions focused on emotional extremes and were characterized by complexity, exploration, and excitement. The interests of the period were expressed in larger, more complex vocal melodies and more colorful harmonies. In addition, instrumentation was expanded to enhance the overall possibilities of tone color in the music, and rhythms became freer and more flexible.

Many Romantic compositions reflect the period's spirit of **nationalism,** *pride in a country's historical and legendary past.* Composers based both instrumental and vocal works on traditional legends or on

COMPOSERS

Ludwig van Beethoven (1770–1827)
Franz Schubert (1797–1828)
Hector Berlioz (1803–1869)
Felix Mendelssohn (1809–1847)
Frédéric Chopin (1810–1849)
Robert Schumann (1810–1856)
Bedvrich Smetana (1824–1884)
Franz Liszt (1811–1886)
Richard Wagner (1813–1883)
Giuseppe Verdi (1813–1901)
Clara Schumann (1819–1896)
Bedřich Smetana (1824–1884)
Johann Strauss (1825–1899)
Stephen Foster (1826–1864)
Johannes Brahms (1833–1897)
Peter Ilyich Tchaikovsky (1840–1893)
Giacomo Puccini (1858–1924)

ARTISTS

Élisabeth Vigée-Lebrun (1755–1842)
Joseph Mallard William Turner (1775–1851)
John Constable (1776–1837)
Rosa Bonheur (1822–1899)
Edouard Manet (1832–1883)
James A. McNeill Whistler (1834–1903)
Edgar Degas (1834–1917)
Paul Cezanne (1839–1906)
Claude Monet (1840–1926)
Berthe Morisot (1841–1895)
Pierre Auguste Renoir (1841–1919)
Mary Cassatt (1845–1926)
Vincent van Gogh (1853–1890)
Georges Seurat (1859–1891)

AUTHORS

Noah Webster (1758–1843)
Sir Walter Scott (1771–1832)
Mary Wollstonecraft Shelley (1797–1851)
Ralph Waldo Emerson (1803–1882)
Elizabeth Barrett Browning (1806–1861)

CHORAL MUSIC TERMS

art song
nationalism

Hay Wain

Painted by John Constable in 1821, *Hay Wain* reflects the emphasis of artists during the Romantic period on the beauty of nature. Not only is the landscape a new source of inspiration during the Romantic period, the sense of warmth and peace reflected by use of light attempts to express a mood as well as a scene. This love of nature is reflected in poetry and musical texts of the period. *Hay Wain* was painted before the invention of the camera. As soon as the camera began to be popular, the horizon became less straight in paintings, and soon moved out of the picture completely. Constable's comfortable, lush painting reflects a calm serenity that would soon lead to the popular styles of Impressionism and pointalism.

Suggested Teaching Sequence

1. Examine the Romantic period.
Have students:
- Read the text on pages 195–197.
- Share what they know about the composers, artists, and authors listed on this page.
- Read, discuss, and answer the review questions on page 197.
- Discuss their answers with the whole group, clarifying misunderstandings.

2. Examine the Romantic period in historical perspective.
Have students:
- Turn to the time line on pages 196 and 197 and read the citations.
- Discuss why these events and people are significant to the Romantic period.
- Compare each of these events to what they know occurred before and after the Romantic period.
- Discuss both how these events and people affected music and the other arts, and how music and the other arts may have led to new ideas.
- Identify any factors that may have led to new ideas and signaled the beginning of the Contemporary period.

3. Define the musical aspects of the Romantic period.
Have students:
- Review the changes in music from the Classical to the Romantic period.
- Identify the musical styles and forms that dominated the period.
- Review the characteristics of vocal music during the period.
- Identify well-known musical figures of the period.
- Listen to music from the period, pointing out characteristics of Romantic music.

Assessment

Informal Assessment

During this lesson, students showed the ability to:

- Share what they know about the Romantic period.
- Describe musical characteristics, styles, forms, and personalities of the Romantic period.
- Describe specific performance characteristics of Romantic choral music.
- Describe and compare characteristics of Romantic art.
- Describe the social, historical, and cultural environment of the Romantic period.
- Identify events, people, and ideas that foreshadowed the Contemporary period.

Student Self-Assessment

Have students:

- Review the questions in Check Your Understanding on page 197.
- Write a paragraph describing how much they understand about the development of music during the Romantic period.

Individual Performance Assessment

To further demonstrate accomplishment, have each student:

- Select a Romantic vocal composition.
- Review the piece, identifying the characteristics of the Romantic period that appear in the piece.
- Prepare a performance guide, discussing the performance style appropriate for the piece, based on characteristics of Romantic vocal music performance.
- Optional: Rehearse and prepare an ensemble to perform the piece, and conduct it during the concert.

Louisiana Purchase transacted **1803**

1804 Napoleon crowned Emperor

Abraham Lincoln **1809–1865**

1812–1814 War of 1812

Frederick Douglass **c. 1817–1895**

Mary Baker Eddy **1821–1910**

1821 Jean Champollion deciphers Egyptian hieroglyphics using the Rosetta Stone

1823 Monroe Doctrine created

Although the Belamy Mansion was built during the years designated as the Romantic period, architect Rufus G. Bunnell chose the Classical revival style. The Corinthian columns uphold a monumental cornice and pediment, making a dramatic statement. Similarly, music of the Romantic period was often monumental and dramatic.

1859. The Belamy Mansion, Wilmington, North Carolina. Rufus G. Bunnell.

nationalistic dramas and novels. Operas, particularly the works of Richard Wagner and Giuseppe Verdi, were the most notable musical vehicles of nationalism. Dance music also grew in popularity. Some of these dance compositions reflected the period's nationalism, imitating and echoing traditional folk tunes.

During the Romantic period, instrumental music became more elaborate and overtly expressive. Symphonies gained in popularity. Ludwig van Beethoven—often considered the world's greatest musical genius—expanded the symphony in both length and content. Each of Beethoven's nine symphonies is unique, and all are challenging to the performing musicians. Beethoven's *Ninth Symphony* even includes a chorus and four vocal soloists.

Of the Romantic vocal forms, the most important was the **art song,** *an expressive song about life, love, and human relationships for solo voice and piano.* The German name for these works is *lieder,* and their most famous composers were German-speakers. Austrian Franz Schubert wrote more than 600 songs, as well as symphonies, string quartets, and other works, before his death at the age of 31. German composers Robert Schumann and Johannes Brahms are also known for their *lieder.* The choral music of the Romantic period was characterized by exaggeration and emotion. The flamboyance of these works was expressed in their meter and stress, tempo, dynamics, texture, expressive aspects, and tone quality.

Romantic choral works exhibited contemporary musicians' particular interest in rhythm. Many of these creations were marked by intricate rhythmic patterns and unusual rhythmic surprises. Unlike the choral works of earlier periods, Romantic works

The Belamy Mansion, Wilmington, North Carolina

Designed by Rufus G. Bunnell in 1859, this building reflects a completely different perspective of the Romantic period. The Industrial Revolution led to great wealth for some, and the ostentatious, oversized characteristics of this structure reflect the grandiose, extravagant personal expression of the time.

Looking back, this structure resembles the Virginia State Capitol; however, it is the residence of one family, rather than an entire state legislature. Still, it is easy to see the Classical influences, this time with more flair and embellishment.

Mary Mason Lyon founds Mt. Holyoke Female Seminary — 1837

1835–1910 — Mark Twain

1844–1900 — Friedrich Nietzsche

American Civil War — 1861–1865

1889 — Jane Addams and Ellen Starr found Hull House

Wireless telegraph developed by Guglielmo Marconi — 1895

1898 — Motion picture camera patented by Thomas Edison; sound recording developed

employed extremes in meter tempo, and stress. The changes of tempo within compositions typically reflected changes in mood; often these tempo and mood changes were quite abrupt.

The dynamics of Romantic choral works evidenced extremes as well. Crescendo and decrescendo were widely and expressively used. In many instances, crescendo was combined with a gradual quickening of tempo and decrescendo with a gradual slowing; these combinations heightened the excitement created by choral works. The climax of a work was more likely to be sudden, and accents were employed more frequently. The combination of a large choir and a large orchestra often contributed to a sense of dynamic opulence. The texture of Romantic choral works was often thick, with an emphasis on rich sound. Most works emphasized harmony rather than counterpoint, and there was a new use of chromatic harmony.

In response to the formality and tradition of Classical works, the expressive aspects of Romantic choral works displayed the domination of expression over form. Individual and personal emotion were given free expression, and unusual harmonic, rhythmic, and dynamic effects were frequently used. Composers focused on the use of tone color and the presentation of "singable" melodies. The tone quality of Romantic works also showed the period's reaction against the standards of Classical compositions. There was a return of vibrato to add warmth and emotion to the tone. Tones were varied in response to the mood of the music; in general, however, fullness of tone was emphasized and beauty of tone was considered essential.

Check Your Understanding

Recall

1. How did the Industrial Revolution affect composers of the Romantic period?
2. List at least three adjectives you might use to describe Romantic music.
3. What is nationalism? How was it expressed in Romantic music?
4. What changes did Beethoven make in the composition of symphonies?
5. What is an art song? Name at least two Romantic composers of these works.
6. How did the meter and stress of Romantic choral works differ from those used in Classical choral music?
7. What one quality was typical of Romantic choral works?

Thinking It Through

1. Compare Romantic choral music with Baroque choral music. Discuss the similarities and differences you can identify.
2. To what extent do you think the Romantic period was simply a reaction against the constraints of the Classical period? Which Romantic changes would you consider "action" rather than "reaction"? Explain your ideas.

ANSWERS TO RECALL QUESTIONS

1. Instruments could be mass produced, which resulted in new avenues of musical composition.
2. Responses will vary.
3. Pride in a country's historical and legendary past. Composers based instrumental and vocal works on traditional legends or on nationalistic dramas and novels.
4. He expanded it in length and content.
5. An expressive song about life, love, and human relationships for solo voice and piano. Schubert, Schumann, and Brahms.
6. Intricate rhythm patterns and rhythmic surprises; the stress resulted in dynamic opulence.
7. Melodies were "singable."

Extension

Networking with Your Community

Romantic music is performed today by most performing ensembles, both vocal and instrumental. The lush harmonies and emotional content make them concert favorites, and they are expected on most concert programs. Romantic music encompasses a wide range of styles and genres, so one concert is not likely to provide the range of experiences. A piano or solo vocal recital, a symphony orchestra concert, a ballet, and an opera would give a broader picture of the Romantic musical landscape. Have students:

- Explore the newspapers, radio and television schedules, and performing group programs to find information about local performances of Romantic music.
- Attend a performance of Romantic music.
- Discuss and critique the performance upon return to the ensemble, identifying positive features of the composition and performance, and making suggestions for improvement or change.

Non-European Cultures and Music During the Romantic Period

Have students:

- Identify the dates of the Romantic period in Europe.
- Research what was happening in at least one non-European culture during those years.
- Research what non-European music was being performed and created at the time of the Romantic period, and where European music was being introduced as a result of military conquest, colonization, or trade.

Listening to... Romantic Music

This feature is designed to expand students' appreciation of choral and instrumental music of the Romantic period.

CHORAL SELECTION: A *German Requiem*, Fourth Movement, by Brahms
Have students:

- Read the information on this page to learn more about *A German Requiem.*
- Watch as you follow a transparency of Blackline Master, Listening Map 7.

Using the Listening Map
Start at the upper left-hand corner on the first page. Note the SATB descriptors at the left-hand side of each line. These indicate which voice parts are heard as the line continues. Follow the German words.
Have students:

- Listen as you play the main theme of the piece from the recording.
- Look at the listening map and predict where this main theme can be expected to be heard again.
- Listen to the recording as you point to the transparency.

ROMANTIC CONNECTIONS

Listening to... Romantic Music

CHORAL SELECTION

Brahms — *A German Requiem,* Fourth Movement

Johannes Brahms (1833–1897) lived most of his life in Hamburg, Germany. He composed almost every kind of music, except opera, and composed during the Romantic period when music began to move from the more traditional forms as represented by Beethoven to more "discordant" and unusual material as represented by Wagner. Not a religious man, he was moved nonetheless to compose a special work, or *German Requiem*, containing seven movements after the death of his teacher, Robert Schumann, and then of his own mother. The requiem was one of the main genres of choral music during the nineteenth century. Brahms intended to portray death as a time of peace and rest and this "Fourth Movement" was the centerpiece of his beautiful compositional effort. Psalm 84 is the text used for this piece.

INSTRUMENTAL SELECTION

Smetana — "The Moldau"

Bedřich Smetana (1824–1884) was a leading composer of Bohemia (later called Czechoslovakia). Smetana had a passion for music and composed in spite of his father's desire for him to become a lawyer. His musical efforts were mainly focused on trying to produce a Bohemian national music based on the folk songs and dances which already existed. Smetana, awoke one morning to find himself totally deaf, which created a depression that stayed with him through the remainder of his life. "The Moldau" represents Smetana's deep feeling about the beauty and significance of the river that flows through the city of Prague.

TEACHER'S RESOURCE BINDER
Blackline Master, Listening Map 7
Blackline Master, Listening Map 8

Optional Listening Selections:
Music: An Appreciation, 6th edition
A German Requiem, Fourth Movement: CD 6, Track 19
"The Moldau": CD 6, Track 1

National Standards
This lesson addresses the following National Standard:

6. Listening to, analyzing, and describing music. **(c)**

Introducing . . .

"So Wahr Die Sonne Scheinet"

Robert Schumann

Setting the Stage

This art song has a strongly Romantic text, using analogies between nature and love, and suggesting that it does not matter what natural disasters may occur, the love between these two people will endure. The structure is deceptively simple and homophonic, but extremely intimate and effective. The use of layering voices, altered tones, melodic skips, and overlapping phrases push the piece always forward. Use of traditional harmonic progressions is applied to the text, suggesting everlasting love, while dissonant and chromatic exploration sneak into the suggestions that nature might fail to be as constant. Dynamics and tempo are critical to successful performance of the piece.

Meeting the Composer

Robert Schumann

Robert Schumann (1810–1856) was a great German Romantic composer. Son of a bookkeeper, he was sent to study law, but instead devoted himself to literature and music. He founded a magazine which explored the most modern trends in the arts, and composed first piano pieces, then art songs, and finally, orchestral pieces. He was intrigued with mystification: secret references hidden in the music that are felt rather than observed by the listener. His literary interest shines through in the settings of Romantic poetry in his art songs. He initially studied piano and later turned to composing. He was a prolific songwriter. In 1840, for example, he wrote over one hundred songs.

INSTRUMENTAL SELECTION: "The Moldau" by Smetana

Have students:

- Read the information on page 198 to learn more about "The Moldau."
- Watch as you follow a transparency of Blackline Master, Listening Map 8.

Using the Listening Map

Begin at the word *start.* Follow each picture, bottom left and up, and then over toward the right and back down. Main themes are indicated along the sequence.

- Listen as you play the theme for the major sections on the piano.
- Listen to the recording as you point to the transparency.

INTRODUCING. . . "So Wahr Die Sonne Scheinet"

This feature is designed to introduce students to the Romantic Lesson on the following pages. Have students:

- Read Setting the Stage on this page to learn more about "So Wahr Die Sonne Scheinet."
- Read Meeting the Composer to learn more about Robert Schumann.
- Turn the page and begin the Romantic Lesson.

ASSESSMENT

Individual Performance Assessment

Have each student:

- With a partner, discuss how the main theme of "The Moldau" is contrasted with other melodic phrases to support the notion of heaven being a safe and comforting place.
- In a small group, discuss the compositional devices and techniques used to provide unity and variety in "The Moldau." Suggest that students think of tempo, voicing, and so on. Identify songs they have studied that use these same techniques.
- In a small group, compare Smetana's techniques for unity and variety to those used in Copland's *Appalachian Spring* or to Mozart's Piano Concerto No. 23 in A Major, First Movement.

ROMANTIC LESSON

So Wahr Die Sonne Scheinet

COMPOSER: Robert Schumann (1810–1856)

TRANSLATORS: Alice and Kurt Bergel

EDITED BY: William D. Hall

Focus

OVERVIEW

Melodic steps and skips; shaping phrases with dynamics.

OBJECTIVES

After completing this lesson, students will be able to:

- Sing melodic steps and skips accurately.
- Use dynamics to shape phrases.
- Sing with correct German pronunciation.

CHORAL MUSIC TERMS

Define the Choral Music Terms for students, giving pronunciation, and answering any questions that may arise.

Warming Up

Vocal Warm-Up

This Vocal Warm-Up is designed to prepare students to:

- Identify and sing melodic steps and skips.
- Sing patterns with a rest on the first beat.
- Sing with pitch accuracy.

Have students:

- Read through the Vocal Warm-Up directions.
- Sing, following your demonstration.

CHORAL MUSIC TERMS

dynamic shaping
melodic skips
melodic steps
phrases
Romantic

So Wahr Die Sonne Scheinet

COMPOSER: *Robert Schumann* (1810–1856)
TRANSLATORS: *Alice and Kurt Bergel*
EDITED BY: *William D. Hall*

VOICING

SATB

PERFORMANCE STYLE

Andante
Accompanied by piano

FOCUS

- Sing melodic steps and skips accurately.
- Use dynamics to shape phrases.
- Sing with correct German pronunciation.

Warming Up

Vocal Warm-Up

Sing this exercise on *no*. Move up or down by half steps on each repeat. Give the quarter rest its full value. Notice the melodic steps and skips, and tune each pitch carefully.

Sight-Singing

Sight-sing this exercise using solfège and hand signs or numbers. First sight-read your part inside your head, then sight-sing in four parts. Can you sing it all the way through the first time? How many phrases are there in this exercise? Where do you think each phrase begins and ends? How will you shape these phrases?

TEACHER'S RESOURCE BINDER

Blackline Master 16, *Translation and Pronunciation Guide for "So Wahr Die Sonne Scheinet,"* page 97

National Standards

1. Singing, alone and with others, a varied repertoire of music. **(a, b, c, f)**
5. Reading and notating music. **(a, b)**
6. Listening to, analyzing, and describing music. **(a, b, c, f)**
7. Evaluating music and music performances. **(a)**
8. Understanding relationships between music, the other arts, and disciplines outside the arts. **(c)**
9. Understanding music in relation to history and culture. **(a, d)**

Singing: "So Wahr Die Sonne Scheinet"

What makes a piece of music "Romantic"? The Romantic period was a time of extravagance, exaggeration, and expression. Read the English translation of the text in "So Wahr Die Sonne Scheinet" on page 202. Do you think it is extravagant, exaggerated, or expressive? Explain your answer with examples from the music.

Now sing to the music for "So Wahr Die Sonne Scheinet."

HOW DID YOU DO? ? ?

Did you do justice to this Romantic piece? Think about your preparation and performance of "So Wahr Die Sonne Scheinet."

1. How accurately do you sing in tune when other parts are being sung? What makes it more difficult? When is it easy?

2. Discuss the phrasing in "So Wahr Die Sonne Scheinet" and how you shape phrases using dynamics. Demonstrate by singing your voice part in the Sight-Singing exercise.

3. How well did you pronounce the German text?

4. If your ensemble were to get a grade for sight-singing, what would it be? What would your individual grade be? Why?

Sight-Singing

This Sight-Singing exercise is designed to prepare students to:

- Sight-sing using solfège and hand signs or numbers.
- Read pitches in the head before singing them.
- Identify and shape phrases.

Have students:

- Read through the Sight-Singing exercise directions.
- Read each voice part rhythmically, using rhythm syllables.
- Sight-sing through each part separately using solfège and hand signs or numbers.
- Sing all parts together.

Singing: "So Wahr Die Sonne Scheinet"

Identify characteristics of the Romantic period in the text.
Have students:

- Read the text on page 201.
- Discuss the characteristics of the Romantic period.
- Distinguish between the concept of romantic as having to do with love, and Romantic as a period during which sentimentality was expected.
- Read the text of "So Wahr Die Sonne Scheinet" in English, deciding whether it is extravagant, exaggerated, or expressive. (Accept any viable opinion that is supported by fact.)

Suggested Teaching Sequence

1. Review Vocal Warm-Up.
Warm-up voice and body. Sing with pitch accuracy.
Have students:

- Review the Vocal Warm-Up on page 200.
- Identify the quarter rest, and make a silent gesture to give it full value if necessary. (nod or wink)
- Identify the melodic steps and skips, and tune them carefully.
- Preview their voice part of "So Wahr Die Sonne Scheinet" for melodic steps and skips, isolating and practicing any that look like a potential problem.

2. Review Sight-Singing.
Read and sight-sing. Identify and interpret phrases.
Have students:

- Review the Sight-Singing exercise on page 200.
- Distinguish between sight-reading, which can be silent, and sight-singing, which must be done out loud.
- Sing the exercise all the way through without stopping.
- Identify the phrases and determine how many phrases are in the piece. (It is possible to see this exercise as having two or four phrases, with two being the more sophisticated answer.)
- Discuss how to shape phrases by making a crescendo from the beginning to the peak, and then releasing tension to the end of the phrase.
- Determine where they will perform the peak and ending of each phrase, and practice shaping the phrases.
- Look at the notation for "So Wahr Die Sonne Scheinet" to determine that they have learned the notation for the first page.

So Wahr Die Sonne Scheinet

(As Surely as the Sun Shines)

Robert Schumann, Op. 101, No. 8, Edited by William D. Hall
English Text: Alice and Kurt Bergel

SATB and Piano

202 *Choral Connections Level 4 Mixed Voices*

TEACHING STRATEGY

Shaping with Dynamics—The Next Level

Have students:

- Add another level of sophistication to their performance of "So Wahr Die Sonne Scheinet" by making a small crescendo and decrescendo on every dotted quarter and eighth combination.
- Identify these as falling dynamics within the larger shaping of the whole phrase.

p
Früh - ling blüht,
blooms the Spring,
so wahr
As sure - ly
hab' ich em-pfun - den,
as I have felt it,
Früh - ling blüht,
blooms the Spring,
mf
Früh - ling blüht,
blooms the Spring,
wie ich dich
Hold - ing you
Früh - ling blüht,
blooms the Spring,
p
mf
du liebst mich,
you love me,
wie ich dich,
I love you,
halt' um-wun - den,
so close in my arms,
mf
dich lieb' ich,
I love you,
3

3. Sight-sing "So Wahr Die Sonne Scheinet" using solfège and hand signs or numbers.

Have students:

- In full ensemble, slowly sight-sing the piece as far as they are able without stopping.
- Divide into voice sections (SATB) and read each part rhythmically, using rhythm syllables, adding dynamics to shape the phrases.
- Still in sections, sing with solfège and hand signs or numbers, identifying and working on problem areas.
- Sing the piece through, using solfège and hand signs or numbers, with full ensemble.

4. Learn the German pronunciation.

Have students:

- Using Blackline Master 16, *Translation and Pronunciation Guide for "So Wahr Die Sonne Scheinet,"* echo the text by phrases.
- Read through the piece, speaking the German text in rhythm.
- Sing the piece with correct German pronunciation.

5. Working through the piece for melodic and harmonic pitch accuracy.

Have students:

- Sing the piece slowly on *loo,* tuning each pitch and chord carefully.
- Sing the entire piece in full ensemble, shaping phrases using dynamics, singing accurate pitches and using correct German pronunciation.

VOCAL DEVELOPMENT

To encourage vocal development, have students:

- Demonstrate good vocal tone by singing with tall, open vowels and clearly articulated consonants in German and in English.
- Create a resonant sound by keeping consistently large spaces in the mouth and pharynx. Feel the stretch of the throat when beginning a yawn.
- Energize sustained tones by increasing the breath support and dynamic level.
- Sustain phrases with controlled breath, using the rests for dramatic effect. Move forward through the phrases.
- Perform the rhythms precisely while conducting and speaking rhythm or speaking the text in rhythm.
- Emphasize the two-note phrases by "leaning into" the first note and tapering off on the second note.
- Listen for diphthongs in *shines, I,* and *my*. Sing or sustain the first vowel sound and barely sing the second vowel sound with the next syllable.
- Demonstrate the correct singing of the *r* consonant after a vowel when singing in English. It should be almost silent, as in *other* and *ever.*
- Feel the arched contour of each musical phrase as it begins, builds, then tapers off. The dynamics are constantly changing and should reflect the melodic contour.
- Balance the chords between the parts by listening to them. Try adding more weight to one part to determine the effect on the chord.

Music after Beethoven

Beethoven was a towering figure at the beginning of the Romantic period, and explored the Classical forms and styles as far as anyone could imagine.

Have students:

- Imagine what the next new style of popular music might be.
- Think about the problem Schumann and other Romantic composers had after Beethoven had "used up" all the possibilities for the symphony and large choral works.
- Discuss the need for great vision and perseverance to create a new style or genre of music.
- Apply this to the creative vision of the Romantic painters. (van Gogh, Matisse, Degas, Lautrec, Manet, and Monet)

Assessment

Informal Assessment

During this lesson, students showed the ability to:

- Identify and sing melodic steps and skips in the Vocal Warm-Up exercise.
- Sight-read and sight-sing using solfège and hand signs or numbers in the Sight-Singing exercise.
- Identify and shape phrases using dynamics in the Sight-Singing exercise.
- Sing with pitch accuracy, shaping phrases and dynamics, and using correct German pronunciation in "So Wahr Die Sonne Scheinet."

Student Self-Assessment

Have students:

- Evaluate their performance with the How Did You Do? section on page 201.
- Answer the questions individually. Discuss them in pairs or small groups and/or write their responses on a sheet of paper.

Individual Performance Assessment

To further demonstrate accomplishment, have each student:

- Into a tape recorder in an isolated space, sing their voice part to the Sight-Singing exercise, demonstrating pitch accuracy with melodic steps and skips.
- In a quartet, sing measures 1–8 of "So Wahr Die Sonne Scheinet" while being videotaped or audiotaped, demonstrating dynamic shaping of phrases.
- In a quartet, sight-read, then sight-sing a section of any piece from this book.

Extension

Romantic Characteristics
Have students:

- Describe the musical characteristics of "So Wahr Die Sonne Scheinet."
- Recall the musical characteristics typical of music in the Romantic period.
- Construct a Venn diagram, demonstrating the overlapping characteristics of the two that define the piece as an example of Romantic music.
- Identify the characteristics of music of the Classical period that have been used by Schumann in this piece.

Listening to Schumann and His Contemporaries
Have students:

- Research the life and compositions of Schumann.
- Listen to his compositions, and learn more about each composition from record jackets or in listening guides.
- Listen also to music by Schubert, Mendelssohn, Chopin, Liszt, and other Romantic composers.
- Read Schumann's writings from *Die Neue Zeitschrift fur Musik*, his publication and journal of advanced musical trends of the Romantic period.
- Share findings with the class through an oral report or a creative presentation.

National Standards

The following National Standards are addressed through the Extension and bottom-page activities:

1. Singing, alone and with others, a varied repertoire of music. **(a, b, c)**
5. Reading and notating music. **(a, b, c)**
6. Listening to, analyzing, and describing music. **(a, b, c, e, f)**
7. Evaluating music and music performances. **(a, b, c)**
8. Understanding relationships between music, the other arts, and disciplines outside the arts. **(a, b, c, d)**
9. Understanding music in relation to history and culture. **(a, b, c, d)**

Preparing a Performance of "So Wahr Die Sonne Scheinet"

Have students:

- Sight-read and sing through the piece once.
- Individually or in groups, review the musical characteristics of choral music of the Romantic period on page 197.
- Review the piece, determining how it should be interpreted to provide a convincing and authentic Romantic performance.
- Write their ideas as recommendations to the conductor.
- Optional: Have five groups of students each prepare one of the pieces from this section of the text, Making Historical Connections. Students should introduce, rehearse, and prepare the ensemble with your guidance, and then conduct the piece in concert.

mp
wie du mich,
I love you,
wie du mich, du mich,
And I love you,
wie du mich,
I love you,
wie du mich, du mich,
And I love you,
wie du mich,
I love you,
wie du mich, du mich,
And I love you,
wie du mich,
I love you,
wie du mich, du mich,
And I love you,
f
p
wie du mich!
You love me!
wie du mich!
You love me!
wie du mich!
You love me!
wie du mich!
You love me!
dim.

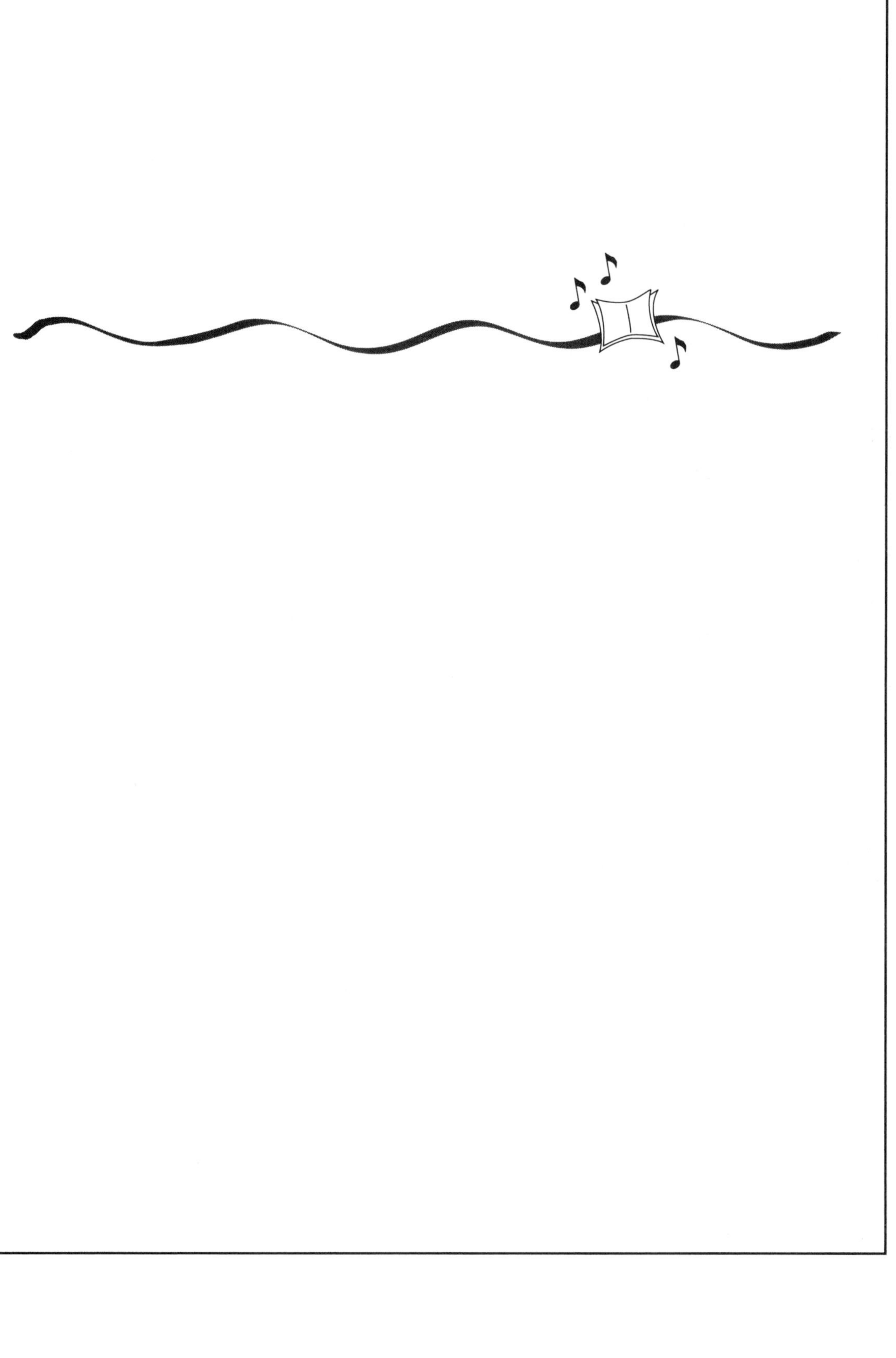

1900–Present

Contemporary Period

Focus

OVERVIEW

Understanding the development of choral music during the Contemporary period.

OBJECTIVES

After completing this lesson, students will be able to:

- Identify musical forms, figures, and developments of the Contemporary period.
- Identify specific performance characteristics to be used in Contemporary choral music.
- Describe the relationship between music and the prevailing social, cultural, and historical events and ideas during the Contemporary period.
- Describe characteristics of Contemporary art and music.
- Identify popular Contemporary music forms and figures.

CHORAL MUSIC TERMS

Define the Choral Music Terms for students, giving pronunciation, and answering questions.

Introducing the Lesson

Introduce the Contemporary period through visual art.

Analyze the painting by Flack on page 210 and the architecture on page 212 of the text.

Have students:

- Study the painting and opera house.
- Discuss the information provided at the bottom of pages 211 and 212 in your Teacher's Wraparound Edition.

***Hannah: Who She Is* is an example of Photorealism by Audrey Flack, (1931–). Throughout her career, Flack has experimented with new techniques, just as contemporary musicians have adopted new techniques for their works. This is a portrait of Flack's daughter, depicted as the goddess-heroine of a Joe Pintauro poem. Composer John Cage (1912–1992) and others continually seek new media for their compositions during the twentieth century.**

1982. *Who She Is.* Audrey Flack. Oil over acrylic on canvas. 17.78 x 12.7 cm (7 x 5'). National Museum of Women in the Arts, Washington D.C.

TEACHER'S RESOURCE BINDER

Fine Art Transparency 5, *Hannah: Who She Is,* by Audrey Flack

Optional Listening Selections:

Music: An Appreciation, 6th edition

Symphony of Psalms, First Movement: CD 7, Track 23

"Sacrificial Dance": CD 7, Track 20

National Standards

6. Listening to, analyzing, and describing music. **(a, b, c, d, e, f)**
7. Evaluating music and music performances. **(a, b)**
8. Understanding relationships between music, the other arts, and disciplines outside the arts. **(a, b, c, d, e)**
9. Understanding music in relation to history and culture. **(a, c, d, e)**

Contemporary Period

1900–Present

After completing this lesson, you will be able to:

- *Discuss the importance of the political changes that have taken place during the Contemporary period.*
- *Describe the effects of technological changes on the musical interests of the public.*
- *Identify at least four experimental approaches developed during the Contemporary period.*
- *Discuss some of the characteristics of Contemporary choral music.*

Change, experimentation, innovation, and reaction—these have been the central features of life and the arts during the Contemporary period, the time from 1900 until right now.

Changes During the Contemporary Period

The twentieth century has been a time of political change and upheaval. The Contemporary period has seen two world wars; many localized wars; revolutions in Russia, China, and many other countries; the Great Depression; the Cold War; and the rise and fall of Communism in many countries. These political events have brought repeated and often radical changes in the lives and ideas of people around the world.

Predictably, change has been a characteristic of the artworks created during the Contemporary period. Painters have experimented with Expressionism, Fauvism, Nonobjectivism, Cubism, Futurism, Fantasy, Surrealism, Abstract Expressionism, Op Art, Pop Art, and many other styles. Photography has developed as a new and varied art form. Sculptors have created works ranging from abstract to super-real. Architects have worked in such varied materials as steel-and-glass and poured concrete, as well as more traditional brick, stone, and wood.

Contemporary Music

Technological developments during the Contemporary period have had an unusually strong effect on music and on the musical interests of the public. Early in the century, phonographs and records made music readily available to anyone who wanted to hear it. As the century progressed, radio and then television brought news and entertainment—including news about music, live musical performances, and new musical recordings—into most homes. Now tapes, CDs, and computers with interactive software have brought higher quality sounds and images to the public. In addition, synthesizers are making it easier and less expensive for everyone to become involved in making and listening to music.

COMPOSERS

Richard Strauss (1864–1949)
Ralph Vaughan Williams (1872–1958)
Arnold Schoenberg (1874–1951)
Charles Ives (1874–1954)
Béla Bartók (1881–1945)
Igor Stravinsky (1882–1971)
Sergei Prokofiev (1891–1952)
Paul Hindemith (1895–1963)
George Gershwin (1898–1937)
Aaron Copland (1900–1990)
Samuel Barber (1910–1981)
Gian Carlo Menotti (1911–)
Benjamin Britten (1913–1976)
Leonard Bernstein (1918–1990)
Philip Glass (1937–)
André Thomas (unknown)

ARTISTS

Henri Rousseau (1844–1910)
Edvard Munch (1863–1944)
Wassily Kandinsky (1866–1944)
Henri Matisse (1869–1954)
Pablo Picasso (1881–1973)
Georgia O'Keeffe (1887–1986)
Jackson Pollock (1912–1956)
Andrew Wyeth (1917–)
Andy Warhol (1930–1987)
Audrey Flack (1931–)

AUTHORS

George Bernard Shaw (1856–1950)
Sir Arthur Conan Doyle (1859–1930)
Edith Wharton (1862–1937)
Beatrix Potter (1866–1943)
Gertrude Stein (1874–1946)
Robert Frost (1874–1963)

CHORAL MUSIC TERMS

abstract
aleatoric music
dissonance
Expressionism
fusion
Impressionism
twelve-tone music

Suggested Teaching Sequence

1. Examine the Contemporary period.

Have students:

- Read the text on pages 211–215.
- Share what they know about the composers, artists, and authors listed on this page.
- Read, discuss, and answer the review questions on page 215 individually, in pairs, or in small groups.
- Discuss their answers with the whole group, clarifying misunderstandings.

2. Examine the Contemporary period in historical perspective.

Have students:

- Turn to the time line on pages 212–215 and read the citations.
- Discuss why these events and people are significant to the Contemporary period.
- Compare each of these events to what they know occurred before and after the Contemporary period.
- Discuss both how these events have affected music and the other arts, and how music and the other arts may have led to new ideas.
- Identify the current state of music and the arts, and what trends seem to be emerging toward the future.

Hannah: Who She Is

Audrey Flack created *Hannah: Who She Is* in 1982. Currently it hangs in the National Museum of Women in the Arts in Washington, D.C. This piece reflects the Contemporary period's blending of physical and emotional, popular and high culture, and concrete and abstract. At this time, it would be interesting to note the similarities and differences between the fine art pieces of all five periods, particularly the portrait of the Renaissance and the representation of women as the artist's subject.

3. Define the musical aspects of the Contemporary period.

Have students:

- Review the changes in music from the Romantic to the Contemporary period.
- Identify the musical styles and forms that dominated the period.
- Review the characteristics of vocal music during the period.
- Identify well-known musical figures of the period.
- Listen to music from the period, analyzing and pointing out characteristics of the music as they are heard.

Wright Brothers' flight **1903**

1905 First motion picture theater opens

Model T Ford introduced **1908**

1914–1918 World War I

The New York Metropolitan Opera House in Lincoln Center, built in the 1960s, blends traditional forms of architecture with a contemporary interest in emphasizing starkness of decoration.

c. 1960. The New York Metropolitan Opera House, Lincoln Center. New York, New York.

This public involvement in music has encouraged change, experimentation, and innovation. Like visual artists, Contemporary composers have developed many different styles. Most have used and adapted music forms from the Romantic period, including the opera, symphony, and art song, but have adapted those forms to new styles and to new musical ideas. Two major stylistic developments of the century have been **Impressionism,** *works that create a musical picture with a dreamy quality through chromaticism,* and **Expressionism,** *bold and dynamic musical expression of mood with great dissonance.*

The New York Metropolitan Opera House

The Metropolitan Opera House is one of several theaters and arts structures that comprise Lincoln Center, a contemporary arts complex in New York City. The building has a contemporary design, with an abundance of glass and a soaring feeling. Behind the glass windows, on both sides, are large Chagall abstract paintings created especially for this space. It would be interesting to again compare the architecture of all five periods, noting similarities and differences. Each period builds on the previous, while also consciously breaking into new avenues of creative expression.

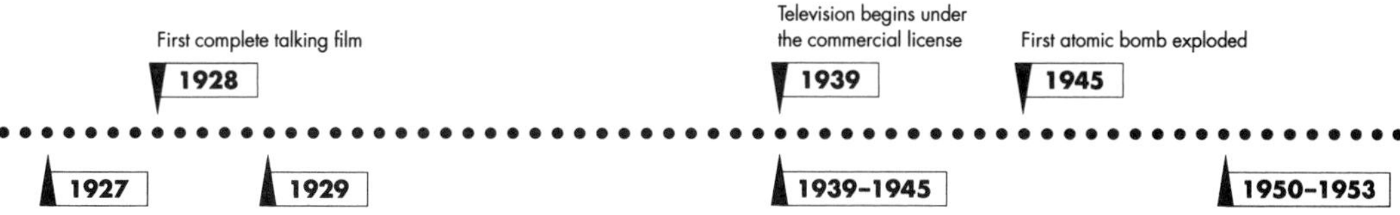

Many kinds of experimentation have been part of the musical development of the Contemporary period. Some composers have worked in an objective style, emphasizing music for its own sake. Their compositions are **abstract,** *focusing on lines, rows, angles, clusters, textures, and form.*

Contemporary composers have also experimented with **dissonance,** *chords using seconds, fourths, fifths, and sevenths,* rather than with traditional chords built on intervals of a third. These compositions lack a tonal center and a scale-oriented organization of pitch.

Another area of experimentation has been **twelve-tone music.** In this organization, *the twelve tones of the chromatic scale are arranged in a tone row, then the piece is composed by rearranging and arranging the "row" in different ways—backward, forward, in clusters of three or four pitches, and so on.* Many critics consider this approach more satisfying for composers than for listeners.

Composers of the Contemporary period have also experimented with **aleatoric**—or chance—**music,** *works that have only a beginning and an end, with the rest left to chance.* An aleatoric composition usually does have a score, but each performer is given the freedom to make many choices, including which pitch to begin on, how long to hold each pitch, how fast to play, and when to stop playing.

Fusion, *a blending of musical styles,* has been an important part of musical experimentation and change during the Contemporary period. Traditional and folk styles from all parts of the world have blended with each other and with new, popular styles. Popular music and art music have also been blended; pop singers, for example, perform with professional orchestras and choirs, and symphony orchestras perform special arrangements of folk songs.

The Contemporary period is still evolving, and the changes and experiments of the period are ongoing.

Contemporary Pop Styles

Listed below are some American styles that have emerged during the twentieth century. Some of them are still thriving, and new ones are being created every day.

- *Ragtime*—an early style of jazz, very rhythmic and syncopated.
- *Musical Stage Music*—centered around Broadway and Hollywood musicals.
- *Blues*—simple, harmonious melodies with two phrases the same, then one different.
- *Spiritual*—songs originating in the slave culture, usually religious in theme.
- *Jazz*—strong but rhythmic understructure supporting solo and ensemble improvisation.
- *Rock*—strong, steady beat.
- *Country*—based on the folk style of the southern rural United States or on the music of the cowboy.

Assessment

Informal Assessment

During this lesson, students showed the ability to:

- Share what they know about the Contemporary period.
- Describe musical characteristics, styles, forms, and personalities of the Contemporary period.
- Describe specific performance characteristics of Contemporary choral music.
- Describe and compare characteristics of several arts of the Contemporary period.
- Describe the social, historical, and cultural environment of the Contemporary period.
- Describe and identify Contemporary music styles.

Student Self-Assessment

Have students:

- Review the questions in Check Your Understanding on page 215.
- Write a paragraph describing how much they understand about the development of music during the Contemporary period.

Individual Performance Assessment

To further demonstrate accomplishment, have each student:

- Select a Contemporary vocal composition.
- Review the piece, identifying the characteristics of the Contemporary period that appear in the piece.
- Prepare a performance guide, discussing the performance style appropriate for the piece, based on characteristics of Contemporary vocal music performance.
- Optional: Rehearse and prepare an ensemble to perform the piece, and conduct it during the concert.

Extension

Comparing Contemporary Music to the Other Arts of the Period

Have students:

- Define the characteristics of Contemporary art and architecture.
- Compare the characteristics of music and one or more other arts within the Contemporary period, comparing uses of characteristic elements, artistic processes, and organizing principles.

Networking with Your Community

Contemporary music is performed today by most performing ensembles, both vocal and instrumental. Experimental music and multimedia presentations are frequently being staged, and many are created for video formats only. Popular music concerts of many styles are frequent. Have students:

- Explore the newspapers, radio and television schedules, and performing group programs to find information about local performances of many styles of Contemporary music.
- Attend a performance of a Contemporary music style that is out of the ordinary or unfamiliar.
- Discuss and critique the performance upon return to the ensemble, identifying positive features of the composition and performance, and making suggestions for improvement or change.

1957 First Earth satellite put into orbit by USSR

1958 U.S. satellite put into orbit

1961 Soviet cosmonaut orbits the Earth

1962 U.S. astronaut John Glenn orbits the earth

1969 U.S. astronauts land on the Moon

1971 Voting age lowered from 21 to 18

- *Folk*—folk songs and composed songs that tell a story or sometimes have a social message.
- *Reggae*—a fusion of rock and Jamaican rhythms, instruments, and language.
- *Calypso*—an island style with strong chords and syncopation.
- *Tejano*—a fusion of Mexican and country music.
- *Zydeco*—a fusion of African-American, Cajun, and French Canadian rhythms, instruments, and lyrics.

Characteristics of Choral Music During the Contemporary Period

The Contemporary period does not have a characteristic style of music. Still, it is possible to consider major trends in the meter and stress, tempo, dynamics, texture, expressive aspects, and tone quality of Contemporary choral music.

In many Contemporary choral works, meter and stress are an important area of experimentation. A strong rhythmic drive is part of many modern choral works, and unusual changes in meter are often used. The influence of jazz can be heard in the rhythms of many Contemporary choral compositions.

Composers have also experimented with the tempo of their works. The use of various tempos to emphasize changes in mood is common. Dramatic pauses are also used by some composers to heighten the effect of changes in tempo and mood.

The dynamics of most Contemporary choral works reflect an increased use of extremes. Rapid changes and strong accents are often used.

The texture of many Contemporary choral works is developed through dissonance and different methods of resolution. Again, there is much variety in the texture of Contemporary choral music.

The expressive aspects of modern choral works also show unusual variety. In some works, objectivity is very important; in others, personal emotions are dramatically expressed.

The tone quality of Contemporary choral works is typically not extreme. Vibrato is used infrequently and usually with restraint. The skills, control, and exact tuning so important in Renaissance music is again a major feature in the successful performance of Contemporary choral works.

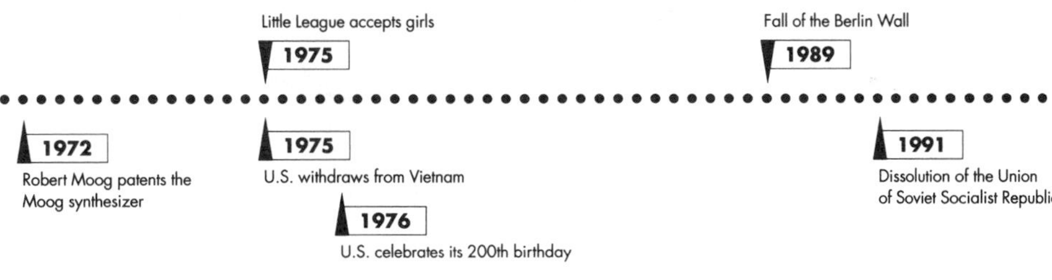

Check Your Understanding

Recall

1. What technological developments have affected public involvement in music during the Contemporary period?
2. What is Impressionism?
3. What is abstract music?
4. What is dissonance?
5. Identify two choices that a performer of aleatoric music might be required to make.
6. What is fusion?
7. What style of music has influenced the rhythm of many Contemporary choral works?
8. What tone quality is typically used in Contemporary choral works?

Thinking It Through

1. Eventually, what we call the Contemporary period will be given a new name that reflects the most important trends and developments of the era. What name do you think it will be given? Why?
2. "The more things change, the more they stay the same." What relevance, if any, do you think this statement has for the development of music during the Contemporary period? Explain and defend your opinion.

ANSWERS TO RECALL QUESTIONS

1. Phonographs, radio, television, audio- and video tapes, CDs, computers, and synthesizers.
2. A style of works that create a musical picture with a dreamy quality through chromaticism.
3. Music that focuses on lines, rows, angles, clusters, textures, and form.
4. Chords using seconds, fourths, fifths, and sevenths.
5. Beginning pitch, duration of each pitch, tempo, and when to end the piece.
6. A blending of musical styles.
7. Jazz.
8. Not extreme, with infrequent vibrato and usually with restraint.

Non-European Cultures and Music During the Contemporary Period

Have students:

- Identify the dates of the Contemporary period.
- Research what has been happening in at least one non-European culture during those years. Possible other cultures are Asian (Asian Russia, China, Middle East, India, Indonesia, Polynesia, and so on); African (any of the African countries or tribal cultures); Hispanic (music of the Spanish-speaking Caribbean Islands, Central America, and South America); and Native and Aboriginal (including Native American, Native Alaskan, Mayan, Aztec and other Native cultures that migrated across the Bering Strait; and Aboriginal of Australia).
- Research what non-European music is being performed in your community or presented through the media, and observe or participate in non-European musical experiences.

The Contemporary in Depth

The Contemporary period is an exciting theme for a unit of study, providing an opportunity for students to interact with their arts community. Have students identify areas of interest individually, in pairs, or in groups. Have them write a contract or proposal with you, describing the topic to be researched, a time line describing methodology, stages, and completion dates, and the nature of the final product to be presented. (paper, performance, lecture, multimedia presentation, and so on)

Each student should be encouraged to choose some task where learning and rigor will be required. Students should also be aware of all other projects going on, and link ideas together whenever possible.

CONTEMPORARY CONNECTIONS

Listening to... Contemporary Music

This feature is designed to expand students' appreciation of choral and instrumental music of the Contemporary period.

CHORAL SELECTION: *Symphony of Psalms*, First Movement, by Stravinsky
Have students:

- Read the information on this page to learn more about Stravinsky's *Symphony of Psalms.*
- Watch as you follow a transparency of Blackline Master, Listening Map 9.

Using the Listening Map
Move from top to bottom, following the melodic representations.
Have students:

- Listen as you "bang" on the piano. Discuss whether your "banging" is music or nonmusic.
- Listen as you describe Contemporary music as being quite varied. Discussion can include ideas such as atonal (music without a definite key or tonal center), ragtime (precursor to jazz), jazz (allows for improvisation and has much syncopation), new ways to play instruments (i.e., Cage's compositions for plucked piano strings), and so on. Tell students about Stravinsky's works.
- Look at a piece of abstract Contemporary art and discuss the similarities and differences between Contemporary art and music. List the qualities.
- Listen to the recording as you point to the transparency.

CONTEMPORARY CONNECTIONS

Listening to . . . Contemporary Music

CHORAL SELECTION

Stravinsky — *Symphony of Psalms,* First Movement

Igor Stravinsky (1882–1971), a Russian composer, was a leader of contemporary music for over 50 years. His *Symphony of Psalms* (1930) is a masterpiece for chorus and an orchestra with no violins, violas, or clarinets, but including two pianos. It is chantlike in its melodies. He used power as well as humor to produce diversity in his work.

INSTRUMENTAL SELECTION

Stravinsky — "Sacrificial Dance" from *Le Sacre du printemps*

In 1912, the director of the Russian ballet, Sergei Diaghilev, commissioned Stravinsky to write for his troupe. *The Rite of Spring* was a story of a solemn pagan rite: wise elders, seated in a circle, watching a young girl dance herself to death as a sacrifice to the god of spring. At its premiere in 1913, a riot erupted because the audience was so shocked by the pagan primitivism of the dancing and the harsh dissonance and pounding rhythms of the music.

TEACHER'S RESOURCE BINDER
Blackline Master, Listening Map 9
Blackline Master, Listening Map 10

Optional Listening Selections:
Music: An Appreciation, 6th edition
Symphony of Psalms, First Movement: CD 7, Track 23
"Sacrificial Dance": CD 7, Track 20

National Standards

This lesson addresses the following National Standard:

8. Understanding relationships between music, the other arts, and disciplines outside the arts. **(a)**

Introducing . . .

"I Hear America Singing"

André J. Thomas

Setting the Stage

You will enjoy singing "I Hear America Singing" because of its positive text and lively syncopated rhythms. It shows the freedom of contemporary composers who have taken the older form (the spiritual) and reshaped it to fit modern thought. The spiritual expressed the hope of the slaves for release from oppression. Similarly, this piece expresses the hope that America will someday be freed from the oppressions of racism and bigotry and be able to "sing together. . . ," "walk together. . . ," and "shout together. . .," as one nation and one people.

Meeting the Composer

André J. Thomas

Dr. André J. Thomas is currently Director of Choral Activities and Associate Professor of Music Education at Florida State University in Tallahassee, Florida. Previously, he was on the faculty at the University of Texas in Austin, Texas. In addition to composing and arranging music, he is constantly in demand as an adjudicator, clinician, and director of honor choirs.

INSTRUMENTAL SELECTION: "Sacrificial Dance" from *Le Sacre du printemps* by Stravinsky

Have students:

- Read the information on page 216 to learn more about "Sacrificial Dance."
- Watch as you follow a transparency of Blackline Master, Listening Map 10.

Using the Listening Map

Start at the first "explosive" section and follow the sections to the end. Listen for the low, pulsating strings playing softly to move to the "piercing" section. Note: The first "explosive" and "piercing" sections are very long.

Have students:

- Predict visual qualities of the ballet that accompanies this story. (bold colorful costumes, and fast, chaotic dancing)
- Look at the listening map as you point out the different sections and the adjectives used to describe these sections. (explosive, piercing, frenzied)
- Listen to the recording as you point to the transparency. Then make a list of the qualities of the music. (dissonant, rhythmic, disjunct, strong use of dynamics)

INTRODUCING. . .
"I Hear America Singing"

This feature is designed to introduce students to the Contemporary Lesson on the following pages.

Have students:

- Read Setting the Stage on this page to learn more about "I Hear America Singing."
- Read Meeting the Composer to learn more about André J. Thomas.
- Turn the page and begin the Contemporary Lesson.

ASSESSMENT

Individual Performance Assessment

To further demonstrate understanding of Contemporary music, have each student:

- Demonstrate the relationship between Contemporary art and Contemporary music, using the worksheet that accompanies *Symphony of Psalms.*
- Use the worksheet that accompanies "Sacrificial Dance" to show the relationship between Contemporary ballet and Contemporary music.

CONTEMPORARY LESSON

I Hear America Singing

Quoting the Spiritual "Walk Together, Children"

COMPOSER: André J. Thomas

Focus

OVERVIEW

Syncopated rhythm; accurate pitches; exuberant spiritual style.

OBJECTIVES

After completing this lesson, students will be able to:

- Identify and perform syncopated rhythms.
- Sing pitches accurately.
- Sing in exuberant spiritual style.

CHORAL MUSIC TERMS

Define the Choral Music Terms for students, giving pronunciation, and answering any questions that may arise.

Warming Up

Vocal Warm-Up

This Vocal Warm-Up is designed to prepare students to:

- Sing with activated breathing and diaphragmatic control.
- Warm-up with movement.
- Sing with pitch accuracy.

Have students:

- Read through the Vocal Warm-Up directions.
- Sing, following your demonstration.

CONTEMPORARY
LESSON

I Hear America Singing

CHORAL MUSIC TERMS

accurate pitches
exuberant style
spiritual
syncopated rhythms

Quoting the Spiritual "Walk Together, Children"

COMPOSER: *André J. Thomas*

VOICING

SATB

PERFORMANCE STYLE

Exuberantly
Accompanied by piano

FOCUS

- Identify and perform syncopated rhythms.
- Sing pitches accurately.
- Sing in exuberant spiritual style.

Warming Up

Vocal Warm-Up

Sing this exercise first on *yo-ho-ho*. Keep the jaw lowered when forming the *y* and form *ee* with your tongue, making the *y* sound free of excess motion.

Now add body movement. Begin with both fists up in front of your shoulders. Extend the fists straight up on beat 1, down on beat 2, and continue alternating through the exercise. Add marching in place after you have mastered the arm motion. Check yourself for pitch accuracy.

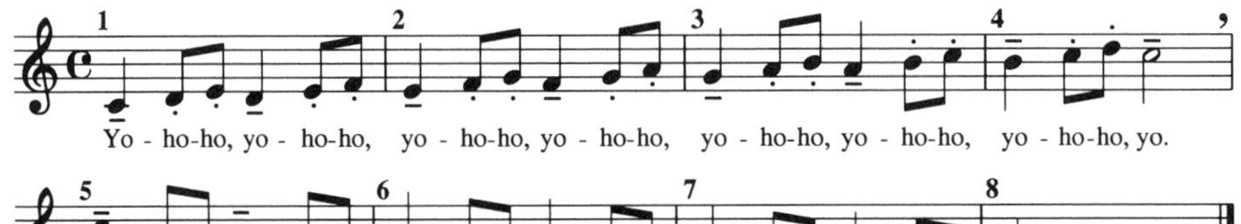

1 2 3 4
Yo - ho-ho, yo - ho-ho, yo - ho-ho, yo - ho-ho, yo - ho-ho, yo - ho-ho, yo - ho-ho, yo.
5 6 7 8
Yo - ho-ho, yo - ho-ho, yo - ho-ho, yo - ho-ho, yo - ho-ho, yo - ho-ho, yo - ho-ho, yo.

Sight-Singing

Sight-sing this exercise using solfège and hand signs or numbers. You can sing the parts separately or in combination. Rotate the parts, so everyone has a chance to sing the syncopations in Part I against the straighter rhythm of the harmony parts. Tune your pitches accurately.

Sing this exercise in an exuberant, spiritual style. How is this different than just reading the notes?

TEACHER'S RESOURCE BINDER

Blackline Master 17, *Syncopated Rhythms*, page 99

National Standards

1. Singing, alone and with others, a varied repertoire of music. **(a, b, c)**
5. Reading and notating music. **(a, b)**
6. Listening to, analyzing, and describing music. **(a, b, c, e, f)**
7. Evaluating music and music performances. **(a)**
9. Understanding music in relation to history and culture. **(a, d)**

Singing: "I Hear America Singing"

Music from Africa has made a great impact on music around the world. One of the early forms of African-American music was the spiritual. Combining rhythms and melodic elements of African music with the English language, the early slaves used songs to keep their spirits up. These songs have become symbols of the struggle for equality that still continues around the world.

Find the spirit of "I Hear America Singing" in the combination of old and new, rhythm and melody, music and text. Let that spirit guide your singing style.

Now turn to the music for "I Hear America Singing" on page 220.

HOW DID YOU DO?

Music has the power to communicate the message of a people. Think about your preparation and performance of "I Hear America Singing."

1. How are syncopated rhythms important to this piece? Sing Part I of the Sight-Singing exercise to demonstrate your ability to sing syncopated rhythms.

2. Even when you sing in exuberant style, the pitches must be accurate. Choose a section of "I Hear America Singing" that you can perform in tune, and demonstrate your ability. Choose the most difficult part you can sing accurately.

3. How is exuberant spiritual style different from plain singing? What do you need to do the same, and what is different? Demonstrate with a small group by singing first without this style, then with it.

4. Describe your feelings when you perform "I Hear America Singing" then tell, as best you can, what makes you feel that way.

Sight-Singing

This Sight-Singing exercise is designed to prepare students to:

- Sight-sing using solfège and hand signs or numbers.
- Read and sing syncopated rhythms against more straight ones.
- Sing in exuberant spiritual style.

Have students:

- Read through the Sight-Singing exercise directions.
- Read each voice part rhythmically, using rhythm syllables.
- Sight-sing through each part separately using solfège and hand signs or numbers.
- Sing all parts together.

Singing: "I Hear America Singing"

Discuss the background and style of the spiritual.

Have students:

- Read the text on page 219.
- Discuss the spiritual as one of the early forms of African-American music in the United States.
- Read the text of "I Hear America Singing," identifying the newly composed beginning and ending, and the spiritual, from measures 17–33.

Suggested Teaching Sequence

1. Review Vocal Warm-Up.
Warm-up voice and body. Sing with pitch accuracy.
Have students:

- Review the Vocal Warm-Up on page 218.
- Work on keeping the jaw in place to pronounce the *y*.
- Add the suggested movement, first just the arms, then with marching in place.
- Check for pitch accuracy as they sing.

2. Review Sight-Singing.
Sight-sing using solfège and hand signs or numbers. Identify and sing syncopated rhythms against straighter rhythm. Sing in exuberant spiritual style.
Have students:

- Review the Sight-Singing exercise on page 218.
- Identify the syncopated rhythms.
- Rotate the parts so everyone sings the syncopation against the straighter harmony parts.
- Sing in exuberant spiritual style, identifying the characteristics of this sound. (slightly heavier tone, plenty of breath support throughout, pushing the rhythm a bit, particularly the syncopation, allowing the notation to be a guide)

Dedicated to the 1993 ACDA Honor Choir, Anton Armstrong, Conductor

I Hear America Singing

Also available: Special TRAK-PAK 15 (99/1009)

Duration: approx. 2:45.

The Spiritual

The enslaved Africans brought music with the following elements to the New World: syncopation, polyrhythm, pentatonic and gap scales, and the idea of music combined with body movements.

From the suffering of the ocean crossing and a life of subjugation, they created a new genre, the "spiritual," or religious folk song of the slave. It revealed their unhappiness and suffering, taught facts, sent messages, provided a common language, and shared religious rituals and beliefs. In the spiritual, the singer must express a personal connection with the deity or God. The spiritual reflects a true historical picture of the lives of slaves as told by slaves themselves.

3. Sight-sing "I Hear America Singing" using solfège and hand signs or numbers.

Have students:

- Read and clap the primary rhythmic elements of the piece as a full ensemble, at measures 9–10, 17–18, and 33–34.
- Divide into voice sections (SATB) and read each part rhythmically, using rhythm syllables, adding dynamics to shape the phrases.
- Still in sections, sing with solfège and hand signs or numbers at a much slower tempo than usual, identifying and working on problem areas.
- Divide into sections and recite the text rhythmically for each voice part.
- Sing the piece through in full ensemble, with the text, using appropriate dynamics and phrasing.

4. Work through the piece for accuracy.

Have students:

- Sing the unison sections together, checking for rhythmic and melodic accuracy.
- Work through the three-part treble and three-part, tenor-bass parts at measures 33–40, slowly singing the chordal progressions out of context to perfect tuning.
- Work through the piece for melodic accuracy.
- Sing the piece in full ensemble with rhythmic and melodic accuracy, in exuberant spiritual style.

17

sing - ing to - day. __ O, walk to-geth - er, chil - dren.

17

Don't you __ get wea - ry. Walk to-geth - er, chil - dren.

Don't you get wea - ry. __ Talk to-geth - er, chil - dren.

TEACHING STRATEGY

Accuracy

Have students:

- Sing "I Hear America Singing" through on the staccato syllable *doot.*
- Listen for accuracy of rhythm, pitch, and harmony.
- Work on areas that need attention.

Don't you _ get wea ry. There's a great camp meet - ing in the

Prom-ised Land._ 25 *mp* Sing to-geth - er, chil - dren.

Don't you _ get wea - ry. Sing to-geth - er, chil - dren.

VOCAL DEVELOPMENT

To encourage vocal development, have students:

- Demonstrate exuberant vocal tone by singing with tall, open vowels and clearly articulated consonants, supported by firmly controlled breath.
- Create a full resonant sound by keeping a consistently large space in the mouth and pharynx.
- Energize sustained tones by increasing the breath support and dynamic level.
- Perform the rhythms precisely while conducting and speaking rhythm or speaking the text in rhythm. Emphasize the syncopated and tied rhythm. At measure 17, sing rhythms precisely with a relaxed feeling.
- Feel the arched contour of each musical phrase as it begins, builds, then tapers off. The dynamics should reflect the drama of the text and the excitement of the rhythm.
- Communicate between the voice parts with the quasi call-and-response style of the spiritual.
- Balance the chords between the parts by listening to them. Try adding more weight to one part to determine the effect on the chord. Note the places where the voices sing in unison.

f

Don't you get wea - ry.___ Shout to-geth - er, chil - dren.

Don't you_ get wea - ry. There's a great camp meet - ing in the

33

Prom-ised Land.__ Great camp meet - ing,

A -

CONNECTING THE ARTS

Artistic Freedom in the Contemporary Period

Have students:

- Research how artistic freedom has been the focus of controversy during the Contemporary period, using written sources, interviews with art educators and/or practicing artists in the community, and through electronic mail and Internet research sites.
- Identify ways in which the arts have shaped society and been influenced by social, political, and economic pressures.
- Identify any parallels they may find between the arts as a social tool in the Contemporary period, and in other periods of history, or in other cultures.

Assessment

Informal Assessment

During this lesson, students showed the ability to:

- Sing with melodic accuracy in the Vocal Warm-Up.
- Identify and sing syncopated rhythms in the Sight-Singing exercise.
- Perform in exuberant spiritual style in the Sight-Singing exercise.
- Sing with pitch and rhythmic accuracy, with syncopated rhythms, in exuberant spiritual style in "I Hear America Singing."

Student Self-Assessment

Have students:

- Evaluate their performance with the How Did You Do? section on page 219.
- Answer the questions individually. Discuss them in pairs or small groups and/or write their responses on a sheet of paper.

Individual Performance Assessment

To further demonstrate accomplishment, have each student:

- Into a tape recorder in an isolated space, clap or sing an assigned example from Blackline Master 17, *Syncopated Rhythms,* demonstrating the ability to identify and perform syncopation.
- In a quartet, sing measures 9–17 of "I Hear America Singing" while being videotaped or audiotaped, demonstrating pitch accuracy.
- In full ensemble, sing measures 17–33 of "I Hear America Singing" while being videotaped or audiotaped, demonstrating exuberant spiritual style singing.
- Write a critique of their video- or audiotaped performance, discussing rhythmic and pitch accuracy, and stylistic correctness of the performance.

Extension

Contemporary Characteristics

Have students:

- Describe the musical characteristics of "I Hear America Singing."
- Recall the musical characteristics typical of Contemporary music.
- Construct a Venn diagram, demonstrating the overlapping characteristics of the two that define the piece as an example of Contemporary music. (There will be many characteristics of Contemporary music outside the middle, demonstrating how many styles are available during this period.)
- Identify the characteristics of music of the Contemporary period that have been used by Thomas in this piece.

Adding Instruments to the Performance

Have students:

- Create a guitar line from the piano accompaniment.
- Add electric bass, guitar, and drum parts to the piece.

Listening to Spirituals as Choral Pieces

Have students:

- Research and listen to recordings or live performances of choral literature with spirituals as a source.
- Determine which they think are good, average, or poor, explicitly stating their criteria and the reasons for them.

Walk _ to - geth - er hand _ in hand _ to-geth-er in peace.

Sing! A - mer - i-ca's sing - ing, A - mer - i - ca's sing - ing, A -

SA

45

— We're go-ing to sing

mer - i - ca's sing - ing. Sing!

and nev - er

National Standards

The following National Standards are addressed through the Extension and bottom-page activities:

1. Singing, alone and with others, a varied repertoire of music. **(a, b, c)**
4. Composing and arranging music within specified guidelines. **(b, c)**
5. Reading and notating music. **(a, b, c)**
6. Listening to, analyzing, and describing music. **(a, b, c, e, f)**
7. Evaluating music and music performances. **(a, b, c)**
8. Understanding relationships between music, the other arts, and disciplines outside the arts. **(a, b, c, d)**
9. Understanding music in relation to history and culture. **(a, b, c, d)**

Preparing a Performance of "I Hear America Singing"

Have students:

- Sight-sing through the piece once.
- Individually or in groups, review the musical characteristics of Contemporary choral music on page 213.
- Review the piece, determining how it should be interpreted to provide a convincing and authentic Contemporary performance.
- Write their ideas as recommendations to the conductor.
- Optional: Have five groups of students each prepare one of the pieces from this section of the text, Making Historical Connections. Students should introduce, rehearse, and prepare the ensemble with your guidance, then conduct the piece in concert.

mf
61
There's a great camp meet - ing,
mf
And A - mer - i - ca's sing - ing!
mf
great camp meet - ing.
f
Great camp meet - ing, great camp meet - ing in the Prom-ised
f
f

Land!
great camp meet - ing, A - mer - i - ca's sing - ing,
8vb
Prom-ised Land!
great camp meet - ing, Prom-ised Land!
(8vb)

Additional Performance Selections

WARM-UPS FOR PERFORMANCE SELECTIONS

Over the Rainbow

COMPOSER: Harold Arlen
ARRANGER: Kirby Shaw
TEXT: E. Y. Harburg

Warming Up

Vocal Warm-Up
Have students:
- Read the Vocal Warm-Up directions.
- Identify the octave leap, and be sure to aim a little high, getting over the top of the upper pitch.
- Work to keep a smooth, connected style.

Now turn to page **236**.

Three Canticles for Treble Voices

COMPOSER: Paul Liljestrand
TEXT: Christina Rossetti, Horatius Bonar, and Blanche Mary Kelly

Warming Up

Vocal Warm-Up
Have students:
- Read the Vocal Warm-Up directions.
- Identify the sequenced thirds moving upward and downward.
- Sing with different articulations.

Now turn to page **241**.

WARM-UPS FOR PERFORMANCE SELECTIONS

VOICING
SATB

PERFORMANCE STYLE
Mystical
A cappella

Over the Rainbow

Warming Up

Vocal Warm-Up
Practice the octave leaps in this exercise, striving to keep a smooth and connected style. Move up by half steps on the repeat.

Now turn to page **236.**

VOICING
SSAA

PERFORMANCE STYLE
Slowly
Accompanied by piano

Three Canticles for Treble Voices

Warming Up

Vocal Warm-Up
Sing this exercise using solfège and hand signs or numbers. Move up and down by half steps on the repeats. This exercise will increase your ability to sing ascending and descending intervals of a third in sequence.

Now turn to page **241.**

VOICING
TTBB
PERFORMANCE STYLE
With awe
Accompanied by keyboard

Who Is He in Yonder Stall?

Warming Up

Vocal Warm-Up

Sing this exercise using solfège and hand signs or numbers, then with the text. Move up or down by half steps on the repeats. This broken-chord exercise will prepare you to sing the melody of "Who Is He in Yonder Stall?" Use good diaphragmatic action on the eighth notes.

Now turn to page **248.**

VOICING
SATB
PERFORMANCE STYLE
Swing
Accompanied by piano

42nd Street

Warming Up

Vocal Warm-Up

Sing this exercise on *doot*, keeping your energy throughout. Notice the accents on the upbeats, and minor mode. Move up by whole steps on each repeat. The accented upbeats and minor mode will get you in the mood for "42nd Street."

Now turn to page **254.**

Who Is He in Yonder Stall?

COMPOSER: Robert H. Young
TEXT: Benjamine Hanby

Warming Up

Vocal Warm-Up

Have students:

- Read the Vocal Warm-Up directions.
- Sing the exercise using solfège and hand signs or numbers, then with the text.
- Practice using good diaphragmatic action on the eighth notes.

Now turn to page **248**.

42nd Street

COMPOSER: Harry Warren
ARRANGER: Mark Brymer
TEXT: Al Dubin

Warming Up

Vocal Warm-Up

Have students:

- Read the Vocal Warm-Up directions.
- Sing the pattern on the syllable *doot.*
- Use a quick tempo and clear articulation with a swing style.

Now turn to page **254**.

Blue Moon

COMPOSER: Richard Rodgers
ARRANGER: Ruth Artman
TEXT: Lorenz Hart

Warming Up

Vocal Warm-Up
Have students:

- Read the Vocal Warm-Up directions.
- Sing the pattern on solfège and hand signs or numbers, then on *doo, vah, boh, meh, nee* or any combination of these syllables.
- Improvise using the scat syllables provided to produce a pop feeling.

Now turn to page **265**.

Desde el Fondo de Mi Alma

Spanish Folk Song
COMPOSER: Domingo Santa Cruz
ENGLISH TRANSLATION: Hugh Ross

Warming Up

Vocal Warm-Up
Have students:

- Read the Vocal Warm-Up directions.
- Sing the pattern on solfège and hand signs or numbers, and then on *loo*, using legato articulation.
- Sing the altered tone accurately.

Now turn to page **273**.

VOICING
SATB

PERFORMANCE STYLE
Upbeat swing
Accompanied by guitar, bass, drums, and B♭ trumpet

Blue Moon

Warming Up

Vocal Warm-Up

Sing this exercise first using solfège and hand signs or numbers, then on *doo, vah, boh, meh, nee,* or a combination of these syllables. Articulate the rhythms with impeccable precision. Move up or down by half steps on each repeat.

Now turn to page **265.**

VOICING
SSA

PERFORMANCE STYLE
Tranquilly
A cappella

Desde el Fondo de Mi Alma

Warming Up

Vocal Warm-Up

Sing this exercise first using solfège and hand signs or numbers, then on *loo* with legato articulation. Move up by half steps on each repeat. The tranquil, connected style and altered tone will get you ready for "Desde el Fondo de Mi Alma."

Now turn to page **273.**

VOICING

SATB

PERFORMANCE STYLE

Slow swing
Accompanied by piano with optional bass, drums, and guitar

Georgia on My Mind

Warming Up

Vocal Warm-Up

Sing this exercise in jazz style. Swing the eighth notes into triple feel. Change the scat syllables at will—be creative. Move up or down by half steps on the repeat.

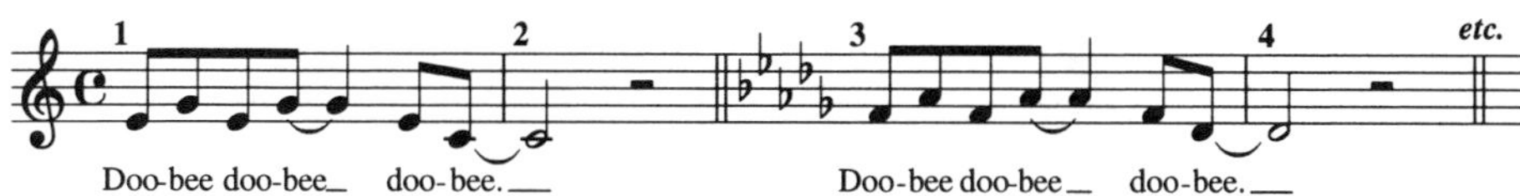

Now turn to page **276.**

VOICING

SATB

PERFORMANCE STYLE

Tenderly
Accompanied by piano

Love Never Ends

Warming Up

Vocal Warm-Up

Sing this exercise first on solfège and hand signs or numbers, then with text, continuing up by half steps on the repeats. Notice the octave leap in preparation for "Love Never Ends." Sing with full, deep breaths and confidence to produce a rich, supported, legato sound.

Now turn to page **283.**

Georgia on My Mind

COMPOSER: Hoagy Carmichael
ARRANGER: Teena Chinn
TEXT: Stuart Gorrell

Warming Up

Vocal Warm-Up

Have students:

- Read the Vocal Warm-Up directions.
- Read and sing the pattern, swinging the rhythm so the first in each set of two eighths gets more time, feeling like a quarter eighth triplet.
- Change the scat singing syllables, continuing long enough to become not only comfortable but inventive.

Now turn to page **276**.

Love Never Ends

Adapted from I Corinthians 13
COMPOSER: Elizabeth Volk

Warming Up

Vocal Warm-Up

Have students:

- Read the Vocal Warm-Up directions.
- Sing, using solfège and hand signs or numbers, and then text.
- Identify the octave leap and be sure to aim a little high, getting over the top of the upper pitch.
- Work on a warm, lyric tone.

Now turn to page **283**.

Over the Rainbow

Performance Tips

Rhythmic Focus

Explain to students:

- The rhythm is straightforward and predictable.
- This would be a good piece to sight-sing for accuracy.

Melodic Focus

Tell students:

- The familiar melody is dominant in the soprano part, but appears in the bass part briefly.
- The expected octave leap occurs in a comfortable and singable range.

Over the Rainbow

Music by Harold Arlen
Lyrics by E.Y. Harburg
Arranged by Kirby Shaw

SATB, A cappella

Mystical (♩ = 80)

Solo
S — *mf* — *stagger breathing to* [B] — Loo loo loo loo loo loo loo loo
A — *mf* — *stagger breathing to* [B] — Loo loo loo loo loo loo loo loo loo loo loo loo loo loo loo loo
T B — *mf* — *stagger breathing to* [B] — Loo loo — Loo loo loo loo

Piano (for rehearsal only) — *mf*

[A] *mf*

Some - where O - ver The Rain - bow way up high,

Loo loo loo loo loo loo loo

Loo loo loo loo loo loo loo loo loo loo loo loo loo loo loo loo

Loo loo loo loo loo loo

"Over the Rainbow"

This piece was composed for and sung in *The Wizard of Oz,* which has become a classic in movie form. Judy Garland's performance of the piece has set the standard by which many show singers measure their talent. The wishful and hopeful message makes it a popular concert tune anytime.

More Ideas

- This arrangement is for a cappella ensemble.
- The first section includes a soloist over SATB choir accompaniment, followed by a traditional four-part style arrangement.
- Keep a smooth and connected style throughout.

Hot Spots

- Measures 30–32 are a modulation. Rehearse them very slowly and gradually build up to performance tempo.

Program Ideas

- This familiar piece makes a good ending or encore number for a spring concert.

"Papillon, Tu Es Volage"—Thompson
"The Prayer of Saint Francis"—Clausen
"The One Who Stands Alone"—Martin
"Over the Rainbow"—Arlen/Shaw

VOCAL DEVELOPMENT

To encourage vocal development, have students:

- Demonstrate good vocal tone by singing with tall vowels and clear consonants.
- Energize sustained tones by increasing the breath support and dynamic level.
- Energize the ostinato of the SATB chorus by staggered breathing and giving a phrase shape to each repetition. Tune the intervals and resulting chords carefully with solfège.
- Sustain phrases by staggering the breathing and moving forward through the phrases.
- Listen for diphthongs (two vowel sounds when one vowel sound is written) in such English words as *way, high, fly, why, I, day,* and *find.* Sing or sustain the first vowel sound and barely sing the second vowel sound with the next syllable.
- Demonstrate the correct singing of the *r* consonant after a vowel in English. It should be almost silent, as in *where, over, there's, heard, birds, star,* and *far.*
- Feel the arched contour of each musical phrase as it begins, builds, then tapers off. The dynamics should reflect the melodic contour and meaning of the text.
- Tune the modulation at measure 30 with solfège and hand signs, leading into the new key.

16 17 18 19

S A: fly.

Some - where O - ver The Rain - bow blue - birds fly, they fly.

20 21 22 23

Birds fly O - ver The Rain - bow, why, then oh why can't I?

unis.

Birds Some

[B] 25 26

Loo loo unis. div sop.

Loo loo loo loo. Where clouds are far be -

day I'll wish up - on a star and wake up where the clouds are far be - hind me.

27
28 loo
29 loo
hind me.
loo loo
loo loo
Where troub-les melt like lem-on drops, a - way a - bove the chim-ney tops, that's
30 cresc.
31 ritard. [C] a tempo f
33
That's where you'll find me. Oh Some - where O - ver The Rain - bow
cresc.
where you'll
a tempo
34 blue - birds fly.
35 36 mf
no breath
blue - birds, blue - birds fly. Birds fly.
fly.

Child-like
unis.
mp
O - ver The Rain - bow, why then, oh why can't I? If
unis.
mp
hap-py lit-tle blue-birds fly be - yond the rain-bow why, oh why can't
no cresc.
1 or 2 voices on each part
mp
I?
no breath
S
Loo loo loo loo loo loo loo.
A
Loo loo loo loo loo loo loo loo loo loo loo loo loo.
T
B
Loo loo
Loo loo loo.

To the Nurses' Choir, West Suburban School of Nursing

Three Canticles for Treble Voices

1. Tune Me, O Lord

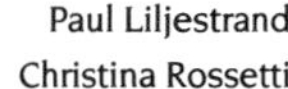

Paul Liljestrand
Christina Rossetti

Three Canticles for Treble Voice

Tune Me, O Lord

Performance Tips

Rhythmic Focus

Explain to students:

- While learning the piece, sing the rhythms in strict rhythm.
- After learning the piece, apply rubato style to the rhythm and tempo. The rhythm will still be performed as notated, but the tempo will allow it to bend.

Melodic Focus

Tell students:

- The melody should dynamically soar to its climax at measure 8, and then fade.

More Ideas

- Sing this piece in an acoustical setting that allows the sound to echo for an unforgettable experience.

Hot Spots

- This piece is a cappella, while the next, "The Master's Touch," has a piano accompaniment. Stay in tune.

Program Ideas

- These three subtle, introspective pieces would fit well toward the beginning of a program.

Composer Paul Liljestrand

Paul Liljestrand is a native of Montclair, New Jersey. He received his musical training primarily through the Juilliard School, graduating from its high school, bachelor's, and master's programs. He resumed his musical training after two years of active service with the armed forces, earning a master of sacred music degree from the School of Sacred Music at New York's Union Theological Seminary.

The Master's Touch

Performance Tips

Rhythmic Focus

Explain to students:

- This piece requires the ability to sustain long notes expressively, shaping them with dynamics.

Melodic Focus

Tell students:

- The flowing lines of this piece require a wide range and excellent tonal production.

2. The Master's Touch

Paul Liljestrand
Horatius Bonar

To wake the mu - sic and the beau - ty needs the
To wake the sound and beau - ty needs the
Mas - ter's touch, The sculp - tor's chis - el keen.
rit.
Mas - ter's touch, The sculp - tor's chis - el keen.
rit.
rit.
a tempo
cresc.
Great Mas - ter, touch me with Thy hand;
a tempo
cresc.
a tempo
cresc.
ped.

More Ideas

- Sing this piece in an acoustical setting that allows the sound to echo for an unforgettable experience.

Hot Spots

- This number requires full range of dynamics and pitch, a rich tone, and stamina.

Program Ideas

- This number could be performed without "Tune Me, O Lord" and "The Mirror." However, when all three are performed together, the experience is more fulfilling.

Let not the mu- sic in me die.
Great Sculp - tor , hew and
Great Sculp-ture,
pol - ish me; Nor let there hid - den, lost, Thy
pol - ish me; Nor let there hid - den, lost, Thy
form with - in me lie.
p

p
Spare not the stroke, Do with me as Thou wilt.
p
Let there be nought un - fin - ished, bro - ken,
marred.
f
Com-plete, O Lord, Thy
marred.
f
Com-plete Thy

cresc.
ff
pur - pose, that I may be-come Thine im - age,
cresc.
ff
cresc.
ff
p
O, my God, and
p
p
a tempo
pp
Lord.
a tempo
pp
a tempo
pp

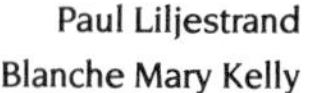

The Mirror

Performance Tips

Rhythmic Focus

Explain to students:

- The rhythms are straight-forward.
- The changing meter complicates the piece.
- Conducting the meters while speaking the words in rhythm, in strict tempo, will make it familiar.

Melodic Focus

Tell students:

- The melodic range is reasonable.
- The dynamics make it more difficult to negotiate the pitch.
- Begin achieving the goal to sing the pitches within the dynamic range by singing the piece on *loo.*

More Ideas

- Set a mystical mood here by slightly shading the stage lights.

Hot Spots

- The parallel motion in this piece must be precisely tuned.

Who Is He in Yonder Stall?

Performance Tips

Rhythmic Focus
Explain to students:

- There are no complicated patterns in this piece.
- The rhythmic flow is steady and sure.
- The meter changes from 3/4 to 4/4 at points that quickly become predictable.

Melodic Focus
Tell students:

- The piece is based on the old hymn tune "Hanby," and flows nicely over the rich harmonies.

For Wesley Gilliland and the Baylor University Men's Glee Club

Who Is He in Yonder Stall?

Based on "Hanby"

Music by Robert H. Young
Text by Benjamine Hanby

TEACHING STRATEGY
Changing Meter

Have students:

- Conduct the meter of this piece as they sing to become familiar with the meter changes.

More Ideas

- There are five verses with keyboard interludes. Each verse is slightly varied, either by voicing or by mood to reflect the text.

Hot Spots

- Although this piece looks easy, it is deceptive. The most challenging aspect is tuning the chords throughout.

Program Ideas

- This piece would make a great tenor-bass festival selection. If there are not enough first tenors, the second alto can handle the range of most of the pitches.

"Ave Maria"—Biebl
"Starlight Lullaby"—Lane
"I Saw Three Ships"—Fissinger
"Who Is He in Yonder Stall?"—Young
"God Rest You Merry, Gentlemen"— Koudelka

VOCAL DEVELOPMENT

To encourage vocal development, have students:

- Demonstrate rich vocal tone by singing with tall, open vowels and clearly articulated consonants, supported by firmly controlled breath.
- Create a full resonant sound by keeping a consistently large space in the mouth and pharynx.
- Carry the phrases through, using adequate breath support and staggered breathing. Feel the forward movement of the melodic line.
- Energize sustained tones into the succeeding tones by increasing the breath support and intensity level.
- Modify vowels to create consistent vocal shape and tone on such words as *wondrous, glory, story, crown* (with diphthong), and *stands.*
- Demonstrate the correct singing of the *r* consonant after a vowel when singing in English. It should be almost silent, as in *Lord, yonder, shepherds,* and *where.*
- Balance the chords between the parts by listening to them. Try adding more weight to one part to determine the effect on the chord. Note the places where the voices sing in unison.

20

He, who stands and weeps, at the grave where Laz - 'rus

sleeps? 'Tis the Lord, O won-drous sto - ry, 'tis the

Lord, O

At His 28 feet we hum-bly

Lord, the King of glo - ry; Mm

Lord, the

Lord, the

fall; Crown Him, crown Him Lord of all! Who is

crown

crown Him

* No breath

33
He in Cal-vary's throes, asks for bless - ings on His
foes? 'Tis the Lord, O won-drous sto - ry, 'tis the
Lord, the King of glo - ry. At His
41
feet we hum - bly
feet we
fall; Crown him, crown Him Lord of all!
crown Him

Who is
He who from the grave comes to seek and help and
He who
save? It is the Lord, O won-drous sto - ry, 'tis the
Lord, O

57
p
Lord, the King of glo - ry. At His feet we hum - bly
Lord, the feet we
fall; Crown Him, crown Him Lord of all! At His
f
slower
pp
crown Him
61
sotto voce
rit.
feet we hum - bly fall; Crown Him, crown Him Lord of all!

42nd Street

Performance Tips

Rhythmic Focus

Explain to students:

- The rhythm drives this piece and is critical.
- The tempo is fast, accents provide excitement, and it is in swing style.
- The rhythm is syncopated.
- Watch for unexpected changes. The first part of the piece is likely to be well known, but there are additional sections which need to be read carefully.
- Keep the rhythm crisp and accurate for maximum effect.

Melodic Focus

Tell students:

- This piece is in a minor key but is upbeat in mood.
- The melody is sung in unison by all in several spots.
- The ranges are comfortable.

42nd Street

Music by Harry Warren
Words by Al Dubin
Arranged by Mark Brymer

SATB* and Piano with Optional Instrumental Accompaniment

1930's Swing-time (♩ = 184)

Dm/A A7♭9 Dm

(Street noise: "Taxi, taxi!"...chatter, laughter, horn honking, cars passing, etc...)

ff

(Drum cues)

Soprano Alto Tenor Bass

7 All mf

Up - town, _

N.C.

(Drums continue) mf

Solo

East Side,

All mf

Down - town, _

Solo

West Side,

*Available for SATB, SAB and SSA Instrumental Pak includes Parts for Trumpet I & II, Tenor Sax/Clarinet, Trombone, Synthesizer, Guitar, Bass and Drums. ShowTrax Cassette also available

TEACHING STRATEGY

Musical Theater

"42nd Street" is from the Broadway musical show of the same title.

Have students:

- Learn more about the musical from which this piece comes.
- Watch a video of the musical.
- Add some simple choreography or costumes to make the piece even more entertaining.

More Ideas

- Although piano accompaniment is adequate, keyboard, bass, and drums would add vitality to this number.

Hot Spots

- The jazz harmonies at measures 29 and 30 are tricky, but the passage is repeated throughout the piece, so students soon master these chordal progressions.
- The almost sudden shift to E minor at measure 71 is tricky at first, but after becoming thoroughly familiar with the preceding interlude, the students will easily prepare for the key change.

Tap Dance Choreography

If you have students who are skilled in tap dancing, have them:

- Watch a performance of "42nd Street" and adapt the choreography to perform with the ensemble, or
- Create a tap dance routine for all or part of the piece.

Program Ideas

- This piece is a perfect opening number in a pop show.

"42nd Street"—Brymer
"Siyahamba"—Moore
"Keep Your Lamps!"—Thomas
"Over the Rainbow"—Shaw
"I Hear America Singing"—Thomas

Unis.
taking you to Forty Second Street.
Dm/A Bb9 Bm7b5/A A7b9#5 Dm Em7b5
Dm/F A7#9/E Dm Em7b5 Dm/F A7#9/E
mf
36
Unis.
Hear the beat of dancing feet,
Unis.
Oo
Dm Em7b5 Dm/F Em7b5 Dm A7#9/E

it's the song I love the mel-o-dy of
Dm/F A7/E Dm C/E F Gm Dm/A B♭9
Unis.
For-ty Sec-ond Street.
Unis.
Bm7♭5/A A7♭9♯5 Dm Em7♭5 Dm/F A7♯9/E
45
Unis.
Lit - tle "nif-ties" from the Fif-ties, in - no - cent and
Unis.
B♭9

sweet; sex - y la - dies from the Eight - ies,
G9
53
f
who are in - dis - creet. They're side by side, they're
Db9 A7#5 Dm Em7b5 Dm/F A7b9/E
glo - ri - fied. Where the un - der - world can
Dm6 A7#9/E Dm/F A7/E Dm C/E F Gm

meet the e - lite,
For - ty
Sec - ond
Street!
Unis.
Dm/A
B♭9
Bm7♭5/A
A7♭9♯5
Dm
Em7♭5
62
Unis.
Come and meet, come and meet, come and meet those danc-
Unis.
N.C.
A7♯5
Dm
- in' feet, those danc - in' feet on the Av - e - nue
Av - e - nue Av-
Dm
Em7♭5
Dm/F
Em7♭5
Dm
Em7♭5

Av - e - nue For - ty Sec - ond Street.
- e - nue
Dm/F Em7♭5 Bm7♭5/A A7♯5 Dm Em7♭5
71
Unis.
Hear the beat, hear the beat, hear the beat of danc-
N.C. B♭7♯5 E♭m
- in' feet of danc - in' feet on the Av - e - nue
Av - e - nue Av-
E♭m Fm7♭5 E♭m/G♭ Fm7♭5 E♭m Fm7♭5

Av - e - nue
For - ty
Sec - ond
For - ty
Sec - ond
- e - nue
Eb♭m/Gb♭
Fm7b5
Cm7b5/Bb
Bb7#5
C#m7b5/B
B7#5
79
Street!
C9
f
C13
C9
A9

* Performance note: Add additional measures for an optional tap dance break.

*pronounced spăwdy

Blue Moon

Music by Richard Rodgers
Lyrics by Lorenz Hart
Arranged by Ruth Artman

SATB, Accompanied with Optional Guitar, Bass, Drums and B♭ trumpet

Blue Moon

Performance Tips

Rhythmic Focus

Explain to students:

- The rhythms are typical pop rhythms and should pose no real problems.
- The rhythm must be felt together, and everyone must be accurate to have a swing feeling.

Melodic Focus

Tell students:

- There is a rather wide range required for basses; however, most of the high notes are doubled by the tenors.
- The close harmonies require careful tuning.
- The solo at measure 38 should be fun to experiment with using scat syllables as in the warm-up.

Rodgers and Hart

The team of Richard Rodgers and Lorenz Hart was quite successful in creating songs for Broadway musicals, movies, and dance bands, before and during World War II. Have students:

- Listen to examples of their music, and identify the characteristics that might have made them so popular.
- Read or watch documentary footage about their collaboration and how they worked together.
- Identify what takes the place of these songs in today's society.

More Ideas

- Add trumpet, drums, string bass, or bass guitar for that dance-band feeling.

Hot Spots

- The finger snaps must be precise, and many good musicians have problems with these offbeats.

Program Ideas

- Dress in 1950s attire for this piece.

"Forest Cool, Thou Forest Quiet"—Brahms
"African Noel"—Thomas
"Blue Moon"—Rodgers/Artman
"The One Who Stands Alone"—Martin

with-out a dream in my heart, —

S. div.

with-out a love of my own, — Oo — Blue — Moon, —

13

— You knew just what I was there — for; —

Blue Moon, — You knew I was the one for

*Guitar Eb maj7 Fm7 Eb maj7 Cm7

mf

Cyms. *ad lib.*

*Guitar: Use chord symbols above piano part.

TEACHING STRATEGY

The Dance-Band Sound

"Blue Moon" was written for a movie in 1934, and became a popular dance band piece during the 1940s and 1950s. It is bound to bring a sense of nostalgia to the older folks in the audience, but continues to be timelessly popular.

Have students:

- Research the movie from which this piece comes.
- Watch a video of the musical.
- Add some simple choreography or costumes to make the piece even more entertaining.
- Consider using a smaller ensemble to sing the piece, or perhaps the first part of the piece.

p unis.
You heard me say-ing a pray'r for Some-one I real-ly could care
p
you, You heard me say-ing a pray'r for
Fm7 Bb Ebmaj7/Bb Bb9/Ab Cm7/G Fm7 Fm7/Bb
p
cresc.
21 mp
for. Oo Oo
cresc.
div. unis. mf
Oo And then there sud-den-ly ap-pear'd be-fore
Eb 21 Fm7/Ab Bb
cresc.
mf
cont. sim. ad lib.
Ah Ah I heard some-
me the on-ly one my arms will ev - er hold;
Eb9 Cm Fm7 Bb7(2) Ebmaj7 Ebmaj7/G Ebmaj7

25
cresc.
bod-y whis-per, "Please a - dore me," And when I looked the moon had turned to gold!
cresc.
25
Ab m/F
Db 9
Gb maj7
Eb m7
Bb/F
F9
cresc.
mf
29
Blue_ Moon,
Now I'm no long-er a - lone,_
mf
Blue Moon,_
Bb 9
N.C.
29
Eb maj7
Fm7(4)
Bb
mf
With-out a dream in my heart,_
Now I'm no long - er a - lone, With-out a dream in my heart,_
Eb maj7
Fm7
Bb
Eb maj7
Cm7/G
Fm7

*Solo may be either trumpet or vocal, either as written or ad lib. Vocalist should ad lib. scat syllables.

end solo
end solo
Fm7(4)/A♭
E♭m
A♭m7/G♭
E♭(6)
47
S.
A.
mf
unis.
And then there sud-den-ly ap - peared be - fore me
T.
B.
unis.
mf
Sud-den-ly ap - peared be - fore me
E♭maj7 Fm/E♭ E♭
Fm7/A♭
B♭
E♭9
Cm
mf
the on-ly one my arms will ev-er hold._
I heard some-bod-y whis - per,
Fm7
B♭9
E♭maj7
Fm7
Gm7
N.C.
Fdim7
D♭9

And when I looked the moon had turned to gold!
"Please a-dore me," And when I looked the moon had turned to gold!
Gb(6)
Ebm7
Bb/F
F9
Bb9
N.C.
56
Blue Moon,
Now I'm no long-er a-lone,
Ebmaj7
Fm7(4)
Bb
With-out a dream in my heart,
Now I'm no long-er a-lone, With-out a dream in my heart,
Ebmaj7
Cm7
Fm7
Gm
Ebmaj7
Cm7
Fm7

Finger Snaps
end snaps
With-out a love of my own, Oh a love of my
F7/B♭
E♭maj7
Fm7
A♭/B♭

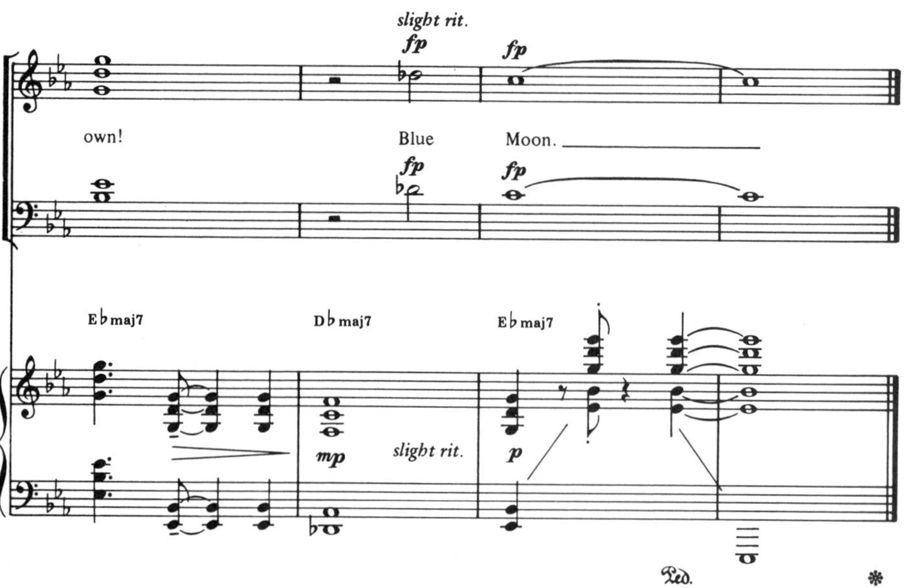
slight rit.
own! Blue Moon.
E♭maj7
D♭maj7
E♭maj7
slight rit.
Ped.

Desde el Fondo de Mi Alma

"Deep Within My Soul's Recesses" (Folk Song)

Music by Domingo Santa Cruz, Op.27
Words Anonymous
English translation by Hugh Ross

SSA with Piano Accompaniment

Desde el Fondo de Mi Alma

Performance Tips

Rhythmic Focus

Explain to students:

- The rhythms of the individual parts are relatively easy.
- Each voice part maintains an independent rhythm.
- Combining all three parts creates the rhythmic challenge for this selection.

Melodic Focus

Tell students:

- The lyrical melody, maintained by soprano I throughout the piece, is challenging because it is very chromatic and contains many challenging intervals.
- The mezzo and alto lines also include many altered tones and interesting leaps which require careful tuning.

TEACHER'S RESOURCE BINDER

Blackline Master 18, *Translation and Pronunciation Guide for "Desde el Fondo de Mi Alma,"* page 100

de to-do el mun - do han di - cho su dul - ce can -
crow with their sweet— cry, Thro' all the world are pro-claim -

— de to-do el mun - do han— di - cho su dul - ce can -
- ing with their sweet cry, Thro'— all the world are pro-claim -

— de to-do el mun - do han di - cho su— dul - ce can -
- ing with their sweet cry, Thro' all the world are pro - claim -

to, en Be - lén Cris - to na - ció — a mi - ti -
ing, That Christ is born in Beth - le - hem,- — To still our

to, en — — Be-lén Cris - to na - ció — a mi - ti -
ing, Christ — — is born in Beth - le - hem,- — To still our

to, en — Be - lén Cris - to na - ció — a mi - ti -
ing, That — Christ is born in Beth - le - hem, — To still our

aumentando

gar— nues-tro llan - to.— — Las mu-si - cas— — ce - les-tia -
mourn-ful com - plain-ing.. — And in the sky— — the mu-si -

gar nues-tro llan - to.— — Las mu - si - cas ce - les-tia -
mourn - ful com - plain - ing.. — And in the sky the mu-si -

gar nues - tro llan - to.— Las mu - si - cas ce - les-tia -
mourn - ful com - plain - ing.— And in the sky the mu-si -

les las a - ves con su tri - no can - tan la glo - ria ce -
cians, Those birds in song are trill - ing, Praise to the glo - ry ce -

les las a - ves con su tri - no can - tan la glo -
cians, Those birds — in song are trill-ing, Praise — to the glo -

les las a - ves con su tri - no can - tan gla -
cians, Those birds in song are trill-ing, Prais - ing the

More Ideas

- This a cappella piece could be performed by a small ensemble of excellent treble singers.
- Have a native Spanish speaker help with the pronunciation, perhaps making a tape to echo.

Hot Spots

- Be prepared for the crossing voice parts at measures 1–2, 8–9, and 23–25.
- The middle section of this ABA selection begins at measure 11 and continues to measure 30, modulating through several keys. This section alone may take several days of isolated rehearsal time.

Program Ideas

- Have one of the singers introduce the piece, discussing the musical characteristics that made this piece a challenge.

TEACHING STRATEGY

Self-Directed Learning

The challenge of this piece offers the students a chance to take part in their own learning and discover how to learn.

Have students:

- Sight-sing through the piece once as far as they can go.
- Identify the difficulties in each part.
- Work in sections to learn their own parts, devising their own strategies, and supporting one another to improve day by day.
- Put the piece together when all sections are ready, having prepared their own parts without help.

VOCAL DEVELOPMENT

To encourage vocal development, have students:

- Demonstrate good vocal tone by singing with pure, tall vowels in Spanish.
- Arch or lift the tone on melodic leaps by increasing the space in the mouth and pharynx.
- Energize sustained tones by increasing the breath support and dynamic level.
- Perform the rhythms precisely while conducting and speaking the rhythm or conducting and speaking the text in rhythm.
- Sustain phrases by staggering the breathing and moving forward through the phrases.
- Increase intensity on the repeated notes to feel forward movement of the melodic lines.
- Tune the chords carefully on the altered notes; follow the melodic line while adjusting the harmony between the parts.

Georgia on My Mind

Performance Tips

Rhythmic Focus

Explain to students:

- This piece has a slow swing feeling, which means the eighths take on a triple feel.
- Lots of quarter triplets and syncopations will keep them on their toes.
- The rhythmic notation is a guide and liberty can be taken, but must be taken as a group, rather than individually.

Melodic Focus

Tell students:

- The melody is mellow and smooth.
- The vocal jazz style requires fades and scoops—everything they would not do in a Mozart piece.

Georgia on My Mind

Music by Hoagy Carmichael
Lyrics by Stuart Gorrell
Arranged by Teena Chinn

SATB, Accompanied, with Optional Bass, Drums and Guitar

Composer Hoagy Carmichael

Born in 1899 in Indiana, Hoagy Carmichael was a jazz and popular music composer, singer, and pianist who earned a law degree before turning to music. His first successful song was "Stardust," composed in 1927. His melodies were slow and graceful with romantic texts, and became standard tunes for jazz musicians. In addition to "Georgia on My Mind," other popular songs include "Heart and Soul" (1938), "Thanks for the Memories" (1938), "Lazy River" (1931), and "The Nearness of You" (1940). Hoagy also composed for Broadway and performed on the radio, in films, and on television into the 1970s.

9

old sweet song__ keeps Geor - gia on my mind.__

9

Eb maj7 C9 Fm9 Bb7(13) Gm7 C7 Gb7

Ride Cym. H.H. Ride Cym. fill

13

Geor - gia,__ Geor-gia,__

Geor-gia,

13

Fm7 Gm7 Abm7 Bb7(b9) Ebmaj7 Cm9 G G9 G/B

Ens.

n.b.

17

a song__ of you,__ comes as sweet and clear__ as

n.b.

17

Cm9 /Bb F6/A Abm7 Db9 Eb6 C9(13) C/E

H.H. fill Ride Cym.

More Ideas

- Have fun with this piece, and let inhibitions go.
- The form is verse, bridge, recapitulation, bridge variation with an altered recapitulation, coda.

Hot Spots

- There are numerous intricate rhythms and jazz licks.
- Be sure to work the style to the maximum.

TEACHING STRATEGY

Swing Style

If students are not familiar with the swing style, and are a bit stiff, have them:

- Listen to swing music.
- Move to swing music.
- Watch video footage of swing style performance.
- Attend a dance-band performance.

Adding Movement

Movement will naturally flow in this lesson, beginning during the Vocal Warm-Up. It is probably impossible to sing this style without moving a bit. Have students:

- Loosen their bodies with some rolling of shoulders, snapping fingers forward and back, and shifting weight from one foot to the other in a carefree way.
- Move as they are comfortable as they sing.
- Interact with one another as they perform the piece.

Program Ideas

- This is an excellent piece for a jazz or show choir.
- Add optional instrumental backup with bass, drums, and guitar if possible.

"42nd Street"—Warren/Brymer
"Blue Moon"—Rodgers/Artman
"Over the Rainbow"—Arlen/Shaw
"Georgia on My Mind"—Carmichael/Chinn
"I Hear America Singing"—Thomas

VOCAL DEVELOPMENT

To encourage vocal development, have students:

- Demonstrate good vocal tone by singing with tall vowels and clear consonants.
- Perform the speech rhythms and sung rhythms precisely with emphasized accents. Note the difference between triplets and hidden syncopations.
- Energize sustained tones by increasing the breath support and dynamic level.
- Note the contrast from unison to part singing. Tune the half steps or minor seconds carefully—they are very close together.
- Balance the chords between the parts by listening to them. Try adding more weight to one part to determine the effect on the chord.
- Perform the rhythms precisely, especially at measure 37. When precise rhythm is understood, relax the rhythm and scoop the melody—feel the style!

37 Sop. div. *mp*

Doo doo doo doo doo doo doo doo

Oth-er arms reach out to me;

G7 F6/A E♭m6/B♭ Bm7(♭5) Cm7 G+/B E♭/B♭ F7/A

Ens. H.H. fill

doo doo doo doo doo doo doo doo

41 unis. *mf*

still in peace - ful

oth-er eyes smile ten - der-ly,

Cm G+/B E♭/B♭ F7/A 41 Cm Dm7 G

fill Ens. Ride Cym.

cresc. n.b.

dreams I see the road leads back to you.

Cm7 Am11(♭5) D7 Gm7 C7 Fm7 B7

fill fill

45
Geor - gia, my Geor - gia no peace I find,
Emaj9
G♯7
C♯m7
/B
Snare Drum
fill
H.H.
49
just an old sweet song keeps Geor - gia on my mind.
cresc.
Am6
D9
Emaj7
C♯9
F♯m7
B7
Ens.
Ride Cym.
S.D.
53
Just an old sweet song
G♯m7
C♯7
F♯m7
Crash Cym.
Ride Cym.
Ens.

* Start fall on second sixteenth after beat 4.

For my sister Barbara on the occasion of her wedding

Love Never Ends

Elizabeth Volk

Adapted from I Corinthians 13

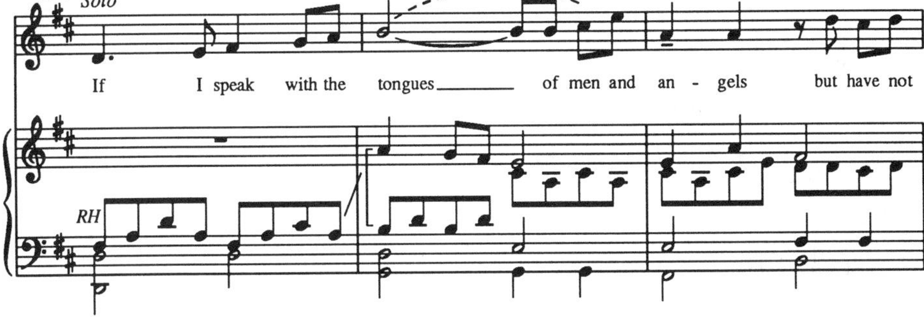

"Love Never Ends"

This piece is dedicated to the composer's sister on the occasion of her wedding.

Love Never Ends

Performance Tips

Rhythmic Focus

Explain to students:

- The piece is uncomplicated rhythmically, with basic rhythmic values dominating.
- Keep the emphasis on phrasing and extending the sound through the longer values.

Melodic Focus

Tell students:

- The lyric melody fits the text well.
- It begins with a soloist, and grows to four parts on the repeat.
- The soloist should prepare for the octave leap in measure 18.

More Ideas

- The form of this piece is strophic, two stanzas, with a modified ending for the second stanza.

Hot Spots

- A keen sense of intonation will be required throughout in the second stanza.
- Measure 30 requires precise unison.
- On measure 32, beat 2, altos and tenors must tune carefully.
- In measure 34, all parts must tune carefully.

23
bears all things, be - lieves all things, hopes all things, en -

dures all things,
love never - er

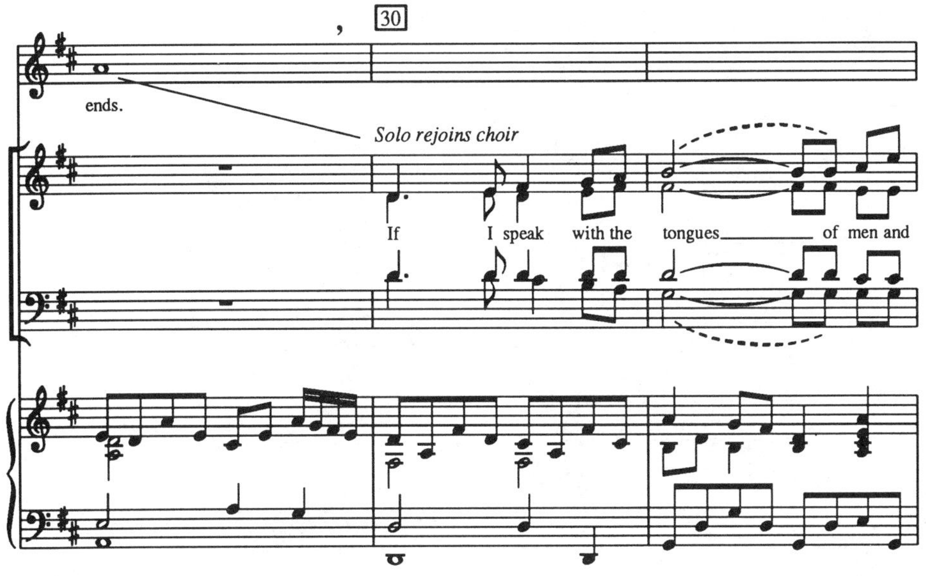
30
ends.
Solo rejoins choir
If I speak with the tongues of men and

Program Ideas

- Use this piece for baccalaureate or graduation.
- It would be great on a program with a Valentine's theme.

"Papillon, Tu Es Volage"—Thompson
"Love Never Ends"—Volk
"Over the Rainbow"—Arlen/Shaw
"Blue Moon"—Rodgers/Artman

VOCAL DEVELOPMENT

To encourage vocal development, have students:

- Demonstrate good vocal tone by singing with tall vowels and clear consonants.
- Energize sustained tones by increasing the breath support and dynamic level.
- Sustain phrases by staggering the breathing and moving forward through the phrases.
- Modify vowel sounds to an open *awh* on such words as *love* and *nothing.*
- Listen for the diphthong (two vowel sounds when one vowel sound is written) in the word *I.* Sing or sustain the first vowel sound and barely sing the second vowel sound with the next syllable.
- Demonstrate the correct singing of the *r* consonant after a vowel when singing in English. It should be almost silent, as in *bears, endures, never,* and *pow'rs.*
- Feel the arched contour of each musical phrase as it begins, builds, then tapers off. The dynamics should reflect the melodic contour and meaning of the text.
- Tune the melodic and harmonic intervals carefully, noting where unison parts grow into chords. Use solfège and hand signs to tune the parts.

or clang - ing

an - gels, but have not love I am as nois - y gong, or

cym - bal. 36

cym - bal. And if I have pro - phe - tic pow'rs and have not

love it pro-fit'h noth - ing, it pro-fit'h noth - ing. Love

41
en -
bears all things, be - lieves all things, hopes all things, en -
en -
dures all things,
love nev - er ends.
48
Faith, hope, love.
rit.
LH

Glossary

Choral Music Terms

a cappella (ah-kah-PEH-lah) [It.] Unaccompanied vocal music.

accelerando (*accel.*) (ah-chel-leh-RAHN-doh) [It.] Gradually increasing the tempo.

accent Indicates the note is to be sung with extra force or stress. (>)

accidentals Signs used to indicate the raising or lowering of a pitch. A sharp (♯) alters a pitch by raising it one-half step; a flat (♭) alters a pitch by lowering it one-half step; a natural (♮) cancels a sharp or a flat.

accompaniment Musical material that supports another; for example, a piano or orchestra accompanying a choir or soloist.

adagio (ah-DAH-jee-oh) [It.] Slow tempo, but not as slow as largo.

ad libitum (ad. lib.) [Lt.] An indication that the performer may vary the tempo, add or delete a vocal or instrumental part. Synonymous with *a piacere*.

al fine (ahl FEE-neh) [It.] To the end.

alla breve Indicates cut time; duple meter in which there are two beats per measure, the half note getting one beat. (¢)

allargando (*allarg.*) (ahl-ahr-GAHN-doh) [It.] To broaden, become slower.

aleatoric or chance music Music in which chance is deliberately used as a compositional component.

allegro (ah-LEH-groh) [It.] Brisk tempo; faster than moderato, slower than *vivace*.

allegro assai (ah-LEH-groh ah-SAH-ee) [It.] Very fast; in seventeenth-century music, the term can also mean "sufficiently fast."

altered pitch A note that does not belong to the scale of the work being performed.

alto The lower female voice; sometimes called contralto or mezzo-soprano.

anacrusis (a-nuh-KROO-suhs) [Gk.] *See* upbeat.

andante (ahn-DAHN-teh) [It.] Moderately slow; a walking tempo.

andante con moto (ahn-DAHN-teh kohn MOH-toh) [It.] A slightly faster tempo, "with motion."

animato Quick, lively; "animated."

anthem A choral composition in English using a sacred text. *See also* motet.

antiphonal Music performed by alternating ensembles, positioned in opposing locations, as in choirs or brass; first brought to prominence by Giovanni Gabrielli at St. Mark's Cathedral, Venice, in the Baroque period.

appassionato (uh-pah-shun-NAHT-oh) [It.] With deep feeling, passionately.

appoggiatura (uh-pah-zhuh-TOOR-uh) [It.] A nonharmonic tone, usually a half or whole step above the harmonic tone, performed on the beat, resolving downward to the harmonic tone.

aria (AHR-ee-uh) [It.] A song for a solo singer and orchestra, usually in an opera, oratorio, or cantata.

arpeggio (ahr-PEH-jee-oh) [It.] A chord in which the pitches are sounded successively, usually from lowest to highest; in broken style.

art song Expressive songs about life, love, and human relationships for solo voice and piano.

articulation Clarity in performance of notes and diction.

a tempo (ah TEM-poh) [It.] Return to the established tempo after a change.

atonality Music not organized around a key center.

augmentation A technique used in composition by which the melody line is repeated in doubled note values; opposite of *diminution*.

augmented The term indicating that a major or perfect interval has been enlarged by one-half step; as in C-F♯ (augmented fourth) or C-G♯ (augmented fifth).

B

balance and symmetry Even and equal.

baritone The male voice between tenor and bass.

bar line (measure bar) A vertical line drawn through the staff to show the end of a measure. Double bar lines show the end of a section or a piece of music.

Baroque period (buh-ROHK) [Fr.] Historic period between c. 1600 and c. 1750 that reflected highly embellished styles in art, architecture, fashion, manners, and music. The period of elaboration.

bass The lowest male voice, below tenor and baritone.

bass clef Symbol at the beginning of the staff for lower voices and instruments, or the piano left hand; usually referring to pitches lower than middle C. The two dots lie on either side of the fourth-line F, thus the term, F clef.

beat A steady pulse.

bel canto (bell KAHN-toh) [It.] Italian vocal technique of the eighteenth century with emphasis on beauty of sound and brilliance of performance.

binary form Defines a form having two sections (A and B), each of which may be repeated.

bitonality The designation of music written in two different keys at the same time.

breath mark A mark placed within a phrase or melody showing where the singer or musician should breathe. (❜)

C

cadence Punctuation or termination of a musical phrase; a breathing break.

caesura (si-ZHUR-uh) [Lt.] A break or pause between two musical phrases. (//)

call and response A song style that follows a simple question-and-answer pattern in which a soloist leads and a group responds.

calypso style Folk-style music from the Caribbean Islands with bright, syncopated rhythm.

cambiata The young male voice that is still developing.

canon A compositional form in which the subject is begun in one group and then is continually and exactly repeated by other groups. Unlike the round, the canon closes with all voices ending together on a common chord.

cantata (kan-TAH-tuh) [It.] A collection of vocal compositions with instrumental accompaniment consisting of several movements based on related secular or sacred text segments.

cantabile In a lyrical, singing style.

cantor A solo singer in the Jewish and Roman Catholic traditions who leads the congregation in worship by introducing responses and other musical portions of the services.

cantus firmus (KAHN-tuhs FUHR-muhs) [Lt.] A previously-composed melody which is used as a basis for a new composition.

chance music *See* aleatoric music.

chantey (SHAN-tee) [Fr.] A song sung by sailors in rhythm with their work.

chant, plainsong Music from the liturgy of the early church, characterized by free rhythms, monophonic texture, and sung *a cappella*.

chorale (kuh-RAL) [Gr.] Congregational song or hymn of the German Protestant (Evangelical) Church.

chord Three or more pitches sounded simultaneously.

chord, block Three or more pitches sounded simultaneously.

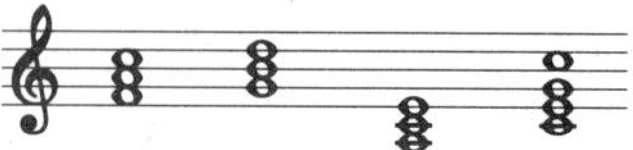

chord, broken Three or more pitches sounded in succession; *see also* arpeggio.

chromatic (kroh-MAT-ik) [Gr.] Moving up or down by half steps. Also the name of a scale composed entirely of half steps.

Classical period The period in Western history beginning around 1750 and lasting until around 1820 that reflected a time when society began looking to the ancient Greeks and Romans for examples of order and ways of looking at life.

clef The symbol at the beginning of the staff that identifies a set of pitches; *see also* bass clef and treble clef.

coda Ending section; a concluding portion of a composition. (𝄌)

common time Another name for 4/4 meter; *see also* cut time. (𝄴)

composer The creator of musical works.

compound meter Meter whose beat can be subdivided into threes and/or sixes.

con (kohn) [It.] With.

con brio (kohn BREE-oh) [It.] With spirit; vigorously.

concerto Composition for solo instrument and an orchestra, usually with three movements.

con moto (kohn MOH-toh) [It.] With motion.

consonance A musical interval or chord that sounds pleasing; opposite of dissonance.

Contemporary period The time from 1900 to right now.

continuo A Baroque tradition in which the bass line is played "continuously," by a cello, double bass, and/or bassoon while a keyboard instrument (harpsichord, organ) plays the bass line and indicated harmonies.

contrapuntal *See* counterpoint.

counterpoint The combination of simultaneous parts; *see* polyphony.

crescendo (*cresc.*) (kreh-SHEN-doh) [It.] To gradually become louder.

cued notes Smaller notes indicating either optional harmony or notes from another voice part.

cut time 2/2 time with the half note getting the beat. (𝄵)

D

da capo (*D.C.*) (dah KAH-poh) [It.] Go back to the beginning and repeat; *see also* dal segno and al fine.

dal segno (*D.S.*) (dahl SAYN-yoh) [It.] Go back to the sign and repeat. (𝄋)

D. C. al fine (dah KAH-poh ahl FEE-neh) [It.] Repeat back to the beginning and end at the "fine."

decrescendo (*decresc.*) (deh-kreh-SHEN-doh) [It.] To gradually become softer.

delicato Delicate; to play or sing delicately.

descant A high, ornamental voice part often lying above the melody.

diaphragm The muscle that separates the chest cavity (thorax) from the abdomen. The primary muscle in the inhalation/exhalation cycle.

diction Clear and correct enunciation.

diminished The term describing an interval that has been descreased by half steps; for example, the *perfect fourth* (3 whole and one half steps) becomes a *diminished fourth* (3 whole steps). Also used for a triad which has a minor third (R, 3) and a diminished fifth (R, 5); for example, C, E♭, G♭.

diminuendo (*dim.*) (duh-min-yoo-WEN-doh) [It.] Gradually getting softer; *see also* decrescendo.

diminution The halving of values; that is, halves become quarters, quarters become eighths, etc. Opposite of *augmentation*.

diphthong A combination of two vowel sounds consisting of a primary vowel sound and a secondary vowel sound. The secondary vowel sound is (usually) at the very end of the diphthong; for example, in the word *toy*, the diphthong starts with the sound of "o," then moves on to "y," in this case pronounced "ee."

dissonance Discord in music, suggesting a state of tension or "seeking"; chords using seconds, fourths, fifths, and sevenths; the opposite of consonance.

divisi (*div.*) (dih-VEE-see) [It.] Divide; the parts divide.

dolce (DOHL-chay) [It.] Sweet; *dolcissimo*, very sweet; *dolcemente*, sweetly.

dominant The fifth degree of a major or minor scale; the triad built on the fifth degree; indicated as V in harmonic analysis.

Dorian mode A scale with the pattern of whole-step, half, whole, whole, whole, half, and whole. For example, D to D on the keyboard.

dotted rhythm A note written with a dot increases its value again by half.

double bar Two vertical lines placed on the staff indicating the end of a section or a composition; used with two dots to enclose repeated sections.

double flat (𝄫) Symbol showing the lowering of a pitch one whole step (two half steps).

double sharp (𝄪) Symbol showing the raising of a pitch one whole step (two half steps).

doubling The performance of the same note by two parts, either at the same pitch or an octave apart.

downbeat The accented first beat in a measure.

D. S. al coda (dahl SAYN-yoh ahl KOH-dah) [It.] Repeat from the symbol (𝄋) and skip to the coda when you see the sign. (𝄌)

D. S. al fine (dahl SAYN-yoh ahl FEE-neh) [It.] Repeat from the symbol (𝄋) and sing to fine or the end.

duple Any time signature or group of beats that is a multiple of two.

duet Composition for two performers.

dynamics The volume of sound, the loudness or softness of a musical passage; intensity, power.

E

enharmonic Identical tones that are named and written differently; for example, C sharp and D flat.

ensemble A group of musicians or singers who perform together.

enunciation Speaking and singing words with distinct vowels and consonants.

espressivo (*espress.*) (es-preh-SEE-vo) [It.] For expression; *con espressione*, with feeling.

ethnomusicology The musical study of specific world cultures.

expressive singing To sing with feeling.

exuberance Joyously unrestrained and enthusiastic.

F

fermata (fur-MAH-tah) [It.] A hold; to hold the note longer. (𝄐)

fine (FEE-neh) Ending; to finish.

flat Symbol (accidental) that lowers a pitch by one half step. (♭)

folk music Uncomplicated music that speaks directly of everyday matters; the first popular music; usually passed down through the oral tradition.

form The structure of a musical composition.

forte (*f*) (FOR-teh) [It.] Loud.

fortissimo (*ff*) (for-TEE-suh-moh) [It.] Very loud.

freely A direction that permits liberties with tempo, dynamics, and style.

fugue (FYOOG) [It.] A polyphonic composition consisting of a series of successive melody imitations; *see also* imitative style.

fusion A combination or blending of different genres of music.

G

gapped scale A scale resulting from leaving out certain tones (the pentatonic scale is an example).

grandioso [It.] Stately, majestic.

grand staff Two staves usually linked together by a long bar line and a bracket.

grave (GRAH-veh) [It.] Slow, solemn.

grazioso (grah-tsee-OH-soh) [It.] Graceful.

half step The smallest distance (interval) between two notes on a keyboard; the chromatic scale is composed entirely of half steps, shown as (v).

half time *See* cut time.

harmonic interval Intervals that are sung or played simultaneously; *see also* melodic interval.

harmony Vertical blocks of different tones sounded simultaneously.

hemiola (hee-mee-OH-lah) [Gk.] A metric flow of two against a metric flow of three.

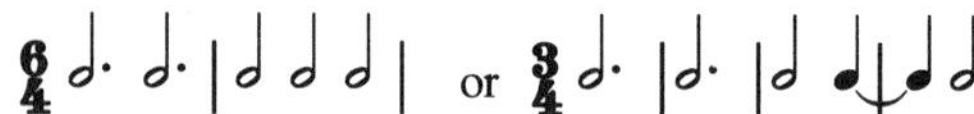

homophonic (hah-muh-FAH-nik) [Gk.] A texture where all parts sing similar rhythm in unison or harmony.

homophony (hah-MAH-fuh-nee) [Gk.] Music that consists of two or more voice parts with similar or identical rhythms. From the Greek words meaning "same sounds," homophony could be described as "hymn-style."

hushed A style marking indicating a soft, whispered tone.

I

imitation, imitative style Restating identical or nearly identical musical material in two or more parts.

improvised Invented on the spur of the moment.

improvisation Spontaneous musical invention, commonly associated with jazz.

interval The distance from one note to another; intervals are measured by the total steps and half steps between the two notes.

intonation The degree to which pitch is accurately produced in tune.

introduction An opening section at the beginning of a movement or work, preparatory to the main body of the form.

inversion May be applied to melody and harmony: *melodic inversion* occurs in an exchange of ascending and descending movement (for instance, a third becomes a sixth, a fourth becomes a fifth, etc.); *harmonic inversion* occurs in the position of the chord tones (that is, root position with the root as lowest tone, first inversion with the third as lowest tone, and second inversion with the fifth as the lowest tone).

key The way tonality is organized around a tonal center; *see also* key signature.

key change Changing an initial key signature in the body of a composition.

key signature Designation of sharps or flats at the beginning of a composition to indicate its basic scale and tonality.

L

leading tone The seventh degree of a scale, so called because of its strong tendency to resolve upward to the tonic.

legato (leh-GAH-toh) [It.] Smooth, connected style.

ledger lines Short lines that appear above, between treble and bass clefs, or below the bass clef, used to expand the notation.

leggiero (leh-JEH-roh) [It.] Articulate lightly; sometimes nonlegato.

lento Slow; a little faster than *largo*, a little slower than *adagio*.

linear flow, line Singing/playing notes in a flowing (smooth) manner, as if in a horizontal line.

liturgical Pertaining to prescribed forms of worship or ritual in various religious services. Western music contains much literature written for the liturgy of the early Roman Catholic Church.

lullaby A cradle song; in Western music, usually sung with a gentle and regular rhythm.

M

madrigal A secular vocal form in several parts, popular in the Renaissance.

maestoso (mah-eh-STOH-soh) [It.] Perform majestically.

major (key, scale, mode) Scale built on the formula of two whole steps, one half step, three whole steps, one half step.

Major 2nd The name for an interval of one whole step or two half steps. For example, from C to D.

Major 6th The name for an interval of four whole steps and one-half step. For example, from C to A.

Major 3rd The name for an interval of two whole steps or four half steps. For example, from C to E.

major triad Three tones that form a major third *do* to *mi* and a minor third *mi* to *so* as in C E G.

marcato (mahr-KAH-toh) [It.] Long but separated pitches; translated as marked.

mass The main religious service of the Roman Catholic Church. There are two divisions of mass: the Proper of the Mass in which the text changes for each day, and the Ordinary of the Mass in which the text remains the same for every mass. Music for the mass includes the Kyrie, Gloria, Credo, Sanctus, and Agnus Dei as well as other chants, hymns, and psalms. For special mass occasions composers through the centuries have created large musical works for choruses, soloists, instrumentalists, and orchestras.

measure The space from one bar line to the next; also called bars.

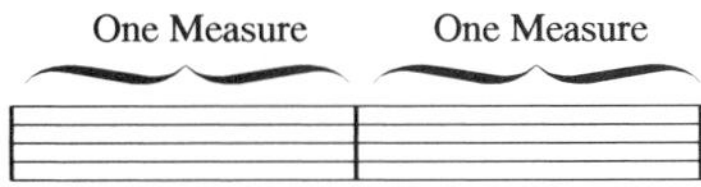

medieval Historical period prior to the Renaissance, c. 500-1450.

medley A group of tunes, linked together and sung consecutively.

melisma (n.) or melismatic (adj.) (muh-LIZ-mah or muh-liz-MAT-ik) [Gk.] A term describing the setting of one syllable of text to several pitches.

melodic interval Intervals that are performed in succession; *see also* harmonic interval.

melody A logical succession of musical tones; also called tune.

meter The pattern into which a steady succession of rhythmic pulses (beats) is organized.

meter signature The divided number at the beginning of a clef; 4/4, 3/4, and so forth; *see also* time signature.

metronome marking A sign that appears over the top line of the treble clef staff at the beginning of a piece indicating the tempo. It shows the kind of note that will get the beat and the numbers of beats per minute as measured by a metronome; for example, ♪ = 100.

mezzo forte (*mf*) (MEHT-soh FOR-teh) [It.] Medium loud.

mezzo piano (*mp*) (MEHT-soh pee-AH-noh) [It.] Medium soft.

mezzo voce (MET-soh VOH-cheh) [It.] With half voice; reduced volume and tone.

middle C The note that is located nearest the center of the piano keyboard; middle C can be written in either the treble or bass clef.

minor (key, scale) Scale built on the formula of one whole step, one half step, two whole steps, one half step, two whole steps.

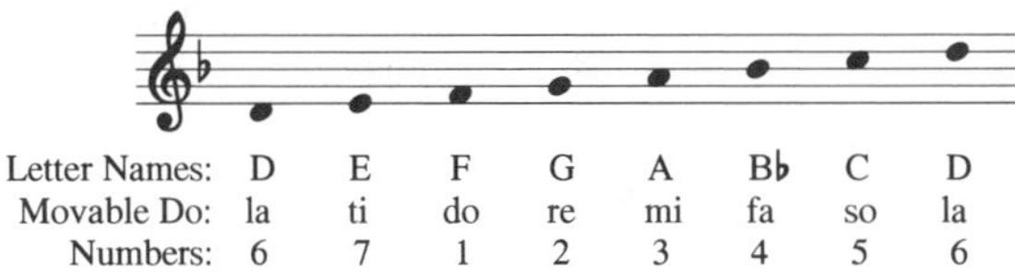

minor mode One of two modes upon which the basic scales of Western music are based, the other being major; using W for a whole step and H for a half step, a minor scale has the pattern W H W W H W W.

minor triad Three tones that form a minor third (bottom) and a major third (top), such as A C E.

minor third The name for an interval of three half steps. For example, from A to C.

mixed meter Frequently changing time signatures or meters.

moderato Moderate.

modulation Adjusting to a change of keys within a song.

molto Very or much; for example, *molto rit.* means "much slower."

monophonic (mah-nuh-FAH-nik) [Gk.] A musical texture having a single melodic line with no accompaniment; monophony.

monophony (muh-NAH-fuh-nee) [Gk.] One sound; music that has a single melody. Gregorian chants or plainsongs exhibit monophony.

motet Originating as a Medieval and Renaissance polyphonic song, this choral form of composition became an unaccompanied work, often in contrapuntal style.

motive A shortened expression, sometimes contained within a phrase.

musical variations Changes in rhythm, pitch, dynamics, style, and tempo to create new statements of the established theme.

mysterioso Perform in a mysterious or haunting way; to create a haunting mood.

N

nationalism Patriotism; pride of country. This feeling influenced many Romantic composers such as Wagner, Tchaikovsky, Dvorák, Chopin, and Brahms.

natural (♮) Cancels a previous sharp (♯) lowering the pitch a half step, or a previous flat (♭), raising the pitch a half step.

no breath mark A direction not to take a breath at a specific place in the composition. (or N.B.)

non-harmonic tones Identifies those pitches outside the harmonic structure of the chord; for example, the *passing tone* and the *appoggiatura*.

non troppo (nahn TROH-poh) [It.] Not too much; for example, allegro non troppo, not too fast.

notation Written notes, symbols, and directions used to represent music within a composition.

nuance Subtle variations in tempo, phrasing, dynamics, etc., to enhance the musical performance.

O

octave An interval of twelve half steps; 8 or 8va = an octave above; 8vb = an octave below.

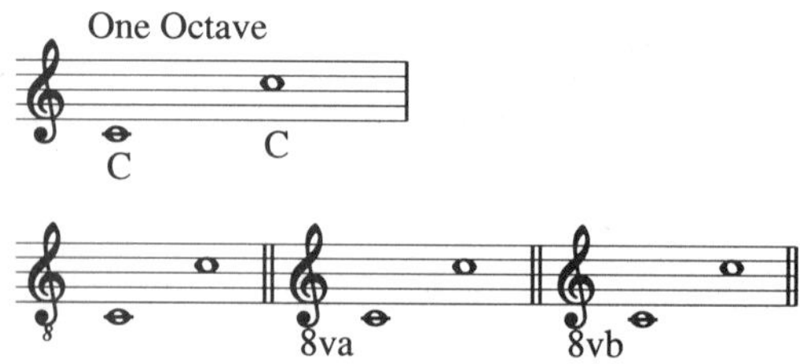

opera A combination of singing, instrumental music, dancing, and drama that tells a story.

operetta A lighter, "popular" style of operatic form, including sung and spoken dialogue, solo, chorus, and dance.

optional divisi (*opt. div.*) Indicating a split in the music into optional harmony, shown by the smaller cued note.

opus, Op. The term, meaning "work," used by composers to show the chronological order of their works; for example, Opus 1, Op. 2.

oratorio A piece for solo voices, chorus, and orchestra, that is an expanded dramatic work on a literary or religious theme presented without theatrical action.

ostinato (ahs-tuh-NAH-toh) [It.] A rhythmic or melodic passage that is repeated continuously.

overtones The almost inaudible higher pitches which occur over the fundamental tone, resulting from the division of the vibrating cycle into smaller segments; compare to partials, harmonics.

P

palate The roof of the mouth; the *hard palate* is forward, the *soft palate* (*velum*) is at the back.

parallel major and minor keys Major and minor keys having the same tonic, such as A major and A minor (A major being the parallel major of A minor and A minor the parallel minor of A major).

parallel motion The movement of two or more voice parts in the same direction, at the same interval from each other.

peak The high point in the course of a development; for example, the high point of a musical phrase or the high point in a movement of instrumental music.

pentatonic scale A five-tone scale constructed of *do, re, mi, so, la* (degrees 1, 2, 3, 5, 6) of a corresponding major scale.

Perfect 5th The name for an interval of three whole steps and one half step. For example, C to G.

Perfect 4th The name for an interval of two whole steps and one half step. For example, C to F.

phrase A musical sentence containing a beginning, middle, and end.

phrase mark In music, an indicator of the length of a phrase in a melody; this mark may also mean that the singer or musician should not take a breath for the duration of the phrase. ( )

phrasing The realization of the phrase structure of a work; largely a function of a performer's articulation and breathing.

pianissimo (***pp***) (pee-uh-NEE-suh-moh) [It.] Very soft.

piano (***p***) (pee-ANN-noh) [It.] Soft.

Picardy third An interval of a major third used in the final, tonic chord of a piece written in a minor key.

pick-up *See* upbeat.

pitch Sound, the result of vibration; the highness or lowness of a tone, determined by the number of vibrations per second.

piu (pew) [It.] More; for example, *piu forte* means "more loudly."

poco (POH-koh) [It.] Little; for example, *poco dim.* means "a little softer."

poco a poco (POH-koh ah POH-koh) [It.] Little by little; for example, *poco a poco cresc.* means "little by little increase in volume."

polyphony (n.) or polyphonic (adj.) (pah-LIH-fuh-nee or pah-lee-FAH-nik) [Gk.] The term that means that each voice part begins at a different place, is independent and important, and that sections often repeat in contrasting dynamic levels.
Poly = many, phony = sounds.

polyrhythmic The simultaneous use of contrasting rhythmic figures.

presto (PREH-stoh) [It.] Very fast.

program music A descriptive style of music composed to relate or illustrate a specific incident, situation, or drama; the form of the piece is often dictated or influenced by the nonmusical program. This style commonly occurs in music composed during the Romantic period. For example, "The Moldau" from *Má Vlast*, by Bedřich Smetana.

progression A succession of two or more pitches or chords; also melodic or harmonic progression.

R

rallentando (*rall.*) (rahl-en-TAHN-doh) [It.] Meaning to "perform more and more slowly." *See also* ritardando.

recitative (res-uh-TAY-teev) [It.] A speechlike style of singing used in opera, oratorio, and cantata.

register, vocal A term used for different parts of a singer's range, such as head register (high notes) and chest register (low notes).

relative major and minor keys The relative minor of any major key or scale, while sharing its key signature and pitches, takes for its tonic the sixth scale degree of that major key or scale. For example, in D major the sixth scale degree is B (or *la* in solfège), *la* then becomes the tonic for A minor.

Renaissance period The historic period in Western Europe from c. 1430 to 1600; the term means "rebirth" or "renewal"; it indicates a period of rapid development in exploration, science, art, and music.

repeat sign A direction to repeat the section of music (𝄆 𝄇); if the first half of this sign is omitted, it means to "go back to the beginning" (𝄇).

repetition The restatement of a musical idea; repeated pitches; repeated "A" section in ABA form.

resolution (*res.*) A progression from a dissonant tone or harmony to a consonant harmony; a sense of completion.

resonance Reinforcement and intensification of sound by vibrations.

rest Symbols used to indicated silence.

rhythm The pattern of sounds and silences.

rhythmic motif A rhythmic pattern that is repeated throughout a movement or composition.

ritardando (*rit.*) The gradual slowing of tempo; also called "ritard."

Rococo Music of the Baroque period so elaborate it was named after a certain type of fancy rock work.

Romantic period A historic period starting c. 1820 and ending c. 1900 in which artists and composers attempted to break with classical music ideas.

rondo form An instrumental form based on an alternation between a repeated (or recurring) section and contrasting episodes (ABACADA).

root The bottom note of a triad in its original position; the note on which the chord is built.

round A composition in which the perpetual theme (sometimes with harmonic parts) begins in one group and is strictly imitated in other groups in an overlapping fashion. Usually the last voice to enter becomes the final voice to complete the song.

rubato (roo-BAH-toh) [It.] Freely; allows the conductor or the performer to vary the tempo.

S

sacred music Of or dealing with religious music; hymns, chorales, early masses; *see* secular music.

scale A pattern of pitches arranged by whole steps and half steps.

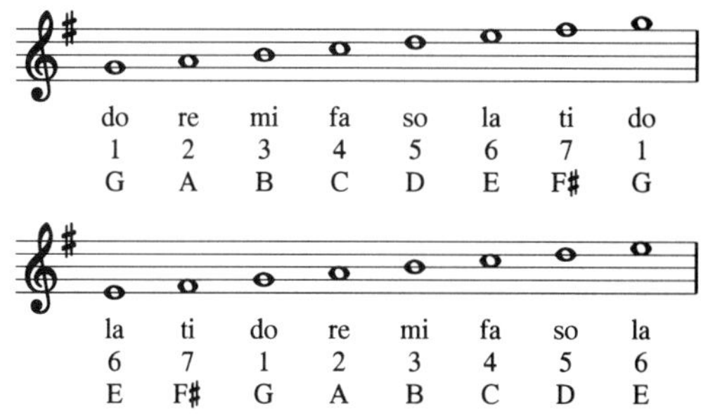

score The arrangement of instrumental and vocal staffs that all sound at the same time.

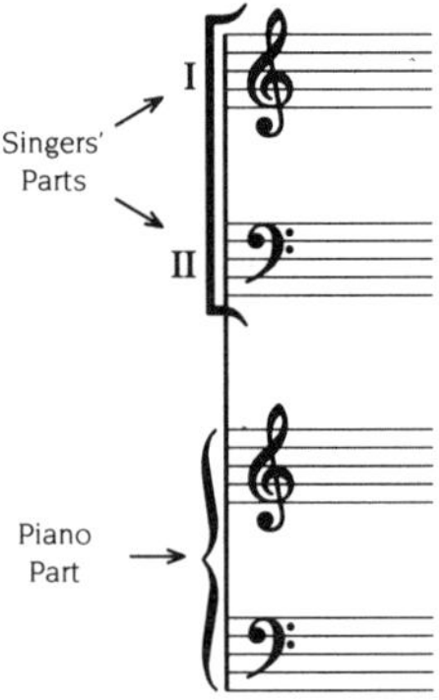

secular music Music without religious content; *see* sacred music.

sempre (SEHM-preh) [It.] Always, continually.

seventh chord By adding a seventh above the root of a triad (R, 3, 5), the result is a four-tone chord (R, 3, 5, 7).

sforzando (*sfz*) (sfohr-TSAHN-doh) [It.] A sudden strong accent on a note or chord.

sharp A symbol (accidental) that raises a pitch by one half step. (♯)

sight-sing Reading and singing of music at first sight.

simile (*sim.*) (SIM-ee-leh) [It.] To continue in the same way.

simple meter Meter in which each beat is divisible by 2.

skip Melodic movement in intervals larger than a whole step.

slur Curved line placed over or under a group of notes to indicate that they are to be performed without a break. ( )

solfège (SOHL-fehj) [Fr.] A method of sight-singing, using the syllables *do, re, mi, fa, so, la, ti,* etc. for pitches of the scale.

solo Composition for one featured performer.

sonata-allegro form (suh-NAH-tuh ah-LEH-groh) [It.] Large A B A form consisting of three sections: exposition, development, and recapitulation.

soprano The higher female voice.

sostenuto (SAHS-tuh-noot-oh) [It.] The sustaining of a tone or the slackening of tempo; the right pedal of a piano, which, when depressed, allows the strings to vibrate.

sotto voce In a quiet, subdued manner; "under" the voice.

spirito (SPEE-ree-toh) [It.] Spirited; for example, *con spirito*, with spirit.

spiritual A type of song created by African Americans who combined African rhythms with melodies they created and heard in America.

staccato (stah-KAH-toh) [It.] Performed in a short, detached manner, as opposed to legato.

staff Series of five horizontal lines and four spaces on which music is written to show pitch.

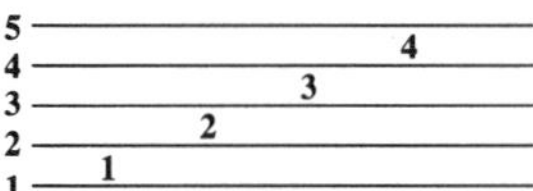

staggered entrances Voice parts or instruments begin singing or playing at different points within the composition.

steady beat A metrical pulse; *see also* beat, meter, rhythm.

step Melodic movement from one note to the next adjacent note, either higher or lower.

stepwise melodic movement Motion from one note to an adjacent one.

stress Emphasis on certain notes or rhythmic elements.

strong beat Naturally accented beats; beats 1 and 3 in 4/4 meter, beat 1 in 3/4 meter.

strophic Description of a song in which all the stanzas of the text are sung to the same music; opposite of *through-composed*.

style The particular character of a musical work; often indicated by words at the beginning of a composition, telling the performer the general manner in which the piece is to be performed.

subito (sub.) (SOO-bee-toh) [It.] Suddenly; for example, *sub. piano* means "suddenly soft."

suspension or suspended tone The tone or tones in a chord that are held as the remainder of the notes change to a new chord. The sustained tones often form a *dissonance* with the new chord, into which they then resolve.

sustained tone A tone sustained in duration; sometimes implying a slowing of tempo; *sostenuto* or *sostenendo*, abbreviated *sost*.

swing This is a performance style in which a pair of eighth notes ( ) are no longer performed evenly, but instead like a triplet ( ), yet they are still written (3); usually indicated at the beginning of a song or a section.

symphony An extended work in several movements, for orchestra; also an orchestra configured to perform symphonic music.

syncopation Deliberate shifts of accent so that a rhythm goes against the steady beat; sometimes referred to as the "offbeat."

T

tactus (TAKT-us) [Lt.] The musical term for "beat" in the fifteenth and sixteenth century; generally related to the speed of the human heart.

tempo A pace with which music moves, based on the speed of the underlying beat.

tempo I or tempo primo Return to the first tempo.

tenor A high male voice, lower than the alto, but higher than bass.

tenuto (teh-NOO-toh) [It.] Stress and extend the marked note. ( )

text Words, usually set in a poetic style, that express a central thought, idea, moral, or narrative.

texture The thickness of the different layers of horizontal and vertical sounds.

theme and variation form A musical form in which variations of the basic theme comprise the composition.

tie A curved line connecting two successive notes of the same pitch, indicating that the second note is not to be articulated. ( )

timbre Tone color; the unique quality produced by a voice or instrument.

time signature The sign placed at the beginning and within a composition to indicate the meter; for example, 4/4, 3/4; *see also* cut time, meter signature.

to coda Skip to the ⊕ or CODA.

tonality The organized relationships of pitches with reference to a definite key center. In Western music, most tonalities are organized by the major and minor scales.

tone A sound quality of a definite pitch.

tone color, quality, or timbre That which distinguishes the voice or tone of one singer or instrument from another; for example, a soprano from an alto or a flute from a clarinet.

tonic chord (TAH-nik kord) [Gk.] The name of a chord built on the tonal center of a scale; for example, C E G or *do, mi, so* for C major.

tonic or tonal center The most important pitch in a scale; *do*; the home tone; the tonal center or root of a key or scale.

tonic triad A three-note chord comprising root, third, and fifth; for example, C E G.

transposition The process of changing the key of a composition.

treble clef The symbol that appears at the beginning of the staff used for higher voices, instruments, or the piano right hand; generally referring to pitches above middle C, it wraps around the line for G, therefore it is also called the G-clef.

triad A three-note chord built in thirds above a root tone.

trill A rapid change between the marked note and the one above it within the same key. (tr~)

triplet A group of notes in which three notes of equal duration are sung in the time normally given to two notes of equal duration.

troppo (TROHP-oh) [It.]Too much; for example, *allegro non troppo*, not too fast.

troubadour A wandering minstrel of noble birth in southern France, Spain, and Italy during the eleventh to thirteenth centuries.

tuning The process of adjusting the tones of voices or instruments so they will sound the proper pitches.

tutti (TOO-tee) [It.] Meaning "all" or "together."

twelve-tone music Twentieth-century system of writing music in which the twelve tones of the chromatic scale are arranged into a tone row (numbered 1 to 12), and then the piece is composed by arranging and rearranging the "row" in different ways; for example, backward, forward, or in clusters of three or four pitches.

U

unison Voice parts or instruments sounding the same pitches in the same rhythm simultaneously.

upbeat A weak beat preceding the downbeat.

V

variation *See* theme and variation form, musical variations.

vivace (vee-VAH-chay) [It.] Very fast; lively.

voice crossing (or voice exchange) When one voice "crosses" above or below another voice part.

W

whole step The combination of two successive half steps. (⌴)

whole tone scale A scale consisting only of whole steps.